E.G. ASPLUND

E.G. ASPLUND

First published in Japan on August 30, 2005
Fourth published on March 30, 2021

TOTO Publishing (TOTO LTD.)
TOTO Nogizaka Bldg., 2F, 1-24-3 Minami-Aoyama,
Minato-ku, Tokyo 107-0062, Japan
[Sales] Telephone: +81-3-3402-7138 Facsimile: +81-3-3402-7187
[Editorial] Telephone: +81-3-3497-1010
URL: https://jp.toto.com/publishing

Copyright	©2005 by TOTO Publishing
Photographs	©2005 by Yukio Yoshimura
Text	©2005 by Yoichi Kawashima
Publisher	Takeshi Ito
Book Designer	Tetsuya Ohta
Printer	Tokyo Inshokan Printing Co., LTD.

Except as permitted under copyright law, this book may not be reproduced, in whole or in part, in any form or by any means, including photocopying, scanning, digitizing, or otherwise, without prior permission. Scanning or digitizing this book through a third party, even for personal or home use, is also strictly prohibited. The list price is indicated on the cover.

ISBN978-4-88706-257-3

アスプルンドの建築 1885–1940

写真＝吉村行雄
文――川島洋一

TOTO出版

エーリック・グンナール・アスプルンド
Erik Gunnar Asplund

1885	9月22日、スウェーデン・ストックホルムに生まれる。 Born in Stockholm, Sweden, on September 22.
1905-09	王立工科大学建築学科で学ぶ。 Studies at School of Architecture, Royal Institute of Technology, Stockholm.
1909-1910	ラーシュ・イスラエル・ヴァールマンの設計事務所で働く。 Works at Lars Israel Wahlman's Architectural Office.
1910	王立芸術大学に入学するが、すぐに仲間と共に退学。 Enters Royal University of Fine Arts, Stockholm. Resigns from the university soon after with his fellow students.
1910-11	仲間5人と共に「クララ・スクール」を設立し、一線級の建築家の指導の下、建築を学ぶ。 Establishes Klara School as a private school of architecture with other five students.
1912-13	独立した設計活動を開始し、5つの設計コンペに入賞。 Starts his own design work. Awarded prizes in five design competitions.
1913-14	パリとイタリアへ見学旅行。 Embarks on a study tour of Paris and Italy.
1915	「ストックホルム南墓地」コンペにシーグルド・レヴェレンツと応募し1等を受賞。 Receives First Prize in the competitions for Stockholm South Cemetery with Sigurd Lewerentz.
1917-20	アーキテクトゥール誌の編集長を務める。 Serves as editor of *Teknisk tidskrift, Arkitektur*.
1918	イェルダ・セルマンと結婚。 Marries Gerda Sellman.
1920	長男ウッレが逝去。 Asplund's first son, Olle, dies.
1928-30	ストックホルム博覧会の主任建築家に任命される。 Named Principal architect of Stockholm Exhibition 1930.
1931-40	王立工科大学建築学科教授。 Serves as professor of architecture, Royal Institute of Technology, Stockholm.
1934	イングリッド・クリングと再婚。 Marries Ingrid Kling.
1940	10月20日、心臓発作のためストックホルムで逝去。 Dies of heart attack in Stockholm on October 20.

Book Design : Tetsuya Ohta

アスプルンドの建築 1885–1940

目次　Contents

序　居心地の良い空間を撮る Preface: Shooting Comfortable Spaces	吉村行雄 Yukio Yoshimura	P.008
アスプルンド　生と建築 Erik Gunnar Asplund: Life and Architecture	川島洋一 Yoichi Kawashima	P.010
アスプルンドの仕事場——元所員、学生、仕事仲間に聞く Asplund at Work—— Interviews with Assistants, Students and Colleagues	クリスティーナ・エングフォーシュ Christina Engfors	P.088

作品紹介	An Introduction to Asplund's Works	
森の礼拝堂／森の墓地	Woodland Chapel, Woodland Cemetery, Stockholm	P.032
森の火葬場／森の墓地	Woodland Crematorium, Woodland Cemetery, Stockholm	P.046
カールスハムンの中学校	Secondary School at Karlshamn, Karlshamn	P.106
スネルマン邸	Villa Snellman, Djursholm	P.114
リステール州裁判所	Lister County Courthouse, Sölvesborg	P.130
スカンディア・シネマ	Skandia Cinema, Stockholm	P.144
カール・ヨーハン学校	Carl Johan School, Göteborg	P.162
ストックホルム市立図書館	Stockholm City Library, Stockholm	P.176
イェーテボリ裁判所増築	Göteborg Law Courts, Göteborg	P.200
国立バクテリア研究所本館	State Bacteriological Laboratory, Solna	P.222
夏の家	E.G. Asplund's Summer House, Stennäs	P.238

作品リスト	List of Works	P.264
略歴	Profiles	P.268
クレジット	Credits	P.270

序　居心地の良い空間を撮る

吉村行雄　建築写真家

　子供のころからカメラに興味をもち、中学・高校時代は写真部、大学に入ってからは自己流で建築写真を撮ってきた私が、建設業の設計部で設計に携わりながら、次第に本格的な建築写真の世界に入り込んでいくきっかけとなったのがヨーロッパ旅行である。

　建築と写真への興味から何度もヨーロッパに行くうちに、自然に足は北欧へと向かっていた。北欧独特の斜光と透明な空気感の中で見る都市や建築は私の撮影意欲を駆り立てた。バイキングの気質をベースにもち、勤勉で穏やかな国民性にも共感を覚えた。以来十数年、毎年のようにスウェーデンに行き、アスプルンドの作品を追い求め、カメラに収める旅が続いている。

　アスプルンドは、ほぼ同時代を生きたル・コルビュジエやミース・ファン・デル・ローエが明快な思想や方法論で近代建築を展開したのとは対照的に、人間の情緒や心理に根ざした建築を目指し、人と環境と建築のかかわりを大切にした作品を生涯つくり続けてきた。このようなアスプルンドの視点は、世界レベルで環境問題が問われ、人間性の復権が叫ばれる動きの中で注目に値するものと思われる。建築写真を考える時のレファレンスとして、アスプルンドの作品は多くの示唆を私に与えてくれた。

　アスプルンドの作品は住宅、学校、礼拝堂、図書館と用途が違っていても、その場に居ると気持ちが安らぎ、長くその場に居たくなる。五感を総動員すると空間は、私の身体感覚に訴えかけてくる。ひとり撮影に没頭していると、いつのまにかアスプルンドに誘われて、カメラを向けているのでは、と感じる時もある。それにしてもこの居心地の良さはどこからくるのだろうか。私はなんとかして居心地の良い空間を撮りたいと思った。この場合、空間とはそこにある空気であって、目に見えないものまでもが含まれる。壁や天井に至る空気の"存在感"をも写し取ることが求められているのだ。その"存在感"をつかむ手がかりとして、空間の形状はもちろんのこと、光と影の存在、石や木や金属、ガラスなどの質感。そしてそれらの硬さや強さ、冷たさや暖かさといった触覚的な感覚も要素のひとつであり、その空間がもつ響きや音、空気のわずかな温度差や流れや澱みといったものも空間に個性を与える。私は五感を総動員して空間を感じ取りながら、それをフィルムに写し込もうとシャッターを切る。

　五感で感じるものを、視覚媒体である写真で表現することの難しさを感じる。私の写真は見る人に心地良さを伝えているだろうか？　今日も果てしない自問自答を繰り返している。

Preface: Shooting Comfortable Spaces

Yukio Yoshimura Architectural Photographer

Ever since I was a child, I have had an interest in cameras. I belonged to photography clubs in junior high and high school, and took my own style of architectural photographs as a university student. Now I work in the design department of a construction company, and have gradually started to make my way as an architectural photographer.

The catalyst for this was Europe. After numerous visits to Europe to pursue my interest in architecture and photography, I found myself heading for Scandinavia. Seeing cities and architecture in the oblique light and transparent skies unique to Scandinavia filled me with an even greater enthusiasm for photography. At this point, I feel a special affinity with the diligent and tranquil nature of the region's people, whose roots lie in the spirit of the Vikings.

For over a decade, I have taken my camera to Scandinavia and almost every year I have gone to Sweden in search of Asplund's work. In contrast to architects of the same generation, like Le Corbusier and Mies van der Rohe, who developed modern architecture through lucid concepts and methodologies, Asplund concentrated on buildings that were rooted in human emotions and sensibilities. And throughout his life, Asplund created work that put an emphasis on the relationship between people, the environment and architecture. I believe Asplund's viewpoint merits special attention in the context of global environmental and human rights issues. Asplund's work has also provided me with countless suggestions for my own architectural photography.

Although the intended purpose of Asplund's residences, schools, chapels and libraries may vary, all of these structures share a relaxed atmosphere that encourages people to stay longer in them. The spaces, drawing on all five senses, appeal to me on a physical level. As I am immersed in taking photographs, I sometimes get the feeling that Asplund has invited me to point my camera in a certain direction. But what is it that makes these spaces so comfortable? I want to somehow convey this feeling in my photographs. Each space consists of the air within it and includes things that are not visible to the eye. My job is to capture the "presence" of the air as far as the walls and ceiling. The key to doing this is, of course, connected to the shape of the space, the existence of light and shadow, and the textures of the stone, wood, metal and glass there. The tactile sensations of these things - their hardness, strength, coldness and hotness - are another element, and the reverberations and sound, slight differences in the temperature, flow and stagnation of the air give the space a unique character. As I experience a space through all of my senses, I click the shutter in the hope that I can capture these things on film.

Expressing what we understand through our senses in a visual medium like photography is a difficult task. Do my photographs communicate the comfortable sensation I felt in the space? This is the question I ask myself over and over again.

アスプルンド　生と建築

川島洋一　建築家・建築史家

　なだらかな丘の斜面に、一本の道が延びている。人影のない風景のなかに見えるのは、芝生の丘、敷石の道、丘の上の十字架、ロッジアの列柱、遠くの暗い森、低く雲の垂れ込めた空、そこにいる自分の存在。この「森の火葬場」を生み出したのが、スウェーデンの建築家エーリック・グンナール・アスプルンド（1885-1940）である。

● ——今、なぜアスプルンドなのか

　これまでアスプルンドは、いわば"知る人ぞ知る"存在であった。たしかに彼の名前は近代建築史の本に出ているし、作品のいくつかは名作とされている。「森の墓地」が、1994年にユネスコの世界遺産に登録されてから、話題になる機会も確実に増えてきた。にもかかわらず彼の仕事が十分に理解され、それに見合う正当な評価がなされてきたとは言いがたい。北欧建築に関する情報が不足していたのも、その理由のひとつであろう。作風もどこかつかみどころがない。とりあえずクラシシズムやモダニズムのラベルを貼って分類できるほど単純ではないから、建築史のどこかにしっくりくる位置が与えられないままだったという事情もあるだろう。コルビュジエやミースのように強烈な影響力があったわけではないし、ライトやアールトほど作品数が多いわけでもない。それでもアスプルンドは設計の名手として、あるいは、なぜか気になる不思議な存在として、その魅力に気づいた建築家たちからひそかに敬愛の対象となってきた。

　アスプルンドの作風に一貫した特徴を見つけにくいのは、当時のスウェーデンでは建築の潮流が次々に変化したためである。これまで彼の作品は、そうした様式的傾向の変遷に基づいて紹介されることが多かった。だが、アスプルンド作品の本当の魅力にたどり着くためには、もっと注目すべき視点がある。作品の設計過程のなかに思考の跡をたどり、"人間"としてのひとりの建築家の生成過程に立ち合うこと。そこにこそ、アスプルンドを知る本当の醍醐味がある。そのとき彼の向こう側に、"建築"という表現の新しい可能性が広がっているのを感じるからである。建築にかかわる喜びと勇気を新たにするために、今こそアスプルンドに注目してみたい。

● ——建築との出会い

　建築家はなぜ建築をつくるのだろうか。"社会が求めるから"では、つくり手の内面を説明したことにならない。建築はかつて信仰や権力の表現手段であったが、20世紀以降はほとんど実用を目的として建てられる。だが、実用性を満たすだけなら特別な苦労はいらないし、実際に街はそうした"建物"で埋めつくされてきた。ここであえて問うのは、それに満足できない建築家が、情熱を傾けて建築をつくるその内面の必然性である。そのとき建築家は、建築

1. アスプルンド自画像。レンブラント自画像に重ね合わせることで、画家に憧れる少年の心情も描いている。（インゲマール・アスプルンド氏蔵）

Figure 1: A self-portrait by Asplund. By superimposing the drawing on a self-portrait by Rembrandt, Asplund tried to render a sense of yearning for his youth. (From Ingemar Asplund's private collection.)

Erik Gunnar Asplund: Life and Architecture

Yoichi Kawashima Architect / Architectural Historian

A road leads up a gently sloping hill. In this scene lacking human forms, one finds a grassy hill, a cobblestone path, a cross on top of the hill, colonnaded loggias, a dark forest in the distance, low-hanging clouds in the sky - and one's own being. The creator of this site, Woodland Crematorium, is the Swedish architect Erik Gunnar Asplund (1885-1940).

Asplund - Why Now?
In the past, Asplund was an architect known only to those "in the know." His name appeared in books on the history of modern architecture and several of his works were considered to be masterpieces. But since Woodland Cemetery was recognized as a UNESCO World Heritage Site in 1994, interest in Asplund has been building. Nevertheless, it would be incorrect to say that his work has been sufficiently understood or that he has received the recognition he deserves. Part of this has do with a lack of information about Scandinavian architecture. It is also difficult to put Asplund's style in context. Since it cannot be easily categorized with a label like classicism or modernism, Asplund's place in the history of architecture remains undefined. He hasn't had the extraordinary influence of a Le Corbusier or a Mies, and neither does he have the body of work of a Wright or an Aalto. Yet, whether as a master of design or a remarkable figure who seems intriguing, Asplund is the subject of great adoration among architects who have fallen under his spell.

Because architectural trends in Sweden at the time underwent a series of rapid changes, it is hard to find a set of uniform characteristics underlying Asplund's style. His work has often been presented on the basis of shifts in stylistic tendencies. But in order to understand the true charm of Asplund's work, there are more important perspectives. These include examining the traces of Asplund's ideas that can be found in the design process, and looking at the evolution of the architect as a "human being." This, more than anything else, is the whole point of studying Asplund, since one always senses that beyond the man there is an expanding horizon of new expressive possibilities in "architecture." Now, more than ever, I would like to focus on Asplund to help renew the joy and courage that are associated with architecture.

Encountering Architecture
Why do architects make buildings? "Because society needs them" is one answer, but this doesn't shed any light on an artist's inner motivations. Architecture was once a means of expressing faith and power, but since the beginning of the 20th century nearly all buildings are made for a practical purpose. Yet, if practicality alone was the goal, no special labor would be necessary and our cities would be teeming with this type of "architecture." The question I

2. アスプルンドによる風景画。スウェーデンならではの水辺の風景は、同国のナショナル・ロマンティシズムの画家が、好んで描いたモティーフである。(インゲマール・アスプルンド氏蔵)

Figure 2: A landscape painting by Asplund. The distinctively Swedish waterfront landscape was a favorite motif of the era's National Romantic painters. (From Ingemar Asplund's private collection.)

でなにを表現したいのだろうか？

　エーリック・グンナール・アスプルンドは、1885年9月22日、北欧スウェーデンの首都ストックホルムに生まれた。翌年生まれのミースや、翌々年に生まれたコルビュジエと同世代ということになる。父親は税務署に勤める役人であったというから、まずまずの中産階級の出である。少年時代から絵を描くことに強い興味を示し、ノッラ・ラテン高校に進んだころには、真剣に画家を志すようになっていた(図1-2)。しかし、少年の夢は周囲の大人たちによって儚く消えていく。父親は息子の将来を案じて反対した。さらに高校の美術教師はこう忠告したという。「才能に恵まれていて、いともたやすく美しい絵が描ける者は画家になる。なかなか才能があって、けっこう上手に描ける者は彫刻家になる。ただ少し絵が好きだ、という程度の者は建築家になる。アスプルンドは建築家になるといい」。

　1905年にアスプルンドは、ストックホルムの王立工科大学に入学し、建築の勉強を始めた。学生時代に最初に出会うのは、ナショナル・ロマンティシズムである。産業革命以降、急速に近代化する社会を背景に、自国のアイデンティティーを追求した文化思潮である。そのなかでスウェーデン人が再発見したものは、ヴァイキングに象徴される英雄的な過去の記憶と、国土を覆う深い森の精神的価値であった。もちろん当時のスウェーデンでも、ほかのヨーロッパ諸国と同様、それまでの様式建築を批判し、変わりゆく社会の現実にふさわしい新しい建築の姿を模索していた。つまり一般に近代建築運動と呼ばれるその動向は、当時の北欧諸国の主導的な建築家の間では、位相も方向性も異なるナショナル・ロマンティシズムという思潮と一体化していたわけである(図3-4)。民族的なアイデンティティーの延長上に、近代的な建築のあるべき姿を追求していたといってもいいだろう。

　アスプルンドが入学した当時の工科大学は、このナショナル・ロマンティシズム派の建築家であるE.ラーレルステッドやL.I.ヴァールマンが指導し、リベラルな雰囲気のなかにあった。アスプルンドは特にヴァールマンを個人的に慕っていたようで、在学中に彼から住宅の仕事をふたつ任されている。当然ヴァールマンの指導を受けながらの設計であっただろうが、アスプルンドにとっては初めての実施作品となった。基本的には伝統的な民家の形式を踏襲した習作ではあるが、安定したプロポーションやシンメトリーの構成をあえて崩した造形手法に、早くもアスプルンドらしさの芽生えが確認できる。

　当時のスウェーデンの建築教育は、工科大学での4年間の後、さらに王立芸術大学における3年間の課程が用意

3. C.ヴェストマン設計の「ストックホルム医師会館」。1906年竣工。国産レンガを用い地域主義に立脚しながら、新時代の現実に応えたナショナル・ロマンティシズムの代表作。

Figure 3: Carl Westman's design for the Medical Society in Stockholm. Construction was completed in 1906. Though the use of domestically produced brick gives the work a regional character, it is a National Romantic work that reflects the reality of a new era.

am asking has to do with the need for a mindset that is not satisfied with practicality alone and passionately believes in the creation of architecture. What is a person like this trying to express through their work?

Erik Gunnar Asplund was born on September 22, 1885 in the Swedish capital of Stockholm. This makes him part of the same generation as Mies, who was born the following year, and Le Corbusier, who was born the year after that. His father was a civil servant employed at the tax office and Asplund was raised in a respectable middle-class environment. As a youth, he had a strong interest in drawing pictures, and by the time he entered Norra Latin High School, he was serious about pursuing a career as an artist. (Figure 1-2.) But his youthful dreams were shattered prematurely by the adults around him. Anxious about his son's future, Asplund's father opposed the idea. His high school art teacher also admonished him, saying: "Those who are blessed with a special gift and can easily draw beautiful pictures become artists. Those with some talent who can draw rather well becomes sculptors. But those who merely have an interest in pictures become architects. Asplund, I think you'd make a good architect."

In 1905, Asplund entered the Royal Institute of Technology in Stockholm and began studying architecture. His first important encounter as a student was with National Romanticism. This cultural trend favored the expression of national identity as a response to the rapid social modernization that followed the Industrial Revolution. In this context, the Swedish people rediscovered the heroic memories of the past as symbolized by the Vikings and came to appreciate the spiritual heritage of the thick forests that covered their nation. Of course, at the time, in Sweden, as in many other European countries, criticism was being leveled at stylized architecture and a search for a new form that was realistically suited to a changing society was underway. In other words, among the leading Scandinavian architects of the day, what was commonly known as the modern architecture movement became associated with National Romanticism, although the latter differed widely in stance and direction. (Figure 3-4.) In a sense, the pursuit of an ideal form of modern architecture was thought to be an extension of ethnic identity.

At the time Asplund entered the institute, National Romantic architects like Erik Lallerstedt and Lars Israel Wahlman were teaching there and a liberal atmosphere pervaded. Asplund was particularly well-liked by Wahlman, who entrusted him with two residential designs during his time as a student. Though it is easy to imagine that Wahlman provided guidance regarding the designs, these were in effect Asplund's first works. Fundamentally, these studies adhered to the traditional house form, but in terms of creative approach, Asplund dared to disrupt stable elements like proportion and symmetry, an early indication of the budding Asplund style.

In Swedish architectural education of the day, it was suggested that four years at a technical university be

4. R.エストベリ設計の「ストックホルム市庁舎」。1904年に設計が開始されたスウェーデンのナショナル・ロマンティシズムを代表する建築。

Figure 4: Ragnar Östberg's design for Stockholm City Hall. The design was began in 1904 on the building which is a prime example of Sweden's National Romanticism.

されており、建築家を志す者はそこに進学するのが一般的であった。工科大学では専門科目以外にも工学系の科目が幅広く課せられ、高度なデザイン教育は芸術大学で行われるという図式である。ところが当時の芸術大学は、依然としてボザール流の保守的な教育を固持していた。建築界における新旧両陣営の対立が、両大学の間で建築教育の矛盾となって表れていたのである。1909年に工科大学を卒業したアスプルンドは、ヴァールマンの事務所で1年間働いた後、1910年秋に芸術大学に入学した。それは、まさに学生たちの不満が頂点に達していた時期であった。ほどなく仲間と共に彼は芸術大学を退学し、S.レヴェレンツ、O.アルムクヴィスト、E.カールストランド、J.エストリン、M.ヴェルンステッドと共に、6人の学生による私設学校「クララ・スクール」を設立する。学生たちの要請に応えて集まった教師は、R.エストベリ、C.ヴェストマン、I.テングボム、C.ベリステンという、同国の第一線級の建築家たちであった。学生が取り組んだ設計課題作品が、当時の『Arkitektur（アーキテクトゥール）』誌に掲載されている。地方都市における集合住宅という現実的な問題に、彼らが真剣に向き合ったことを伝える貴重な記録である。「クララ・スクール」の活動は、約7カ月間で幕を閉じた。芸術大学への反抗から出発した彼らの活動は短期間のうちに終わったが、スウェーデンでナショナル・ロマンティシズムを担った建築家たちが、その理念を求心力のある運動へと十分に組織化できなかったことを思えば、若者たちのささやかな試みの歴史的意義は称賛に値しよう。

　アスプルンドは「クララ・スクール」の時期に、大御所I.G.クラーソンの事務所でも仕事を経験した。担当したのは「アデルスネース城」というマナーハウスであるが、森の木立の間から遠くの景色を眺められるように建物の軸線を振っている。アスプルンドが、一生をかけて追求することになった平面計画の手法を、ここで学んだ痕跡と見ることができる。

●──設計活動の開始とイタリア旅行

　1909年にアスプルンドはふたつの設計コンペに応募しているが、ひとつが選外佳作に選ばれたにすぎなかった。ところが、1912年に「カルマルの小学校」のコンペで2等となり、賞金1000クローナを獲得したのを皮切りに、同年の「大工組合」では応募案の買い上げ賞（500クローナ）、同じく1912年の「カールスハムンの中学校」では1等、翌1913年には「イェーテボリ裁判所増築」で1等、同年の「ヘデムーラ共学学校」で1等（実現せず）と、2年間に応募した5つのコンペすべてに入賞したのである。圧倒的な入賞実績で、建築家としての基盤を築いたわけだ。これらの賞金を手に、彼は1913年12月から南欧へと旅立った。途中で立ち寄ったパリには興味を示していない。だが、イタリアに入ると、

supplemented with a three-year course at the Royal University of Fine Arts, and most people who were serious about going into the profession went on to this level. Along with a specialized subject, a wide range of engineering courses were required at a technical university. The idea was that students would follow this with an advanced art education at an art college. In fact, art colleges at the time persisted with the same conservative, Beaux-Arts curriculum they had been offering for years. It is evident from the contradictory education offered at the two universities Asplund attended that a conflict was brewing between the old and new schools of architecture.

Asplund, who had graduated from technical university in 1909, entered art college in the fall of 1910, after a year of work in Wahlman's office. Dissatisfaction among the students was at a peak, and not long after, Asplund and some of his friends quit the university. Along with Sigurd Lewerentz, Osvald Almqvist, Erik Karlstrand, Josef Östlihn and Melchior Wernstedt, Asplund established the private Klara School. In response to the students' urgings, teachers like Ragnar Östberg, Carl Westman, Ivar Tengbom, Carl Bergsten, some of Sweden's leading architects, agreed to take part in the project. The design work that the students did was published in *Arkitektur*. The magazine is an important record of how the students earnestly tried to address realistic problems such as building housing complexes in regional cities.

After a period of about seven months, Klara School closed its doors. Although the activities of these students, who had begun simply by rebelling against the art college, had proven to be very short-lived, when one considers that even the architects who were behind Sweden's National Romanticism were unable to sufficiently organize their philosophy into a cohesive movement, it is hard not to admire the significance of the younger men's modest attempt.

While he was involved with Klara School, Asplund also had the opportunity to work in the office of the prominent architect, I.G. Clason. He was put in charge of a manor house called Adelsnäs Manor. The axis line of the building was staggered to allow a view of a distant landscape from within a grove of trees. In this, one finds a hint of the type of floor plan Asplund favored for the rest of his life.

Architectural Beginnings and A Trip to Italy

In 1909, Asplund submitted proposals to two design competitions, one of which received nothing more than an honorable mention. In a 1912 competition for Kalmar School, however, he was awarded second prize and 1,000 kronor. This encouraging start was followed by a purchase prize (500 kronor) for his submission to the Carpenters' Union and a first-prize award for Karlshamn Secondary School, both in the same year. In the following year, 1913,

彼のスケッチブックは感激の言葉で埋めつくされていった(図5-6)。ローマ、パレルモ、ナポリ、シラクーサ、タオルミナ、ポンペイ、アッシジ、ボローニャ、ラヴェンナ、ヴェネツィア、フィレンツェ、そしてチュニス……。当時としては、長いとはいえない約半年間の見学旅行で味わった歓びが、生涯にわたり発想の源となっていった(図7-8)。

　1914年5月に帰国したアスプルンドは、その年の9月に告知された「ストックホルム南墓地設計コンペ」に応募することにした。その年にマルメで開催された「バルティック博覧会」では、スウェーデン火葬協会の展示場で、S.レヴェレンツ(1885-1975)とT.ステュベリウス(1883-1963)が、火葬場の計画案を共同で出品していた。それを知ったアスプルンドは、コンペの応募にあたり、このテーマについて一日の長がある、「クララ・スクール」での同級生レヴェレンツに共同を申し入れたのである。新しい墓地のコンペは、ナショナル・ロマンティシズムの時代背景を反映して、敷地を覆う「森」が焦点となっていた。彼らの応募案は敷地の森林には手をつけず、圧倒的な自然の優位を認めて、そこにひっそりと建築をとけ込ませたのが特徴であった(図9-10)。ナイーヴな精神性から生まれた、静かだが鮮烈なコンセプトである。53を数える応募案のなかから、彼らの作品が高い評価を受けて1等を獲得した。ふたりの衝撃的なデビューである。

　この「森の墓地」に彼らが取り組み始めて間もなく、ナショナル・ロマンティシズムの時代はそっと幕を閉じた。それでも手が届かない過去や遠い異国にあこがれるロマンティシズムは、アスプルンドの生き方の特徴となっていく。たとえば「スカンディア・シネマ」(1923)では、若き日のイタリアへの旅で体験した、星空の下でのカーニバルの思い出を再現したものだという。なかなかロマンティックな男であったことはまちがいないようだ。

●──北欧における近代建築の受容とアスプルンドの役割

　「森の墓地」の受賞以来、アスプルンドの影響力は次第に強くなっていく。「森の墓地」のなかの「森の礼拝堂」(1920)や「ストックホルム市立図書館」(1928)などの作品により、スウェーデンのみならず北欧建築界全体のリーダー的な存在になっていった。この時期に、まだ無名だったA.アールト(1898-1976)がアスプルンド事務所に弟子入りを希望した(空席がないため断られた)のには、こうした背景があったのである。

　1920年代に入ると、北欧諸国の建築界の主流はクラシシズムに移った。一般に、北欧新古典主義と呼ばれる動向である。すでに近代建築運動が始まった後でのクラシシズムへの回帰は、時代の流れに逆行したのではなく、アール・デコをはじめとする大陸諸国の新しい動向を意識した結果であろう。北欧諸国にとっては、ナショナル・ロマンティ

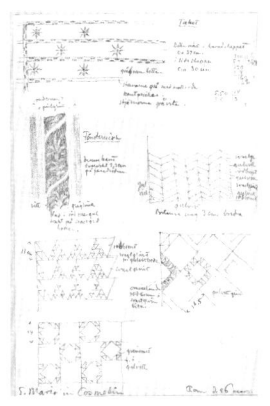

5. アスプルンドの旅のスケッチブックより。ローマで天井や床の仕上げを克明にメモしたもの。のちの「森の火葬場」小礼拝堂待合室の床に、類似の仕上げが見られる。

Figure 5: A page from Asplund's travel sketchbook. In Rome, he made meticulous memos on ceiling and floor finishes. The floor he later created for the waiting room in the Chapel of Faith (at Woodland Crematorium) is very similar in appearance.

6. スパゲッティ！　アスプルンドの旅のスケッチブックより。スパゲッティを勢いよく食べる人物。イタリア旅行の楽しい日々が想像できる。

Figure 6: Spaghetti! Another page from Asplund's travel sketchbook. This drawing of someone energetically eating spaghetti suggests how much Asplund enjoyed himself in Italy.

Asplund won first prize for his Göteborg Law Court expansion and Hedemora Coeducational School (unrealized) designs. Of the five competitions he entered during this two-year period, he won prizes for all of them. With this formidable showing, Asplund was able to establish a foundation for himself as an architect.

Prize money in hand, Asplund decided to travel to southern Europe in December 1913. He wasn't particularly intrigued by Paris, where he stopped off briefly, but once he got to Italy, he added some emotional and inspired notes to his sketchbook. (Figure 5-6.) He saw Rome, Palermo, Naples, Syracuse, Taormina, Pompeii, Assisi, Bologna, Ravenna, Venice, Florence, and Tunis. For the period, Asplund's approximately six-month sightseeing tour wasn't especially long, but the pleasures he found there would serve as a source of inspiration throughout his life. (Figure 7-8.)

In May 1914, he returned to Sweden, and that September, submitted a proposal for the Stockholm South Cemetery Design Competition. At the Sweden Cremation Society display at the Baltic Exhibition (held in Malmö the same year), Sigurd Lewerentz and Torsten Stubelius had shown some collaborative designs for crematoriums. With this in mind, Asplund approached Lewerentz, who he had studied with at Klara School and who was more knowledgeable on the subject, about collaborating for the competition. The main focus of the new cemetery competition, a reflection of the still popular National Romantic movement, was the "forest" that covered the building site. What made Asplund and Lewerentz's proposal so distinctive was their plan to leave the trees on the lot untouched, recognize the overwhelming superiority of nature and quietly slip a building inside. (Figure 9-10.) It was a subdued yet spectacular concept that emerged from their naive sense of spirituality. Of the 53 proposals that were submitted, their plan received great acclaim and was awarded first prize. This marked their startling debut.

Shortly after starting work on the "Woodland Cemetery," the National Romantic era came to a close. Despite this, romanticism, an ethos that favored the unreachable past and distant, foreign lands, remained a unique part of Asplund's way of life. There was, for example, the reproduction based on his memories of the carnival he'd seen under the night sky in Italy which he created for Skandia Cinema (1923). And by all accounts, Asplund was quite a romantic.

The Breakthrough of Modern Architecture in Scandinavia and Asplund's Part in It

After winning the Woodland Cemetery competition, Asplund's influence gradually grew. With works such as Woodland Chapel (1920) and Stockholm City Library (1928), he became a leading presence not only in Sweden but in the wider world of Scandinavian architecture. This explains why the as-yet-unknown Alvar Aalto (1898-1976) attempted to join Asplund's office as an apprentice (he was turned down because there weren't any openings).

Figure 7: A page from Asplund's travel sketchbook. This humorous depiction of a facelike facade was an idea for the elevation surface of Villa Snellman.

Figure 8: The Temple of Juno in Agrigento from Asplund's travel sketchbook. In sketching designs for Woodland Crematorium, Asplund first envisioned an ancient temple along the road.

シズムの地域主義的な発想から抜け出し、クラシシズムという全ヨーロッパ的な文化へ再接近することを意味していた。また、木やれんがなどの素材感や民族の歴史を象徴するイコンに頼る表現から、平滑な壁面によるヴォリュームの構成へと表現の力点が変化したという意味でも、より近代性をめざす移行であったはずである。スウェーデンにおけるこの時期のクラシシズムの特徴は、建築家I.テングボム（1878-1968）の作品に端的に表現されている。添えられたオーダーは本来のプロポーションを逸脱し、建物全体に過剰なまでに優美で繊細な形態を生み出す操作がされている。"スウェディッシュ・グレース"と称賛されたその造形感覚は、クラシシズムのモティーフを便宜的に用いながらも、明らかに近代を指向していた。

　ところが話は複雑になるのだが、アスプルンドのクラシシズムはそうした感覚とも違っていた。「森の礼拝堂」や「リステール州裁判所」などの1910年代末から20年代前半のクラシシズム作品を見ると、ナショナル・ロマンティシズムで身につけた地域主義的な感覚がまだどこかに残り、軽快でユーモラスな味つけによってその泥臭さが脱臭されている。建築の原初の段階までさかのぼって理想形を模索するような、本来の意味でのクラシシズムの発想に近いといえよう。たとえば「森の礼拝堂」は、"プリミティヴ・ハット"のような建築の"原型"をめざした感があるし、「スカンディア・シネマ」は古典の世界そのものへのオマージュとなっている。ところが20年代であっても、より都市的な環境に建てられた「カール・ヨーハン学校」や「ストックホルム市立図書館」の場合は、使われている建築言語はたしかにクラシシズムのものだが、造形上の"見せ場"だと本人が考えるポイントで、アスプルンドは近代を指向する造形を示している。大陸の動向が彼の価値観に無意識に作用したのだろうが、テングボムのように美しい造形そのものを目的とすることには一生無縁であった。新しい様式を追い求めることにも、関心がなかったようだ。あらゆる造形は、彼が表現したい"内容"を表現する手段だったのである。

　1920年代後半にドイツで成立した近代建築は、いうまでもなく北欧の建築界にも大きな刺激を与えた。大陸の動向にただちに追随した建築家も存在したが、北欧建築界が本格的にモダニズムの時代に突入するには、アスプルンドを待たねばならなかった。スウェーデン工芸協会の会長だったG.パウルション（1889-1977）は、1930年開催の「ストックホルム博覧会」のプロデューサーを務めるにあたり、1925年のパリにおけるアール・デコ博や1927年のヴァイセンホフ・ジードルンクに続くストックホルム博覧会を、近代建築が北の地に開花したことを世界に知らしめる一大デモンスト

9. コンペ案に描かれていた「十字架の道」。
Figure 9: Asplund and Lewerentz's proposal for Holy Cross Road.

By the 1920s, the main trend in Scandinavian architecture had become classicism. This movement is commonly known as Scandinavian Classicism. The return to classicism, even after the modernist architecture movement had begun, wasn't a regression to some earlier era, but rather the result of a new awareness of movements like Art Deco in continental Europe. To the Scandinavians, the shift was significant because they had broken free of the regional concepts of National Romanticism and reconnected with the pan-European culture of classicism. In addition, the transition from a reliance on the materiality of wood and brick, and icons symbolizing ethnic history to an emphasis on volume through the use of smooth, flat walls alone indicated a shift toward something more modern.

The main characteristics of Swedish classicism during this period can be found in an extreme form in the work of Ivar Tengbom (1878-1968). Unmatched column orders are made to deviate from their original proportions and the entire building is manipulated to create an overly graceful and delicate form. This creative notion, acclaimed as "Swedish grace," made the best use of classical motifs while clearly aiming for a modern design.

Though the reasons are a bit complicated, Asplund's classicism was based on a different concept. In Asplund's works made between the late 1910s and the early 1920s, such as Woodland Chapel and Lister County Courthouse, there are still remnants of the regional mindset of National Romanticism, but his use of light and humorous touches provide the buildings with a touch of sophistication. One might view this as an exploration of the original concept of classicism, or Asplund's attempt to return to the primordial stage of architecture and find an ideal form. There is an element of this in Woodland Chapel, where Asplund seems to have been searching for the archetype of architecture or a "primitive hut," and also in Skandia Cinema, which was an outright homage to the classical world. Although he was working in the 1920s, buildings like Carl Johan School and the Stockholm City Library make use of an architectural language that is clearly classical. But in terms of what Asplund himself saw as the "focus" of the works, his orientation was clearly modern. Continental European trends had exerted an unconscious influence on his values, but striving like Tengbom to create beautiful work was something that remained alien to Asplund until the end of his life. Neither does he seem to have been interested in the pursuit of new styles. Every creation was a means of expressing his desired "content."

Modern German architecture of the late 1920s, needless to say, exerted a huge influence on Scandinavian architecture. Some architects immediately followed continental trends, but Scandinavian architecture wouldn't have entered a full-fledged era of modernism unless Asplund had first led the way.

10. アスプルンドとレヴェレンツによる「ストックホルム南墓地コンペ」の応募案。森林をそのまま残し、道や建物をひかえめに表現した。

Figure 10: Asplund and Lewerentz's proposal for the Stockholm South Cemetery Competition. The plan was distinguished by their modest design for the road and building and the idea to leave the forest intact.

レーションにしようと計画した。彼は迷わずアスプルンドを主任建築家に指名する。その下で協力した建築家は、U.オレーン(1897-1977)、S.マルケリウス(1889-1972)、S.レヴェレンツ、O.アルムクヴィスト(1884-1950)、W.ガーン(1890-1985)、E.スンダール(1897-1974)らであった。

　パウルションは、大陸の実態を視察するためにアスプルンドを連れ出した。ふたりはブルノとシュトゥトゥガルトの博覧会を訪れ、J.ホフマンやS.ギーディオンに面会した。本人は海外に出ていて不在だったが、パリのコルビュジエも訪ねている。帰国したアスプルンドは、確信をもって新時代の表現の可能性を謳い上げた。ストックホルムのユールゴーデン湾の両岸に建ち並んだ目新しい形の建築と斬新な広告塔、風になびく無数の旗、空に浮かぶ飛行船、水上を行き交うボート、新し物好きの観客のすべては、「真昼の花火」と呼ばれた衝撃的で華やかな夏を歴史に刻んだのである(図11-12)。

　残された写真が証言するのは、アスプルンドが初めて挑戦するこの新しい造形言語の性質をすでにだれよりも理解し、たちまち自在に使いこなせた事実である(図13-14)。G.パウルションが自らの野心を実現するために、必要としたのはこの才能だった(図15)。だが、初めからアスプルンドの関心は、造形よりもこの新しい建築空間が表現できる"内容"に向いていたようだ。

　彼は生涯を通して作品をつくることに専念したので、自身の建築理念をまとまった形で書き残すことには興味がなかった。したがって、翌1931年に王立工科大学の教授に就任した際の記念講演は貴重である。その記録によると、新しい建築の性質が"空間の解体と変化"という以前にはなかった建築理念を生む、と主張するのだが、そのとき彼が念頭においていたのは、なんと日本建築だというのである。軽快な壁を必要に応じて動かして設えを変えること、内部と外部の空間が一体化すること、の両者を結びつけて彼が語るとき、"われわれの時代の建築が日本建築に近づく"とアスプルンドは主張したのであった(図16)。彼は新しい建築表現を単なる造形手法としてとらえるのではなく、空間の性質として理解し、それがおよぼす人間の行為にまで思考を進めていたのはまちがいない。

　しかし当時の人々は、「ストックホルム博覧会」を近代建築の偉大な躍進として、必ずしも歓迎したわけではなかった。会期中からさまざまな批判が容赦なく浴びせられたが、C.マルムステーン、R.エストベリ、C.ベリステン、C.ミレスらのように、アスプルンドが尊敬する建築家や芸術家からの厳しい評価は、特につらいものだったにちがいない。とはい

11. ストックホルム博覧会のスケッチ・パース。アスプルンド画と思われる。
Figure 11: A sketch for a pass to the Stockholm Exhibition. The picture is thought to be Asplund's work.

Gregor Paulsson (1889-1977), the head of the Swedish Arts and Crafts Association, served as the organizer of the 1930 Stockholm Exhibition. He saw the event as a successor to the 1925 Art Deco Expo in Paris and the 1927 Weissenhofsiedlung, and planned a huge demonstration to inform the world that modern architecture was flourishing in the North. Paulsson had no doubt that Asplund should serve as the principal architect of the event. Other architects who took part in the exhibition included Uno Åhrén (1897-1977), Sven Markelius (1889-1972), Lewerentz (1885-1975), O. Almvist (1884-1950), Wolter Gahn (1890-1985) and Eskil Sundahl (1870-1974).

Paulsson invited Asplund along to find out what was happening on the Continent. The two of them saw the expos in Brno and Stuttgart, and met with Josef Hoffmann and Sigfried Giedion. And although the man himself was away, they also tried to visit Le Corbusier in Paris. On his return to Sweden, Asplund spoke with confidence about the expressive possibilities of the new era. Held on either shore of Stockholm's Djurgården Bay, the exhibition included groundbreaking buildings and innovative advertising towers, countless flags flapping in the breeze, airships floating through the sky, boats going back and forth across the water, and countless visitors in search of the new. All of these became a part of history during that impressive and glitzy event known as "Fireworks at Noon." (Figure 11-12.)

Photographs prove that Asplund understood the essence of the new creative language, which he used here for the first time, better than anyone, and that he had came to have a full command of it almost instantly. (Figure 13-14.) To realize Paulsson's own ambition, this talent was necessary. (Figure 15.) But from the outset, Asplund's interest seems to have been less in the work than the "content" that could be expressed with the new architecture.

Throughout his life, Asplund dedicated himself to making architecture, but had no interest in leaving a written record of his creative philosophy in any concrete form. This is why the commemorative lecture he delivered the next year, 1931, while serving as a professor at the Royal Institute of Technology is such a valuable document. According to the record, Asplund asserted that the nature of the new architecture had given birth to a previously unknown architectural ethos which "dismantled and altered space." At the time, he was preoccupied with Japanese architecture - of all things. Asplund cited the ability to move and alter light walls according to one's needs and related this to the unification of interior and exterior spaces, maintaining that "architecture in our time is becoming more like Japanese architecture." (Figure 16.) Asplund wasn't merely trying to capture a creative method as a new architectural expression; he had clearly come to understand the essence of space and consider how it might affect people's activities.

12. ストックホルム博覧会の広告塔。アスプルンド設計。斬新なロゴのデザインは、ロシア構成主義を意識したものだろう。

Figure 12: An Asplund-designed ad tower at the Stockholm Exhibition. The innovative logo design was probably inspired by Russian Constructivism.

え、翌1931年にパウルションを筆頭に、いわば近代派のアスプルンド、マルケリウス、ガーン、スンダール、オレーンの6人が共著で『Acceptera（受け入れよ）』という本を出版したのは、彼らが主張する新しい考え方が、好むと好まざるとにかかわらず、新時代の現実となることを確信していたことを証明している。この本における個々の役割分担を正確に知ることは困難であるが、よくいわれるようにアスプルンドの関与を限定的だとみなすのは、彼がモダニストではなかったとする偏見に基づくものであろう。

批判した側の顔ぶれを見れば、それが建築や工芸をめぐる新旧両陣営の対立という図式であったことは想像がつくが、問題は双方の論点が初めからずれていたことにあった。近代建築は、北欧ではなにより"機能主義（Funktionalism）"として（彼らはフンキス"funkis"という愛称で呼んだ）導入されたのであり、それは字義通りには「形態を機能から導き出す態度」を意味する。だが、いうまでもなくこの論理には矛盾が含まれる。"機能"が限定されたとしても、そこには形態をひとつに決定する根拠が含まれていないから、最終的に形態は設計者の恣意的な意図により決められるからである。つまり機能主義者がある傾向の造形を好んで採用するとき、そこから排除された歴史的な要素に魅力を感じる立場から批判が出たのは当然のことであろう。紙数の関係で結論を急げば、アスプルンドが機能主義者であったことは、実は一度もなかったはずである。

● ── アスプルンドの設計手法とモダニズム

1930年代後半に、アスプルンドが典型的な近代建築の造形を採用しなくなったのは、彼がモダニズムとは距離をおいたからだろうか？　あるいはストックホルム博覧会の時期だけ、G.パウルションにそそのかされて機能主義者と行動を共にしたが、そもそも彼は伝統主義者なのだろうか？　作風が一貫していないことから判断して、あらゆる様式を等価と見なして自由に取捨選択する価値観が、彼の正体なのだろうか？　アスプルンドを理解する上で最も重要な問題であり、また最も難解な部分であるから、こうしたさまざまな見方がされてきたのも無理はない。ここでは、アスプルンド独自の設計手法を手がかりに考えてみよう。

アスプルンドは設計をするにあたって、まずは古典建築の姿を最初にイメージすることが多かった。エスキースをくり返す間に、最初にイメージした形態から歴史様式に由来する要素が姿を消し近代建築の表現に近づいていくのである。

たとえば晩年の「イェーテボリ裁判所増築」は、その典型的な例のひとつである。17世紀に建てられたN.テッシン

13. ストックホルム博覧会のパラダイス・レストラン外観。アスプルンド設計。大胆なガラス面とピロティーによるデザイン。庇は日本建築を意識したものか。
Figure 13: The Asplund-designed exterior of the Paradise Restaurant at the Stockholm Exhibition. The sweeping design makes use of a large glass area and piling. The eaves may have been inspired by Japanese architecture.

14. パラダイス・レストラン内部。ガラスと吹抜けを用いた開放的な空間構成は、アスプルンド自身が言及したように日本建築を意識した結果であろう。
Figure 14: The interior of the Paradise Restaurant. With a large glass area and a breezeway, the expansive structure seems to be the result of Asplund's admitted interest in Japanese architecture.

Yet at the time, not everyone was willing to accept the tremendous breakthroughs that modern architecture had made at the Stockholm Exhibition. During the event, Asplund was subjected to relentless criticism. It must have been particularly painful for him to be judged so harshly by architects and artists he revered such as Carl Malmsten, Ragnar Östberg, Carl Bergsten, and Carl Milles.

Nevertheless, in 1931, with Paulsson in a leading role, six of the so-called Modernists, including Asplund, Markelius, Gahn, Sundahl, and Åhrén published a book called *Acceptera*. The new ideas they put forward, regardless of whether one liked them or not, proved with conviction that a new era had begun. It is difficult to know exactly what part of the book each individual was responsible for, but the reason Asplund's involvement seems to have been limited is probably connected to the prejudice that he was not a modernist.

One might imagine that Asplund's critics would be evenly split between the old and the new camps in architecture and arts and crafts, but the real problem lay in the fact that the contentions of both sides were off the mark from the very start. More than anything, modern architecture introduced "funktionalism" (or "funkis" for short) to Scandinavia. The word literally meant a "stance that derives form from function." Needless to say, this logic contained a contradiction. Even when "function" was limited, because there weren't any grounds for settling on a particular form, it was ultimately decided by the arbitrary intentions of the designer. In other words, when a functionalist favored or adopted a form related to a certain trend, it was natural that criticism would arise from those who were partial to the historical elements that had been eliminated. Space restrictions prevent me from going any further, but suffice to say, there was never a single point in his career when Asplund could have been called a functionalist.

Design Methods and Modernism

In the late 1930s, did Asplund stop espousing work that was typical of modern architecture because he wanted to distance himself from modernism? Or was he basically a traditionalist who Paulsson had talked into working with functionalists for the Stockholm Exhibition? Judging from the fact that no single style underlies his work and that since Asplund considered every style to be equal, his sense of values was based on will or choice, can we consider this to be his true identity? As this is the most important question and also the most difficult part of Asplund to understand, it's not unreasonable to examine a wide range of views. Let's look first at the clues surrounding Asplund's unique design methods. In designing his work, it was common for Asplund to first envision a form of classical architecture. In making repeated sketches, the elements derived from the historical style of the form that

15. ストックホルム博覧会の工事現場で、同博覧会の副会長J.サックスに説明するアスプルンド。

Figure 15: Asplund shows the vice-president of the Stockholm Exhibition, Josef Sachs, the construction site for the event.

の裁判所を増築するにあたり、彼は初期の段階では既存建物のクラシシズムにならい、それと表現を統一した増築棟を構想した。歴史的建築への増築計画としては、ごく自然な発想である。ところが、その後の設計プロセスは特異な経過をたどった。エスキースのなかで徐々に歴史様式に由来する装飾が削ぎ落とされ、単純な幾何学形態にデフォルメされていく。開口部は壁と面を揃えて納められ、直方体の全体ヴォリュームが強調される。(P.205参照)最終的に生み出された形態は「白い無装飾な箱形」ではなかったものの、現代のわれわれの目から見るとまぎれもない近代建築の表現になっている。それでも既存建物の高さ方向のスケール感は尊重されており、淡いイエローに塗られた壁のスタッコの色もお揃いだし、なによりピラスターで分割されたファサードの、各スパンのなかの窓はすべて既存建物の側に寄り添うように配置されているのである。増築部分のデザインは、"隣のクラシシズムの建築が大好き"だという設計者の感情を伝えている。歴史のなかで役割を果たしてきた建物に敬意を払い、その美しさを損なうことを慎重に避けながら、増築棟には新時代のリアリティにしっかりと応える解決がなされているのだ。もし彼が単なる伝統主義者であり、モダニストでなかったならば、こうした解答を選んだだろうか？ ただ、アスプルンドはあらゆる様式に対し、教条主義的な態度を取らなかっただけなのである。

　近代建築史を書物で学ぶ非ヨーロッパ圏のわれわれは、ともすれば近代建築運動に対して誤解しがちになる。様式建築が否定されたのは、第一にそれが新しい時代の現実に合わなくなったからであって、過去の文化がすべて否定されたわけではない。実際に今でもヨーロッパの都市に行けば、街を形作る建築の大半は様式建築時代のものである。それらを次々に破壊してまで、彼らは近代建築を建てることはしない。過去の文化に対する誇りは当然ある。その上で、近代建築はあくまでも20世紀の現実に即した表現として受け入れられてきた。アスプルンドの設計過程に見られる思考の跡は、彼がこうした意味でのモダニストであったことを証明している。過去の文化を愛し敬意を払うことと、近代建築による現実的な解決を選ぶこととは、本来異なる次元に属することであって、けっして矛盾しないことを彼の建築は証明しているのである。

●——建築家の人生の光と影

　晩年にあたる1936年の講演で、アスプルンドは画家を志していた少年時代を懐かしく振り返っている。すでに建築家として名声を確立した彼が、なぜ今さら昔のかなわなかった夢を人に語る必要があったのか。ここに、彼の創作

16. 1931年の講演で示された日本建築の写真。この軒下と驚くほど類似した空間が、パラダイス・レストランにおいて確認できる。

Figure 16: A photograph of Japanese architecture that Asplund used in a 1931 lecture. The amazing similarity between the space under the eaves in this photograph and those at the Paradise Restaurant is clear.

he had imagined would disappear and Asplund's expression would gradually grow to be more like modern architecture.

   The Göteborg Law Court expansion, which he did in his later years, is a typical example. To expand the court building that Tessin had built in the 17th century, Asplund aimed in the initial stages for the classicism of the preexisting building, and conceived of an addition that would be uniform in expression. As an expansion plan for a historical structure, this was a perfectly natural concept. Yet, the design process that unfolded later follows a singular course. Gradually, the historically derived ornamentation in Asplund's sketches falls away, and the simple geometrical shapes grow deformed. The openings are arranged in walls and plains, and the total volume of the rectangle is emphasized. (See p. 205.) The form that ultimately emerged, though, was not a "white, bare box," but to our contemporary eye, an unmistakable expression of modern architecture. Despite this, the heightwise sense of scale was maintained, the pale yellow of the stucco applied to the exterior wall matched and more than anything, the windows in every span of the facade, divided by pilasters, were positioned as if they were nudging up to the preexisting building. The design of the expansion conveys the idea that the architect "loves the classical building next door." While paying respect to the role architecture has played in history, and carefully preventing its beauty from being spoiled, there is a resolve about the expansion that firmly responds to the reality of a new age. If Asplund was merely a traditionalist and not a modernist, would he have chosen such a solution? It's vital to remember that Asplund never took a dogmatic approach in regard to any type of style.

   Those of us non-Europeans who learn the history of modern architecture from books are apt to have some misunderstandings about the modernist movement. The reason stylized architecture was denied is that, first of all, it didn't fit the reality of the new era; all of the culture that went before, however, was not being negated. In fact, in visiting European cities today, the majority of the buildings that shape a town are examples from a stylized architectural period. Europeans have not tried to build modern structures in order to systematically destroy them. They naturally feel a sense of pride about the culture of the past. And in addition, they have also accepted modern architecture as an absolute reality of the 20th century. The traces of thought that we find in Asplund's design process prove that he too was a modernist in this sense. Being able to love and pay respect to a culture from the past while choosing a realistic solution using modern architecture proves that, though these things may have originally existed in entirely different dimensions, there is by no means any contradiction in Asplund's architecture.

の秘密を読み解く重要な鍵があるように思う。生涯を通して設計が続けられた「森の墓地」の設計過程に重ねてみよう。
　「森の墓地」はレヴェレンツとの共同作業によって、ゆっくりと時間をかけて進められた。その主要部分である「森の火葬場」の周辺は、1930年ごろからアスプルンドの手によって具体的にスタディーされ始めた。注目すべきは、墓地のエントランス付近に計画された1本のオベリスク(記念柱)である(図17)。1932年のスケッチでは、そこに添える銘板の文字が検討されている。「今日は私、明日はあなた」。建築家の意図は、衝撃的な言葉でストレートに表現されている。「今日は私が逝った。明日はあなたの番である」。暗い森の墓地を訪れる生者に向けられた、死者からの容赦ない言葉。自らの死と対峙することを迫る言葉には、逃げ場が用意されていない。だれもが日常生活のなかでは目をそむけているが、絶対に避けることができない自然の摂理を、眼前にただ突きつけるのである。
　すでに彼は、1920年ごろに設計した「森の礼拝堂」の門にこう記していた。「今日はあなた、明日は私」(図18)。ちょうどこのころである1920年5月に、アスプルンド夫妻は最初に授かった息子ウッレを幼くして病気で亡くしている。アスプルンドが34歳のときであった。"今日はあなたが逝ってしまった。明日は私の番である"。息子の死との、時期的な前後関係はわからない。ただ、この言葉こそ、アスプルンドが作品に込めようとしたテーマだったのではないか。"人間として生まれてきた以上、死から逃れることはできないのだ"と。時を経た1932年のスケッチで、再びこの言葉がくり返された事実がそう確信させる。「今日は私、明日はあなた」。47歳になったアスプルンドは、もはや自分の順番が近づいたことを意識し始めていた。死に対する過敏なまでのこの感受性は、わが子との間に突然起った悲しい別離がきっかけではなかったか。愛する妻は、その出来事が発端となって精神のバランスを崩し、本来の明るさを取り戻すことがなかったという。やがて彼らの夫婦関係にも、修復できない破綻が訪れた。罪のない幸せな家族を突然襲った暗い死の影。さらに、生涯にわたって与えられた墓地という仕事。彼が「森の墓地」に取り組むにあたって「生と死」というテーマを抱き、建築家としての人生のすべての時間を要したこの設計を通して、思考を研ぎ澄ませていったことは想像に難くない。
　いったい、建築で人生が表現できるものだろうか。文学や絵画や映画ならともかく、建築という芸術形式で表現するには、「生と死」はあまりにも不向きな、無謀なテーマではなかったのか。いや、この難しい課題に挑戦することが、画家になれなかった建築家の夢であり意地であったにちがいない。建築家は与えられた仕事によって育てられる。

17. 1938年10月7日の日付が入ったオベリスクのスケッチ。銘板の文字は、「今日は私、明日はあなた」。

Figure 17: An obelisk sketch dated October 7, 1938. The words on the plaque read: "Today it is me, tomorrow it will be you."

The Life of an Architect: Shadows and Light

Toward the end of his life, in a 1936 lecture, Asplund looked back nostalgically at his youth to the time when he had his sights set on being a painter. Having already achieved renown as an architect, was it necessary for him to talk at this point about unfulfilled dreams of the past? In this, I believe, we find one of the important keys to understanding Asplund's creativity. Let's look at the design process for Woodland Cemetery and how it pertains to Asplund's life.

Woodland Cemetery, a collaborative work with Lewerentz, was carried out at a leisurely pace. Beginning in about 1930, Asplund made concrete studies for the main part of the project, Woodland Crematorium. One detail that should be given special attention is the obelisk that was planned near the entrance to the cemetery. (Figure 17.) In a 1932 sketch, a plaque appears in the design which reads: "Today it is me, tomorrow it will be you." The architect's intention is expressed with powerful words in a straightforward way. "Today I left, but tomorrow it'll be your turn." These unapologetic words of the dead are meant for the living visitors to this dark cemetery in the forest. These words, which force us to confront our own death, leave us with no place to turn. All of us attempt to forget death in our daily life. But here this law of nature, which it is absolutely impossible to avoid, is being leveled at us directly.

Asplund had already left these words on the gate to Woodland Chapel, a 1920 design: "Today it is you, tomorrow it will be me." (Figure 18.) At around this time, in May 1920, Asplund's first son, Olle, fell ill and died at a young age. Asplund was 34. "Today you went on. Tomorrow it will be my turn." We don't know exactly what was happening in Asplund's life at the time of his son's death; only that these words were related to the theme Asplund was attempting to include in his work: "Once you are born as a human being, there is no escape from death." We can also confirm the fact that these words made a reappearance in a later sketch in 1932. "Today it is me, tomorrow it will be you." Having turned 47, Asplund began to be aware that his turn too was approaching. Perhaps the painful and sudden loss of his child inspired this overly sensitive attitude toward death. As a result of this event, Asplund's beloved wife became mentally unstable, and was unable to regain her cheerful temperament. Gradually, an irreparable break in the couple's marriage occurred. An innocent, happy family had suddenly been shrouded in the dark shadow of death. Moreover, Asplund had also been hired to create a cemetery. In taking on the Woodland Cemetery project, Asplund embraced the theme of "life and death," and by devoting all of his time to the design, it is easy to imagine that he emerged with heightened sensibilities.

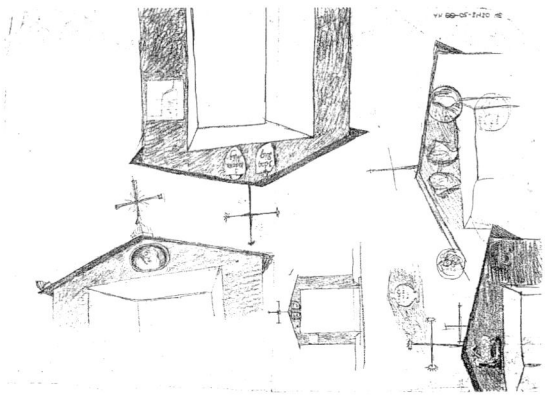

18. 1920年前後に描かれたと思われる「森の礼拝堂」の門のスケッチ。銘板の文字は、「今日はあなた、明日は私」。

Figure 18: A sketch for the gate to Woodland Chapel that was probably drawn around 1920. The words on the plaque read: "Today it is you, tomorrow it will be me."

不動の精神を備えた人間が作品を生み出すのではない。作品をつくる行為のなかで、悩み熟考し試行錯誤をくり返すプロセスを通して、建築家は建築家になっていく。墓地という仕事が生涯与えられて、アスプルンドは自らが志す意味での建築家になっていった。

残された膨大な量のスケッチは、この意図を言葉ではなく、建築で表現することに挑戦した建築家の苦悩と執念を伝えている。このころ墓地の委員会は、この仕事をアスプルンドひとりに依頼することを決定した。レヴェレンツの仕事のやり方に発注者側から批判があったのは事実である。だが、委員会の提案を受け入れたアスプルンドにとって、内面に深まる思考と確信をもつに至ったテーマの実現のためには、もはや他の建築家が入り込む余地がないと判断したのだろう。

あのオベリスクと共に丘の上の火葬場と礼拝堂のスタディーが開始された(図19)。アスプルンドは丘を昇る1本の道の正面に、いつもの彼らしく古代神殿風の建築を最初に描いている。徹底した試行錯誤がくり返されるなかで何通りものプランが練られ、何通りものデザインが検討された(図20-21)。神殿につけられていた装飾は削ぎ落とされ、形態が徐々にシンプルになっていく。オベリスクは丘の中腹に移され、やがて姿を消した。それと同時に、建物は道の正面から引き下げられ、ついには道からほとんど見えない位置に隠された。建築家は自らの建築を隠すことによって、背後の森へ向かってまっすぐに延びる道を生み出したのである。「森の火葬場」のコンセプトが完成した瞬間である。

命あるものはすべて、いつかは森の向こうに還っていかねばならない運命だ。火葬場に向かう道は、無意識のうちに自分の運命を直感的に悟らせる道である。この道を歩いて行く時間は、亡くなったばかりの親しい人の死、そしてやがて迎える自分自身の死を受容していく過程でもある。建築家は、あの強烈な言葉の助けを借りずとも、空間体験という建築本来の手法によってそれを表現したのである。彼は十字架はもはや不要であると考えた。むしろ、あるべきではなかった。最終的には、墓地の委員会が強く要求したようである(図22)。アスプルンドは、人がそこからやってきて、そこへ還っていく"母なる森"にすべてをゆだねることで、自らの運命を告げられた人々の救済さえ意図したのであろう。

アスプルンドは超越的な自然の優位を疑いもしなかったが、最後まで建築の力でできることを追求し続けた。大礼拝堂は故人の尊厳を守り、参列者の注意がピンポイントで柩に集中するように、さまざまな建築的な配慮がなされて

19.「十字架の道」のスケッチ。オベリスクは当初、墓地のエントランスの近くに建てることも検討された。

Figure 19: A sketch for Holy Cross Road. At first, Asplund planned to place an obelisk near the entrance to the cemetery.

Is life something that can actually be expressed in architecture? Literature, painting and film aside, aren't "life and death" ill-suited subjects to try and express in an art form like architecture? No, challenging this difficult subject was the dream and the personal responsibility of this architect who wasn't able to become a painter. Architects mature through the work they are given. People who possess fixed mindsets do not produce works of art. Through the act of creating their work, and the process of repeatedly contemplating acts of trial and error, architects become architects. The cemetery job made Asplund the architect he wanted to be.

The massive amount of sketches that remain tell of an architect's anguish and tenacity, and someone who approached the challenge not with words but through architectural expression. Around this time, the cemetery planning committee made the decision to entrust the job to Asplund alone. It was a fact that the client had criticized the way Lewerentz worked. But the committee must have also known that for Asplund to add the emotional depth and conviction needed to realize the theme, there was no longer any room for a second architect.

He began making studies for the obelisk and the crematorium, and the chapel on the hill. (Figure 19.) Along the road that led up the hill, Asplund first drew an ancient temple-style building in the way that he always started a design. In repeated attempts, he conceived of many plans and considered many designs. (Figure 20-21.) The decorations that had first been on the temple disappeared and gradually the form became simple. The obelisk was moved halfway up the hill, and in time, it disappeared entirely. Simultaneously, the building was pushed back from the front of the road, and at last, it was hidden in a place that was almost invisible from the road. By concealing his own building, the architect came up with the idea to make a road that would stretch straight toward the forest in the background. At this instant, the concept for Woodland Crematorium was complete.

Everything that is given life is fated to someday be returned to a place beyond the forest. Before one is fully aware of it, the road facing the crematorium makes one realize one's own fate. The time spent walking along this road is the process of accepting the loss of those close to you who have just died and one's own death that will arrive by and by. Asplund, without the help of this type of intense language, expressed the idea through an original method of architecture - a spatial experience. He had already begun to think that crosses were unnecessary; or rather, that they weren't appropriate. Ultimately, the cemetery committee demanded one. (Figure 22.) By leaving everything to "Mother Forest," the place from which people come and eventually return, Asplund intended that one's own fate would merely be informed by people's salvation.

Asplund had no doubt about the superiority of a transcendental nature. But he continued to do whatever he

20.「十字架の道」が検討されるプロセス。建築の形態から推測して時系列に並べたもの。建物は、道の正面に妻側をこちらに向けていたが、向きが90度変わり、ペディメントの形態が簡略化されながら、徐々に道から後退した位置に動かされた。

Figure 20: A look at the design process for Holy Cross Road. (The order has been inferred from the changes that were made in the building's form.) First, the building had a gable side that faced the road. Later, it was shifted 90 degrees, and gradually as the shape of the pediment was simplified, the building was moved away from the road.

いる。卓越した設計能力は、たとえば小礼拝堂の待合室で示された。アスプルンド特有の斜めの壁は、入室するときは中庭に注意をそらして最後のお別れの時間に近づく切迫感を和らげ、いよいよ葬儀が始まるときには、礼拝堂への移動をそっと促す。室内にある柱や金物の出隅、壁と天井の入隅など、あらゆるものの角は丸くされ、哀しみに暮れる遺族の心をなにかが不用意に傷つけることのないよう、細心の注意が払われている。しかも、それらの意図は実にさりげなく、遺族にはこの部屋の印象などなにも残らないにちがいない。

晩年の彼は、すでに体調が限界にきていることを自覚していた。だが、異常なまでの仕事のペースを落として、長生きする道は選択しなかった。「森の火葬場」は、残された時間との競争にすべり込んだ最後の作品である。命を削ってまでも建築に向かう情熱が、アスプルンドにとっての生の燃焼であった。ところが、そんな晩年の彼に、つかの間の幸せが訪れたことはあまり語られてこなかった。

1934年に彼は再婚する。これまで自邸を設計したことのなかった彼が、ストックホルム郊外に休日の家を構えた。美しい自然のなかの「夏の家」である。伝統的な農家をモティーフに設計を始めた彼は、あえてラフに仕上げた内装で素朴な農家のたたずまいを演出した。近代の光が差し込む白く明るい空間に、家族と過ごす休日の時間をさりげなくデザインしたのである。限りある人生の時間を意識していた彼は、最後につかんだ平安の瞬間をここで最大に謳歌することで永遠界に触れようとしたのではなかったか。自然の美しさを讃える揺るぎないまなざしに満ちて、その建築は生のすべてを無条件に肯定しながら自然のなかに建っている。ここで最後の夏を楽しんだアスプルンドは、1940年10月20日、あの"母なる森"へひとりで還っていった。

21.「十字架の道」のスケッチ。建物の形態がシンプルになり、最終案に近い状態になっている。

Figure 21: A sketch for Holy Cross Road. The shape of the building is now simpler and the drawing is similar to Asplund's final proposal.

22. 完成に近づいた「森の火葬場」の風景。発注者への説得に使ったのだろうか、説明の文字がついている。丘の上に十字架は見あたらない。

Figure 22: A landscape drawing of Woodland Crematorium in a nearly completed state. Perhaps as an attempt to persuade the client of his ideas, Asplund has included a written explanation of individual elements. No cross is visible on the hill.

could with the power of architecture until the very end. The large chapel is imbued with a variety of architectural considerations such as protecting the dignity of the deceased, and focusing the mourners' attention on the coffin. His eminent design skill is also apparent in, for instance, the waiting room in the small chapel. On entering the room, one's attention is averted to the courtyard, and the sense of urgency regarding the last farewell that is approaching is assuaged by Asplund's characteristic slanting walls. When the funeral finally begins, one is quietly encouraged to move into the chapel. Meticulous attention has been paid to every corner of the room. The columns, external corners of the metallic materials and the reentrant angles of the walls and ceiling have been rounded as if to avoid any unnecessary injury to the deeply grieving hearts of the bereaved. In addition, Asplund's intent is to insure that the bereaved are left with no impression of the room.

In his final years, Asplund had already realized that he was reaching his limits physically. Yet, he didn't choose to slow the extraordinary pace of his work or try to live a long life. Woodland Crematorium, his last work, was just barely completed in this race against time. Even as his time ran out, his passion for architecture spurred Asplund on through life. But in his last years, there were few moments of happiness.

In 1934, Asplund remarried. He had never designed a house of his own until this time, when he built a holiday villa in the suburbs of Stockholm. It was a "summer house," which stood in the middle of a beautiful natural setting. Starting with a traditional farmhouse motif, he gave the house a simple design and a roughly finished interior. Asplund's casual design was meant for family vacations, which were spent in this bright space bathed in modern light. Aware that he didn't have much time left, Asplund's last instants of peace and tranquility in this environment must have taken him to the edge of eternity. Imbued with an enduring appearance that sings the praises of nature, the building is an unconditional affirmation of all life. Here Asplund enjoyed his last summer. He returned alone to "Mother Forest" on October 20, 1940.

主要参考文献　**Selected Bibliography**
E.G.Asplund, Litteratur. Liselund, *Teknisk Tidskrift Arkitektur,* Stockholm, pp.44-47, 1919.
E.G.Asplund, Vår arkitektoniska rumsuppfattning, *Byggmästaren,* Stockholm, pp.203-210, 1931.
E.G.Asplund, Konst och teknik, *Byggmästaren,* Stockholm, pp.166-171, 1936.
Sigfrid Ericson, Arkitekturutbildningens omorganisation, *Teknisk Tidskrift Arkitektur,* Stockholm, pp. 82-86, 1912.
Ivar Tengbom and Cark Bergsten, Ett bidrag till belysning af bostadsfrågan i stad, *Teknisk Tidskrift Arkitektur,* Stockholm, pp. 105-112, 1912.
Nils Blank, Täflan om utvidgning af Stockholms södra begrafningsplats, *Teknisk Tidskrift Arkitektur,* Stockholm, pp.43-68, 1915.
Ulf G. Johansson, De första svenska krematorierna och deras förutsättningar, *Konsthistorisk Tidskrift,* No.15, Stockholm, pp.117-126, 1964.
Hans Edestand and Erik Lundberg, *Isak Gusaf Clason,* Stockholm, 1968.
Claes Caldenby, Början, *Årsbok 1985 Arkitekturmuseet,* Stockholm, pp.11-21, 1985.
Caroline Constant, *The Woodland Cemetery : Toward a Spiritual Landscape,* Stockholm,1994.
Dan Cruickshank ed., *Erik Gunnar Asplund, The Architect's Journal,* London, 1988.
Christina Engfors, *E.G.Asplund : Arkitekt, vän, och kollega,* Stockholm, 1990.
Bengt O.H.Johansson, *Tallum : Gunnar Asplund's & Sigurd Lewerentz's Woodland Cemetery in Stockholm,* Stockholm, 1996.
川島洋一「瑞暉亭と北欧の近代建築」『建築史論聚』、思文閣出版、pp.524-549 2004.
(Yoichi Kawashima, "Zuikitei and Scandinavian Architecture", *Kenchikushironshu,* Kyoto, pp.524-549, 2004)

森の礼拝堂／森の墓地 1918−20 ストックホルム
Woodland Chapel, Woodland Cemetery, Stockholm

　最初の計画案は、4本のオーダーがファサードに並ぶ古代神殿風の石造の建物だった。エンジニアによる設備図まで用意しており、実施を前提に進めていたはずである。この案をまとめた2日後に、アスプルンドはイェルダと結婚する。デンマークへ新婚旅行に出かけ、メーン島にある「リーセルンド」という18世紀の荘園風別荘をサイクリングで訪れた。この幸せな体験が、礼拝堂の設計に重要なヒントをもたらしたようだ。

　ほどなくまったく発想の異なる別の案がまとめられた。大きな寄棟屋根が特徴の木造の建物になり、祭室の天井をドーム型とした最終案へと発展していく。1919年に「リーセルンド」の実測図集が出版されたとき、建築雑誌『Arkitektur（アーキテクトゥール）』の編集長を任されていたアスプルンドは、こう書いている。「これがリーセルンドの本の概要である。これを学んだ人は、新しい紙を取り出し、自分の古い図面を新鮮な感覚でやり直す作業をはじめることだろう」。自身が実践したことの、素直な告白だったにちがいない。

　祭室のドーム屋根にはトップライトが設けられ、さらに8本のオーダーが祭室内に現れた。その後、ポーティコのトスカーナ式の列柱は4本2列だったのが、4本3列になった。さらに「死の天使」像が軒に描かれ、完成形となる。

　高さを抑えたポーティコから祭室に入ると、トップライトからの静かな光が支配する冷厳な雰囲気に包まれる。しかし、キャンドルが灯り故人を囲んで席につくと、親密で清らかな印象さえ漂う追悼の空間が現れる。まだ若さの残る、アスプルンド初期の傑作である。

The original plan for Woodland Chapel called for a stone building that resembled an ancient temple and used four orders. An engineer had already gone as far as preparing a utilities drawing, with the assumption that the plan would be implemented. But two days later, Asplund married Gerda Sellman. For their honeymoon, the couple went to Møn, an island in Denmark, where they cycled to an 18th century manor-style country house called Liselund. This felicitous experience provided Asplund with an important inspiration for the chapel.

　Not long after his return, Asplund conceived an entirely different proposal. The new design centered on a distinctive wooden building with a large, hipped roof. With a domed ceiling, this soon became the final plan. In 1919, when a collection of measured drawings of Liselund was published, Asplund, who was the editor of the architecture magazine, *Arkitekur,* wrote, "This is a brief summary of the book on Liselund. Those who study it will take out a new sheet of paper and begin redoing their old drawings from a fresh perspective." This statement, an honest confession, was undoubtedly what Asplund himself had done.

　There is a skylight in the domed ceiling and eight orders in the chapel. The original plan to use two rows of four Tuscan pillars in the portico was eventually increased to three rows. Then after a depiction of the "Angel of Death" was added to the eaves, the work was complete.

　When entering the chapel from the rather low portico, one is greeted by a solemn air dominated by the quiet sunlight that shines in through the skylight. But once one reaches the seats which surround the deceased among lit candles, the memorial space seems imbued with a sense of intimacy and purity.

小さな門の背後に広がる、圧倒的な高さの樅の樹林。

A grove of breathtakingly tall firs covers the area behind the small front gate.

SKOGSKAPELLET

樅の木立ちの中を歩むと、礼拝堂が姿を現す。トスカーナ様式の素朴な柱列によるポーティコの低い軒をくぐると、黒い扉が参列者を迎える。

Upon entering the grove of firs, the chapel becomes visible. After passing under the low eaves and through the simple, Tuscan-order columns, mourners are greeted by a black door.

Plan

雪を頂いた樅の木立ちの中、小さな門の奥に森の礼拝堂が見える。門から礼拝堂までの道は、わずかに下り勾配で礼拝堂を遠く、小さく見せている。

Woodland Chapel is visible in the forest behind the gate in a clutch of snow-covered firs. A slight incline in the road leading from the gate to the chapel makes the building appear farther and smaller than it is.

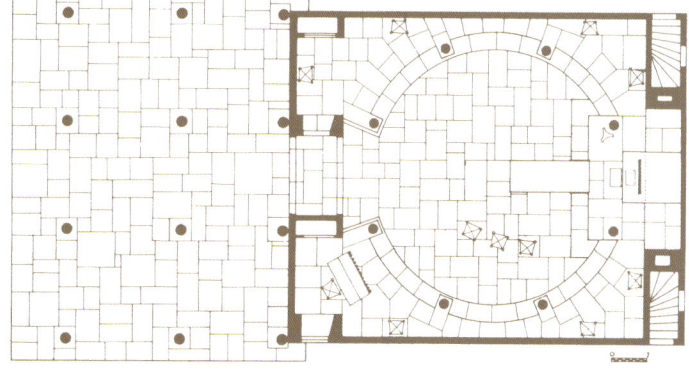

1:200

礼拝堂正面。柿葺きの寄せ棟屋根の先端のカール・ミレスの彫刻「死の天使」が参列者を迎える。

The front entrance to the chapel. At the edge of the shingled, hipped roof, mourners are greeted by Carl Milles's sculpture "The Angel of Death."

Cross section　　　　　　　　　1:200

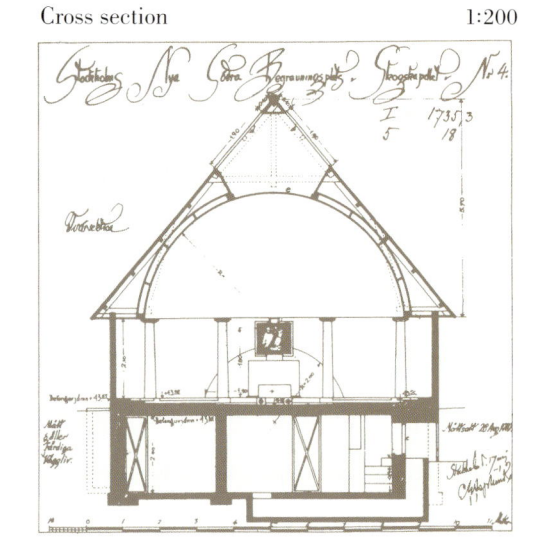

南側面。棟に素朴な丸太を乗せた柿葺きの屋根は苔むしている。小さな窓はパイプオルガン奏者用の採光窓。

The south side of the chapel. The ridges of the shingled roof, with its simple timber-laid design, are covered with moss. The small window is a lighting window for the pipe organist.

Longitudinal section

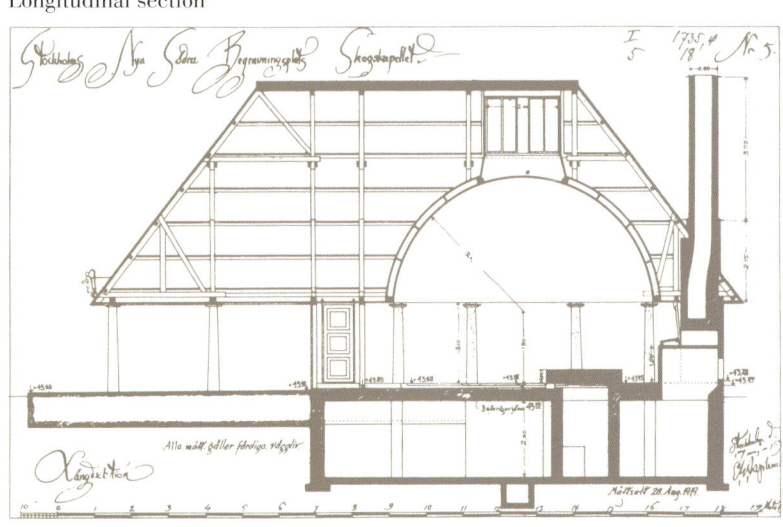

アイアンワークのグリル扉越しに外部を見る。柱列の先に樅の樹幹が続きその先には小さな門が見える。

A view of the exterior ironwork on a grill door. Visible beyond the row of pillars is another section of the fir grove and beyond that the small gate.

礼拝堂内部を見る。優雅な曲線のグリル扉の上半分は騎馬像が天国を、下半分の蛇と髑髏は地獄を表す。

An interior view of the chapel through the grill door. The horse motif in the upper section of the door, with its elegantly curved lines, represents heaven, while the snakes and skulls in the lower section represent hell.

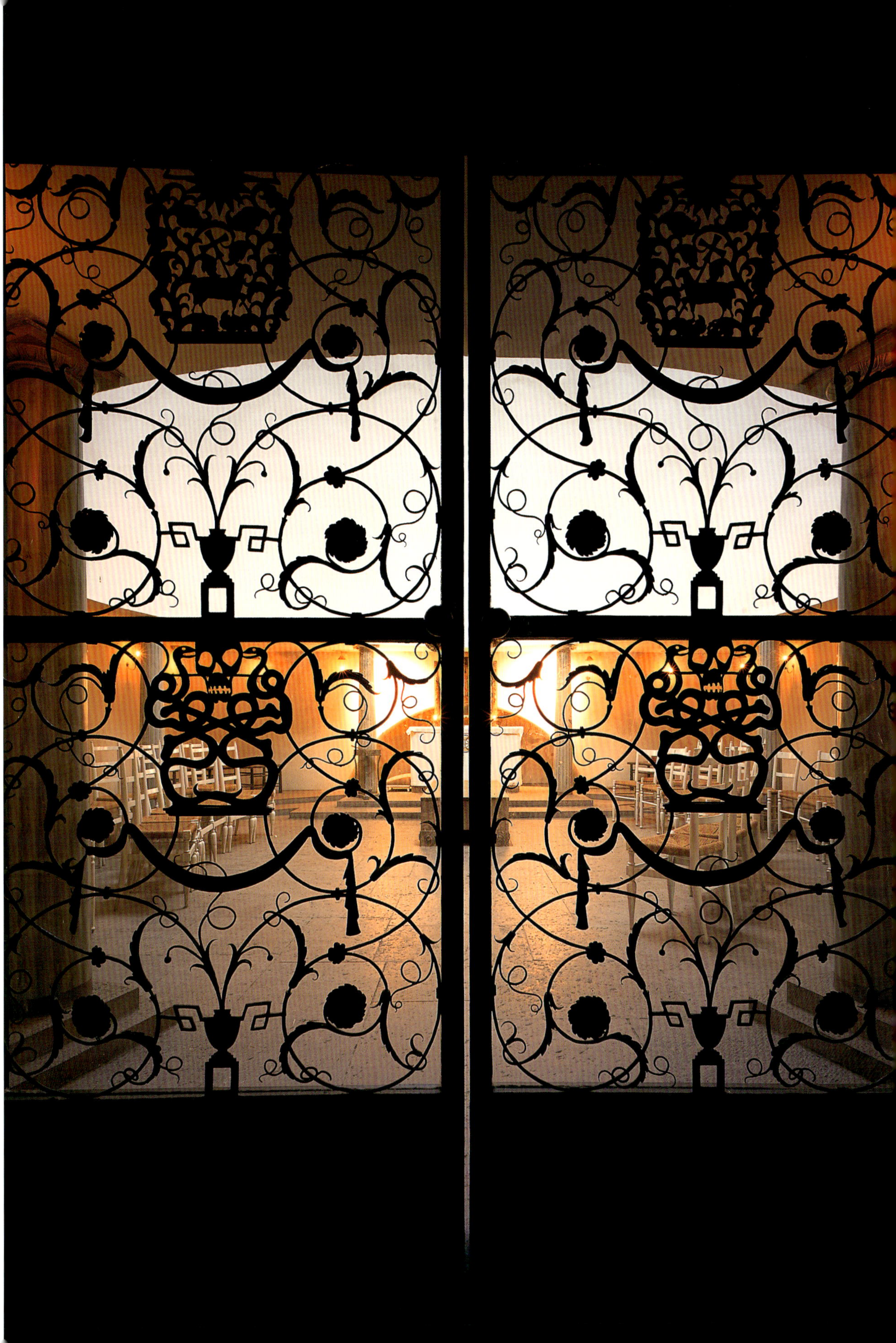

礼拝堂のドームを支えるドリス式円柱。正方形の礼拝堂の中央にあるドーム天井を支える8本の柱は、すべて木製で、柱頭の装飾、リブや石目は絵筆で描かれている。

The Doric columns under the chapel's dome. The eight columns, which support the domed ceiling in the center of the square chapel, are wooden and in the ornamentation on the capital, the lips and right eye have been painted with a brush.

Wrought-iron candlestick

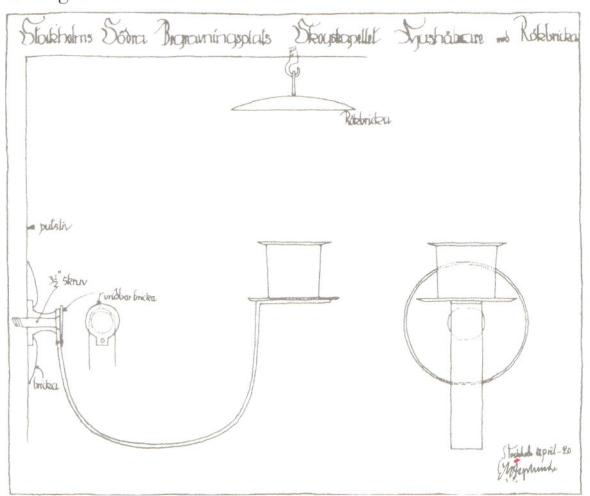

半円形のドーム頂部のトップライトは礼拝堂を真上からソフトに照らす。礼拝堂入り口から礼拝堂祭壇前の棺台に向けて、床にはわずかな下り勾配がつき、参列者がおのずと棺台に集中できるように配慮されている。

The skylight in the top of the semicircular dome softly illuminates the chapel from overhead. When facing the bier in front of the altar from the chapel's entrance, the floor has a slight downward slant to allow mourners to assemble before the coffin.

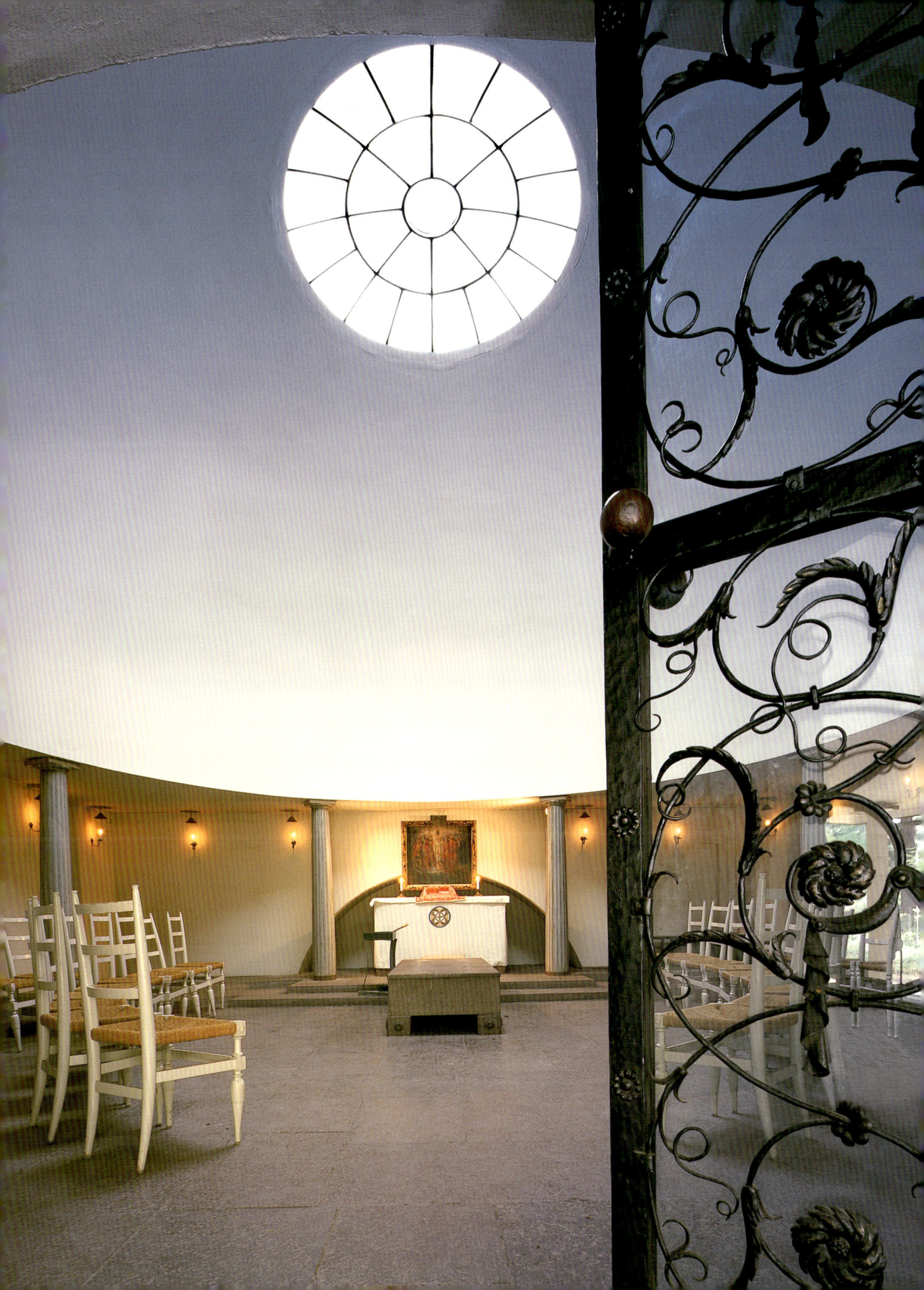

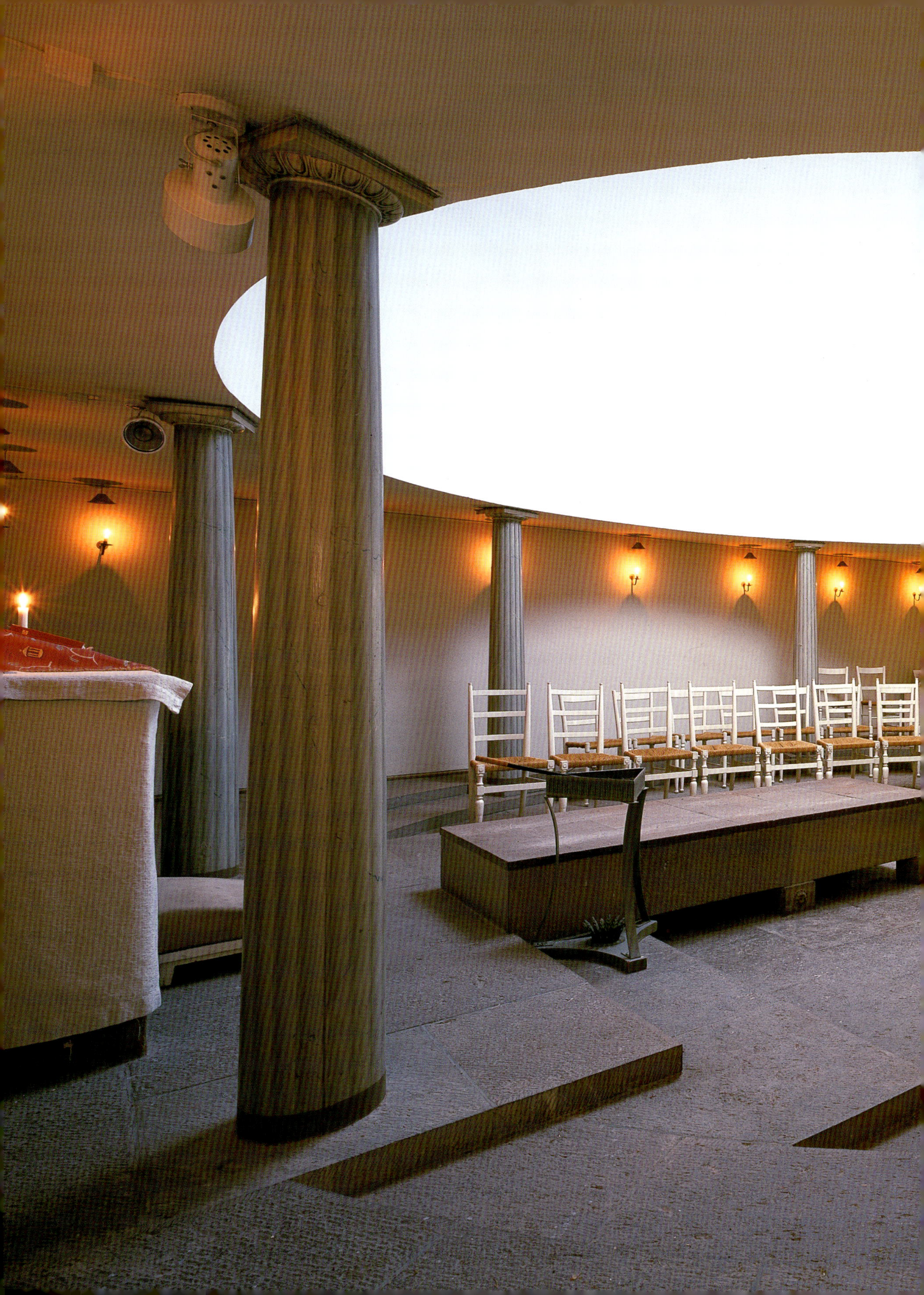

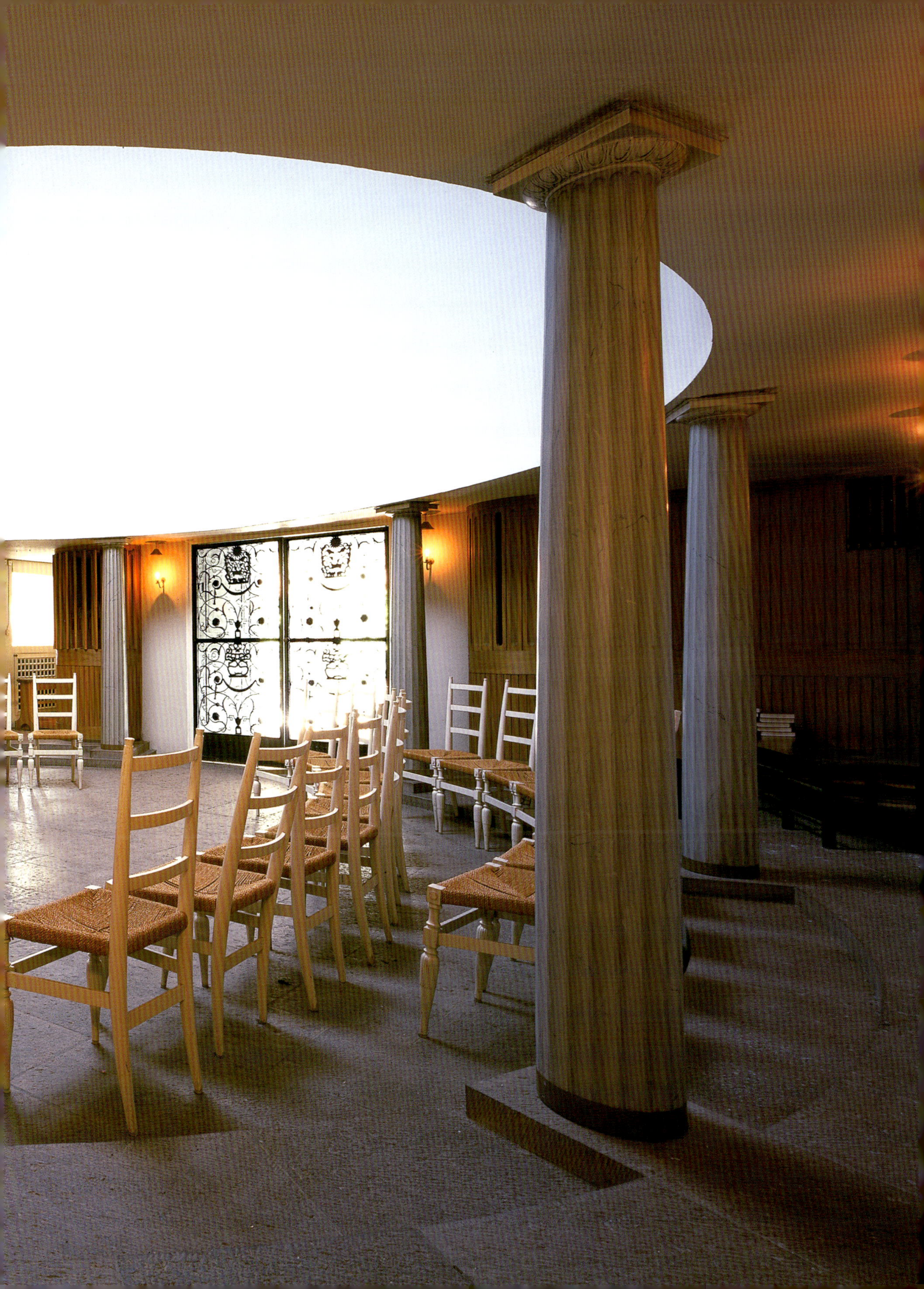

森の火葬場　1935–40／森の墓地　1915–40　ストックホルム
Woodland Crematorium, Woodland Cemetery, Stockholm

　1935年1月に「森の墓地」の建設委員会は、礼拝堂と火葬場からなる主要施設を、アスプルンドひとりに依頼することにした。彼が苦悩の末にこれを了承したため、コンペ以来ずっと続いたS.レヴェレンツとの共同関係は消滅し、ふたりの交友関係も崩壊を迎えた。その後は発注者側の期待どおり、アスプルンドによって「森の火葬場」の建築と周辺のランドスケープが一気に最終形へと向かう。この作品が特別な価値に到達するための、最も本質的な創造行為もこの段階でなされた。「十字架の道」の完成と、それに伴う建物の位置関係の変更である。

　施設本体の計画も、実に巧みである。墓地の入り口から施設の方へは丘を昇る傾斜地になっているが、施設の表側から裏側にかけても敷地に高低差がある。表側が礼拝堂やその待合室など、葬儀の列席者が使う諸室であるのに対し、裏側は主に職員の執務空間となっている。アスプルンドは表と裏でデザインの表現を変えているが、建物にかかわる人々の立場や心理の違いを踏まえてのことだろう。裏側の玄関から建物に入ると、1層分の高低差があるため表の葬儀の気配を感じることがない。職員にとって重苦しくない、日常的な執務空間を確保しているわけだ。一方で、牧師室やオルガン奏者室など葬儀に関係する部屋は、礼拝堂と同じ階に配置されている。

　アスプルンドは、この建物の設計中に体調の悪化を自覚していた。死期を悟った建築家が最後にたどり着いた死生観は、熟練の技術で建築表現に翻訳されていったのである。

In January 1935, the Woodland Cemetery Construction Committee requested that Asplund alone design a facility that would consist primarily of a chapel and crematorium. After a difficult struggle to get his permission, Asplund dissolved the collaborative relationship he had maintained with Sigurd Lewerentz since they won the original design competition. This also led to the collapse of their friendship. After that, the construction of Woodland Crematorium and the surrounding landscape began to move quickly toward completion in exactly the way the architect intended. It was also at this stage that the most essential creative work was carried out, giving the project extraordinary significance. This included the completion of Holy Cross Road and changes in the location of the buildings.

The plan for the facility itself displayed great skill. Leading from the entrance of the cemetery toward the facility is a sloping plot of land on the side of a hill. There is a marked difference in elevation between the front and the back side of the facility. In contrast to the front, where the chapel, waiting room and other spaces used by funeral mourners are located, the back is primarily set aside for employees' offices. Asplund's reason for making two distinct designs probably has to do with the difference in the status and emotional state of the people using the building. When coming through the back entrance, as the elevation is one-level lower, there is little indication of the funeral proceedings. This ensures an ordinary and not overly somber working environment for the staff. On the other hand, the rooms for the priest, organist and others connected to the funerals are located on the same floor as the chapel.

During construction, Asplund found that his physical condition was deteriorating. Using his masterful technique, Asplund translated his final views of life and death into this architectural expression.

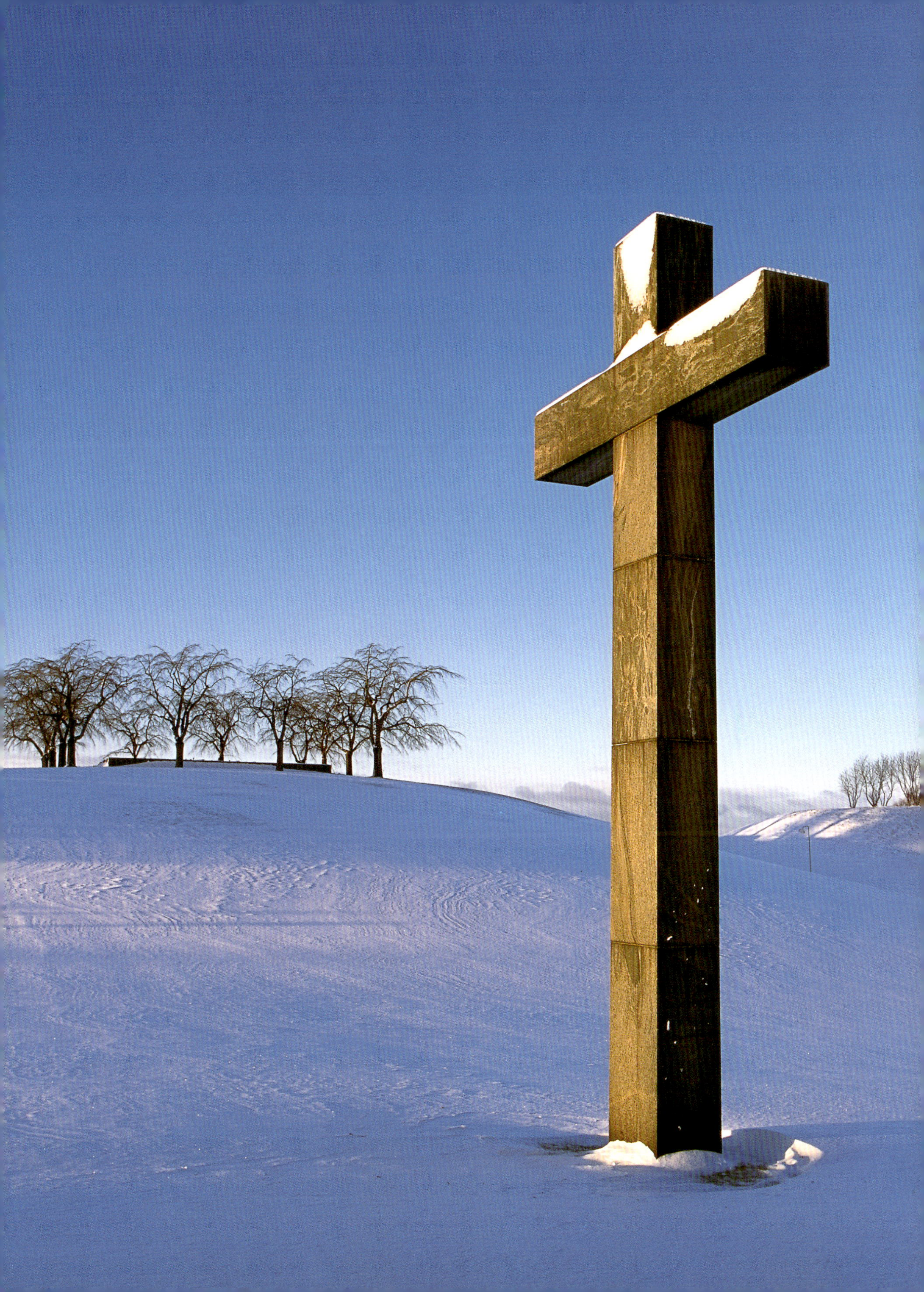

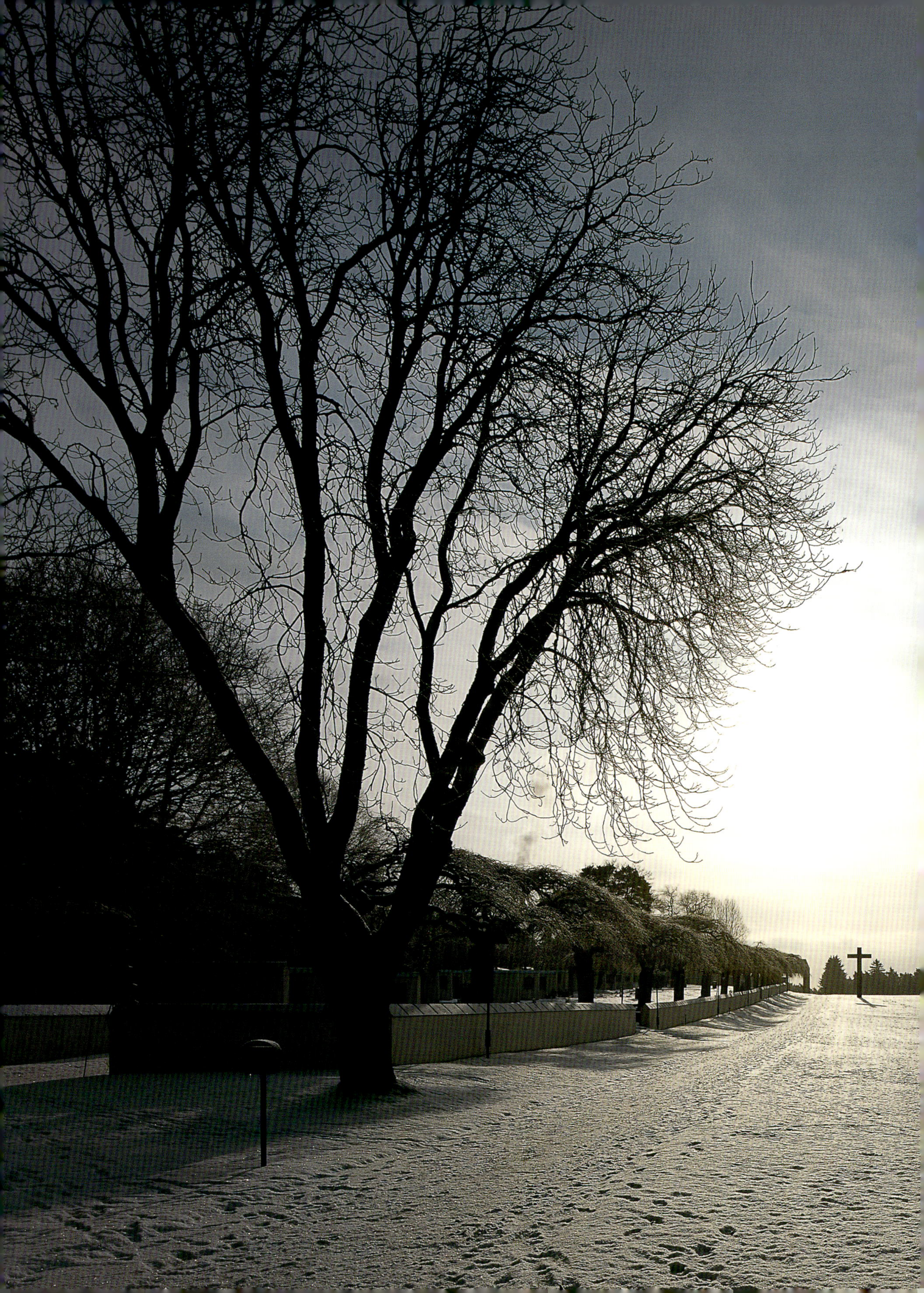

森の墓地入り口より聖なる十字架への道を見る。雪が降り積もった十字架の道からは、葉を落とした木々と逆光の太陽の下に母なる森がシルエットとなる。十字架の背後にはアスプルンドが描いた墓地の風景が広がる。

The road that leads from the entrance of Woodland Cemetery to the Holy Cross. From the snow-covered road next to the cross, a silhouette of the forest appears backlit by the sun. The ground is blanketed with snow and the leaves have fallen from the trees. Behind the cross is the archetypal landscape that inspired Asplund's cemetery.

右に瞑想の丘を臨み、正面の十字架に向かって荒い石の表情を皮膚で感じながら、緩やかな上り勾配の石畳を踏みしめるように歩むとき、死者との思い出がよみがえる。十字架の先に広がる「母なる森」を目前にし、かすかな疲労感とともに左手の森の火葬場へと歩みを進める。

On the right, one sees Meditation Hill while sensing the texture of the rugged rocks underfoot and moving toward the cross up ahead. As one steps firmly on the stone pavement leading up the gentle slope, memories of the dead arise. In a short while, "Mother Forest" comes into view beyond the cross, and with a faint sense of fatigue, one continues on toward the crematorium on the left.

瞑想の丘から森の火葬場を見る。

Woodland Crematorium as seen from Meditation Hill.

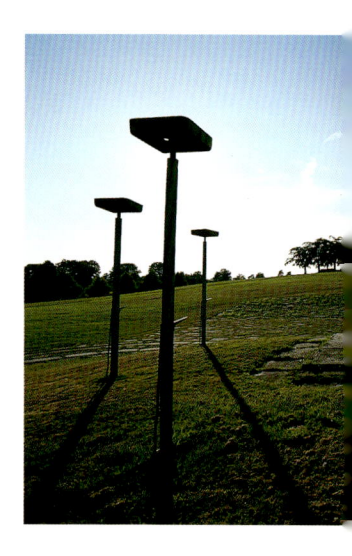

Plan of area

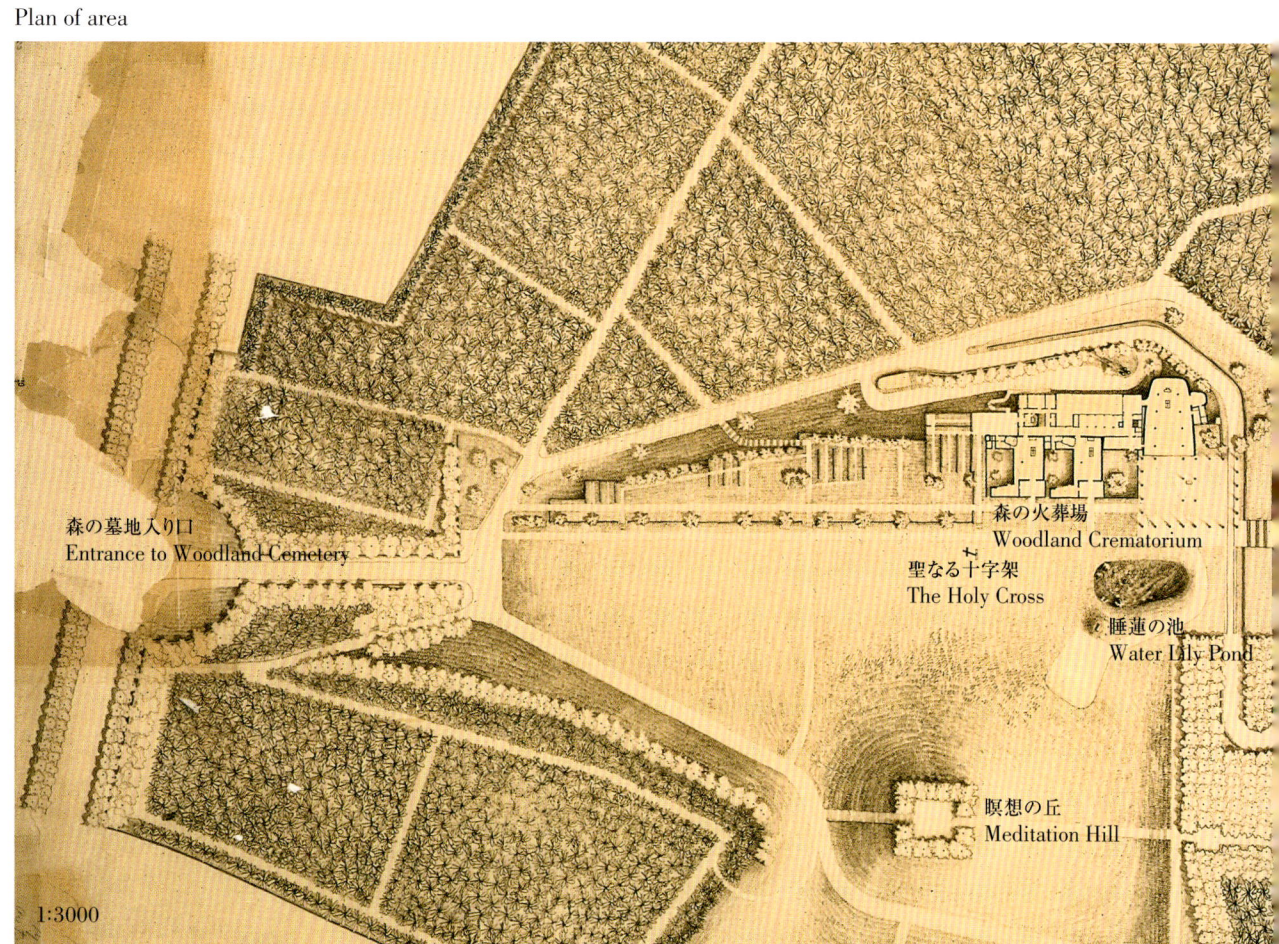

森の墓地入り口
Entrance to Woodland Cemetery

森の火葬場
Woodland Crematorium

聖なる十字架
The Holy Cross

睡蓮の池
Water Lily Pond

瞑想の丘
Meditation Hill

1:3000

森の礼拝堂
Woodland Chapel

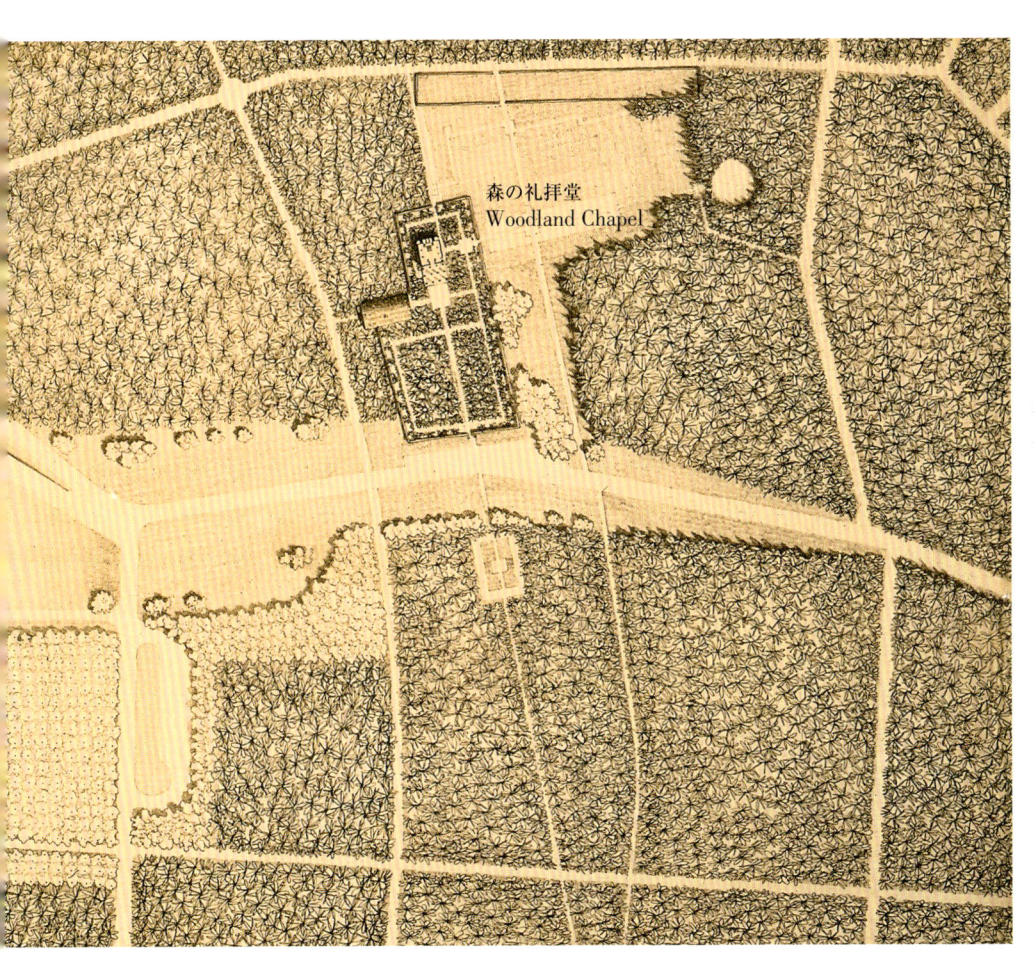

墓地管理棟 →
Administrative Wing

復活の教会 →
（設計：S.レヴェレンツ）
Resurrection Chapel
(Design: Sigurd Lewerentz)

大礼拝堂（聖十字架礼拝堂）前ロッジア
The loggias in front of the Chapel of the Holy Cross.

森の火葬場前の小さな睡蓮の池に、聖なる十字架が映し出される。

The small water-lily pond in front of the Woodland Crematorium reflects the Holy Cross.

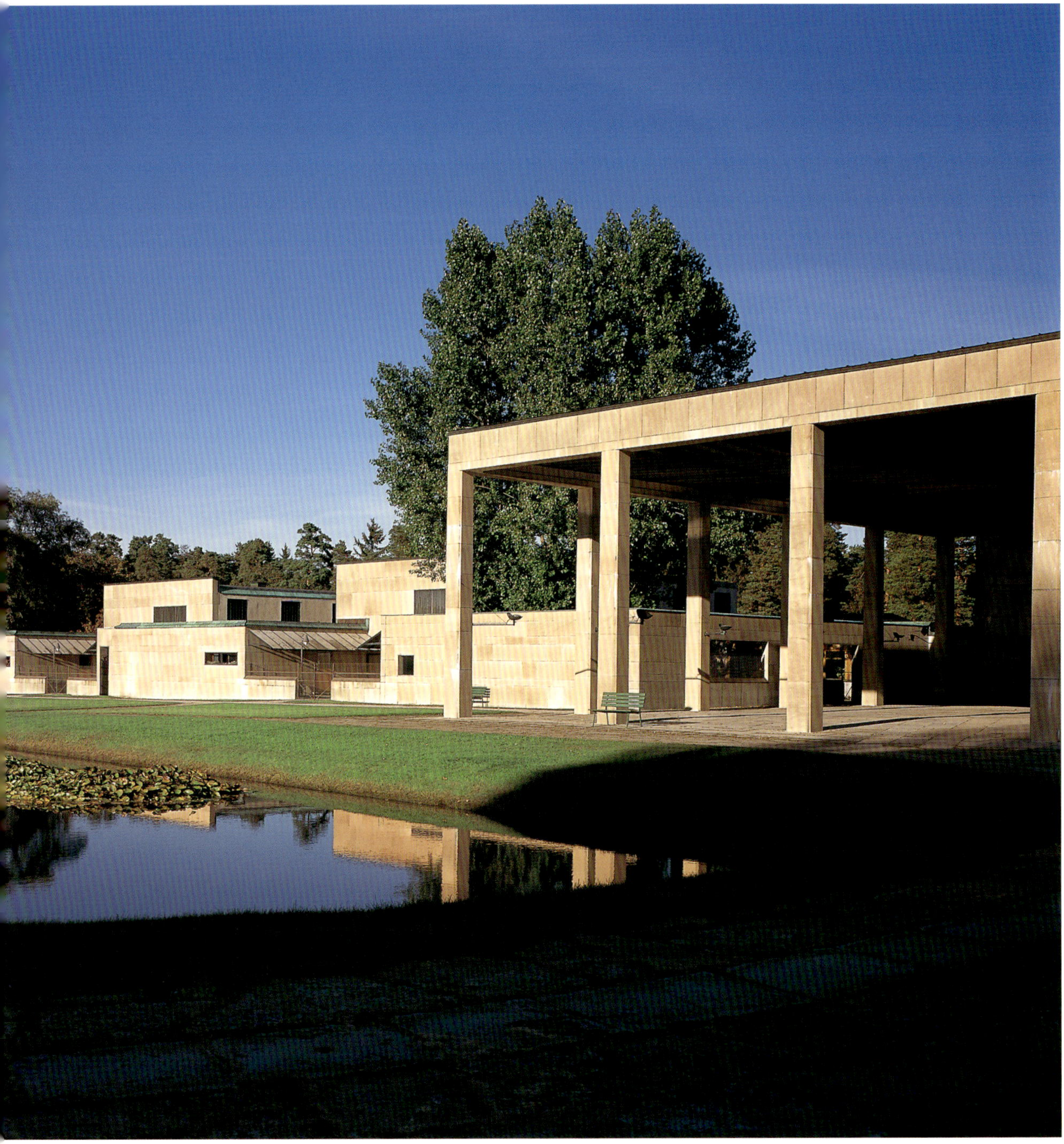

General location plan of Woodland Crematorium

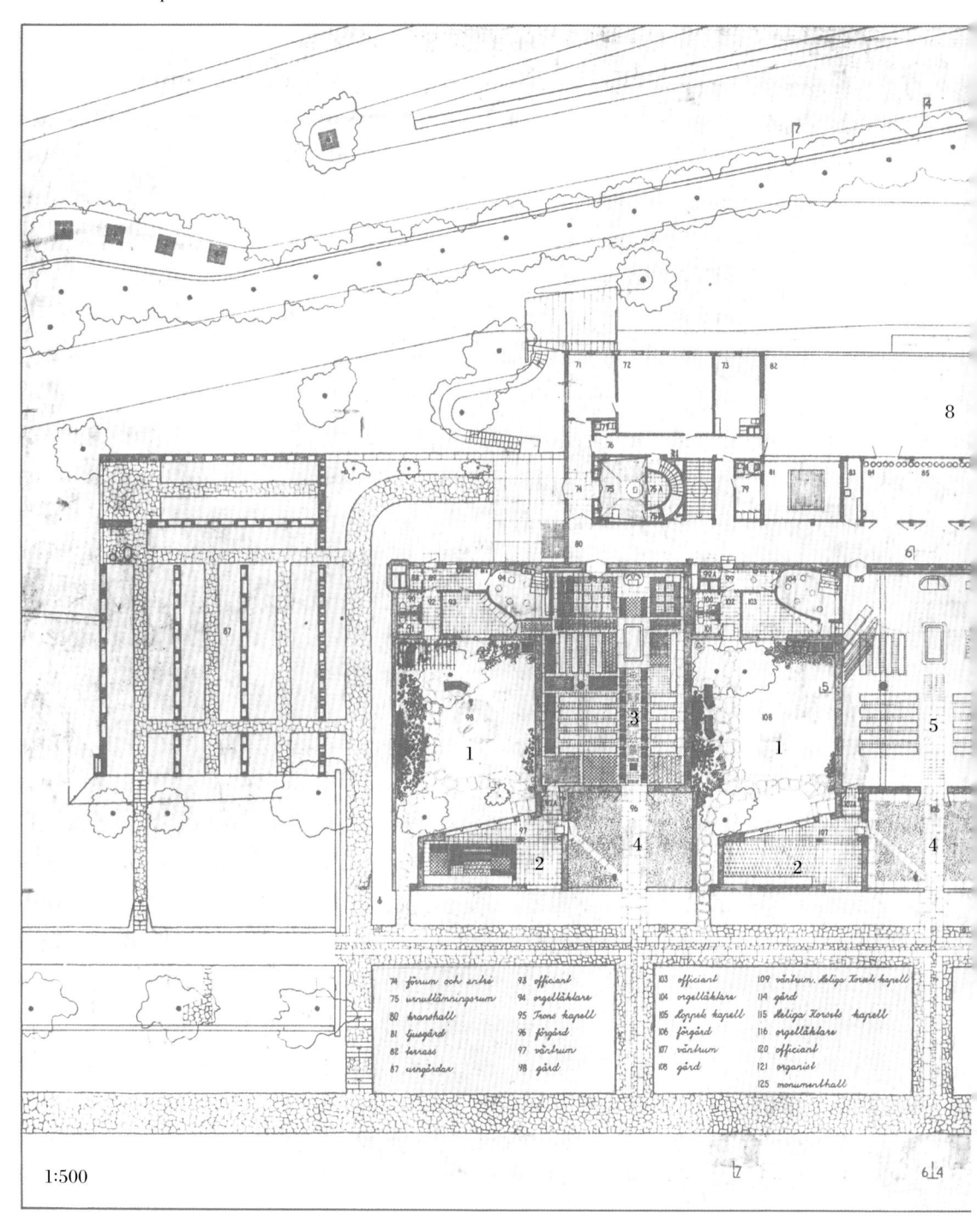

74 förrum och entré	93 officiant
75 urnutlämningsrum	94 orgelläktare
80 kranshall	95 Trons kapell
81 ljusgård	96 förgård
82 terrass	97 väntrum
87 uregårdar	98 gård

103 officiant	109 väntrum. Heliga Korsets kapell
104 orgelläktare	114 gård
105 Hoppets kapell	115 Heliga Korsets kapell
106 förgård	116 orgelläktare
107 väntrum	120 officiant
108 gård	121 organist
	125 monumenthall

1:500

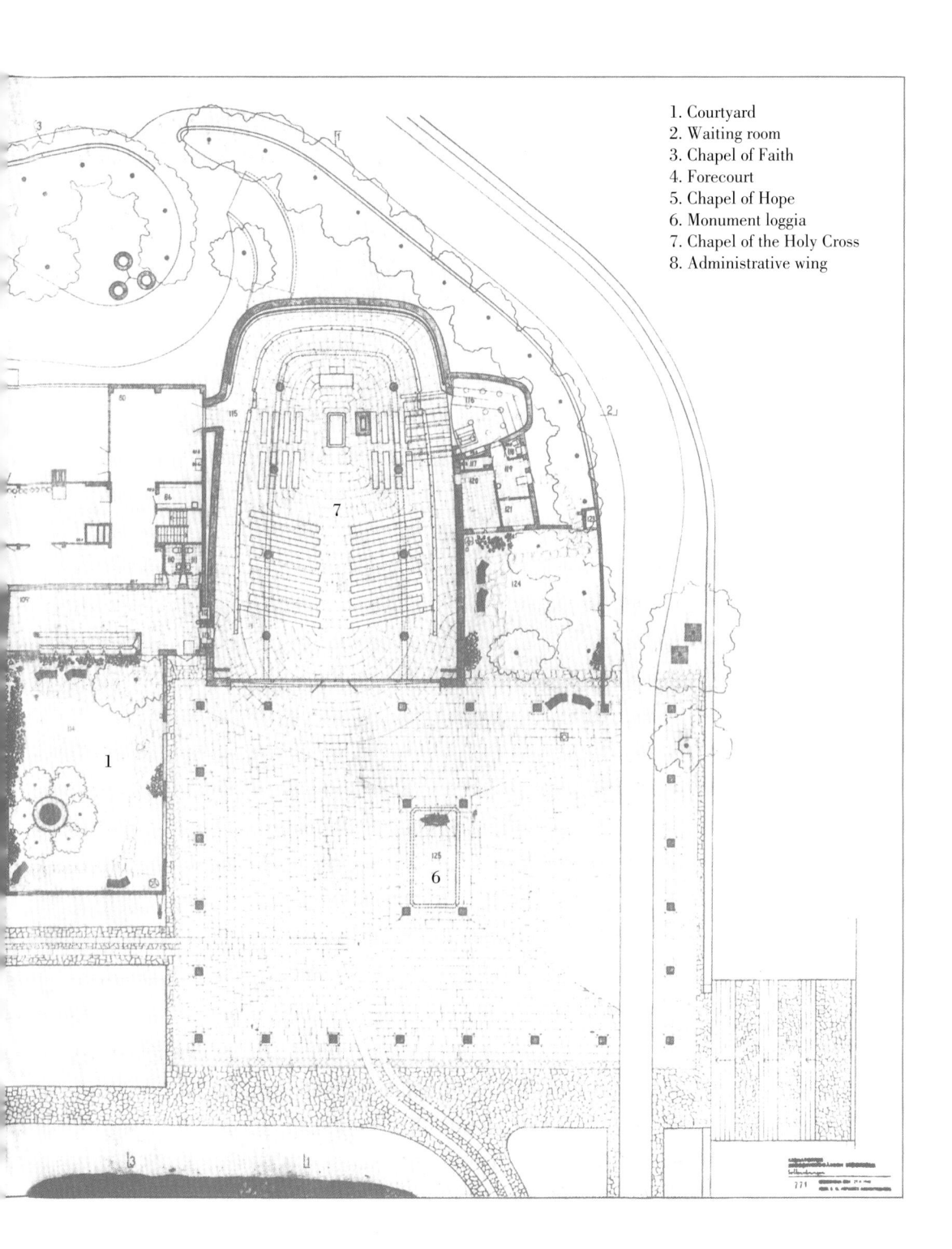

1. Courtyard
2. Waiting room
3. Chapel of Faith
4. Forecourt
5. Chapel of Hope
6. Monument loggia
7. Chapel of the Holy Cross
8. Administrative wing

睡蓮の池から大礼拝堂を見る。
The Chapel of the Holy Cross as seen from the water-lily pond.

大礼拝堂ロッジアより、瞑想の丘を見る。夕方、太陽が黄金色の光を瞑想の丘の向こうから投げかけ、睡蓮の池に光の粒子を反射させる。

Meditation Hill as seen through the loggias of the Chapel of the Holy Cross. At dusk, the sun bathes the hill in golden light and the particles of light are reflected in the water-lily pond.

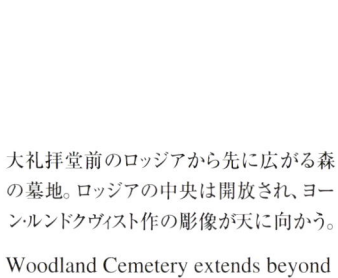

大礼拝堂前のロッジアから先に広がる森の墓地。ロッジアの中央は開放され、ヨーン・ルンドクヴィスト作の彫像が天に向かう。

Woodland Cemetery extends beyond the loggias in front of the Chapel of the Holy Cross. In the open, center space between the loggias, pointing toward the heavens, is a sculpture by John Lundqvist.

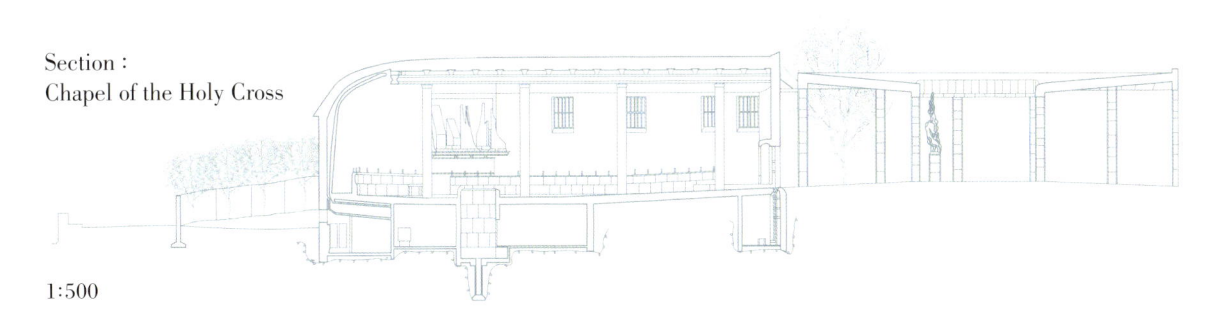

Section:
Chapel of the Holy Cross

1:500

059　E.G. Asplund

火葬場前の床石の組合せ。自然石の乱張りによる十字架への道が大礼拝堂ロッジア前に至る。さまざまな石の形状と、テクスチャーの組合せで、場のヒエラルキーや結界を表している。

The fitted stone pavement in front of the crematorium. The road to the Holy Cross, paved with randomly laid natural stones, stretches before the loggias of the Chapel of the Holy Cross. The combination of various stone shapes and textures expresses a hierarchy of place and the boundary of the sacred area.

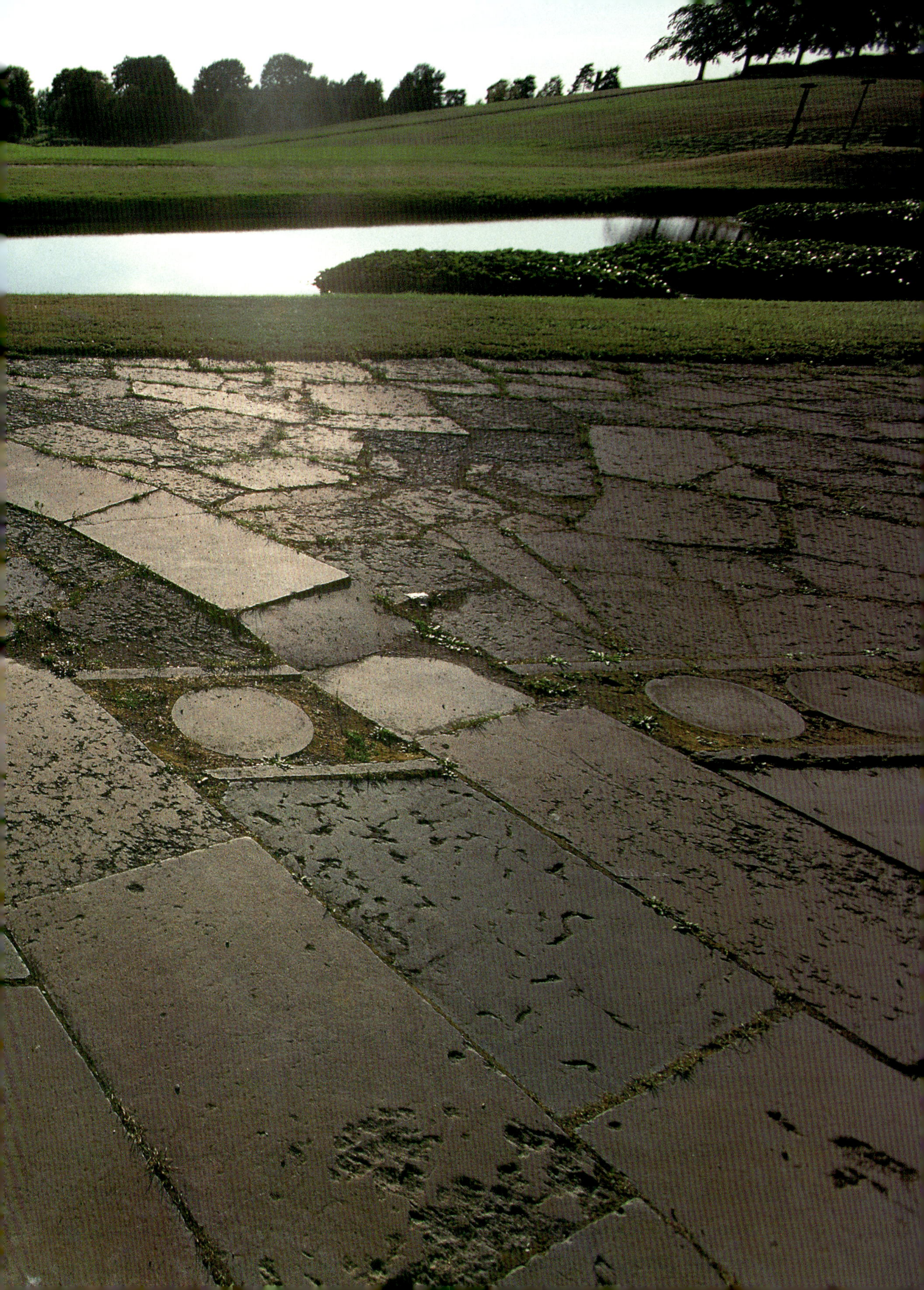

大礼拝堂入り口の格子扉。ロッジアの石床は途中からわずかな下り勾配で格子扉中央に向かって傾斜し、その傾斜は祭壇前の棺台に至る。格子扉は、電動で地下に降下し、ロッジアを含めた大規模な葬儀が可能となっている。

The glazed latticework gate at the entrance to the Chapel of the Holy Cross. In the middle, the pavement around the loggias begins to slope downward toward the center of the gate until it reaches the bier in front of the altar. The gate descends into the ground electronically, making it possible to hold large-scale funerals encompassing the loggia area.

Drawing of glazed latticework gate and descent mechanism between the loggias and the Chapel of the Holy Cross.

1:100

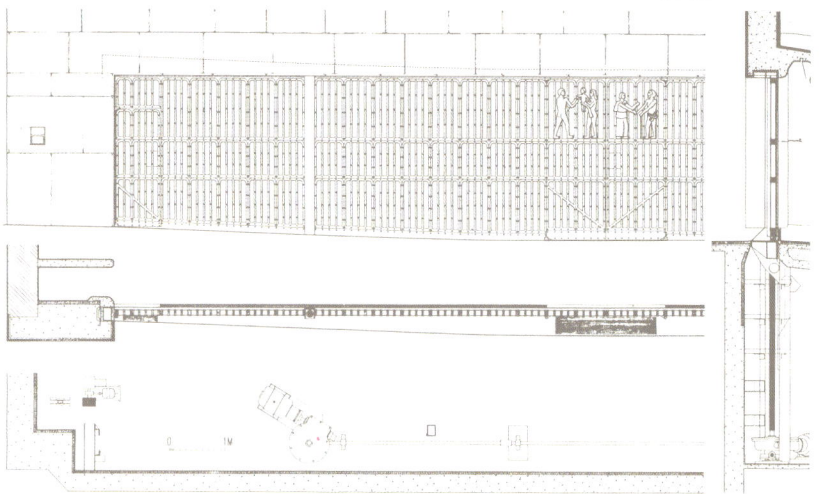

日没直前の太陽は、地を這うように黄金色の光をロッジアの柱や彫像に反射させ、そのシルエットを大礼拝堂の外壁に投影する。

Just before the sun sets, it creates reflections of the loggias and statue in golden light across the ground. These silhouettes are thrown on the exterior wall of the Chapel of the Holy Cross.

大礼拝堂正面内観。内部は緩やかに下がる花崗岩の床、傾斜天井と凹面の壁に描かれた祭壇画の効果で、参列者の視線は自然と祭壇前の棺に集まる。天井を支える梁は二重になっており、その隙間が空間全体に軽やかな印象を与えている。

An interior view of the Chapel of the Holy Cross from the entrance. The granite floor slopes gradually, and due to the slanted ceiling and the frescoes painted on the concave surface of the walls, the mourners' line of vision naturally moves toward the altar where the coffin is.
The eaves that support the ceiling are two-layered, and the space between the layers imbues the entire space with a sense of lightness.

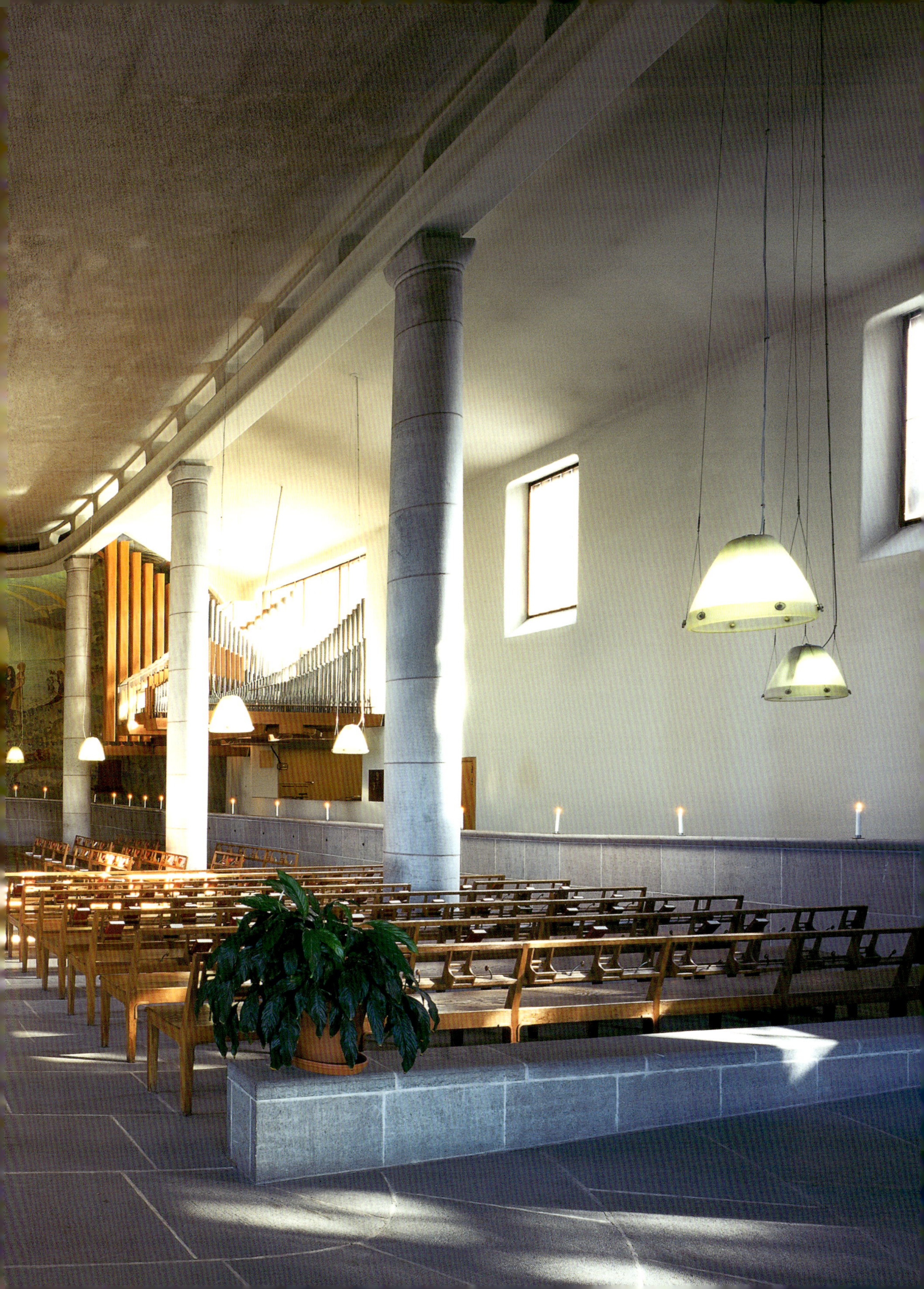

棺台を包み込むように正面、側面に描かれたスヴェン・エーリクソン作のフレスコ画「生・死・生」。

A fresco, "Life - Death - Life" by Sven Erixson, is painted on the inside of both the front and sides of the altar area as if to embrace the bier.

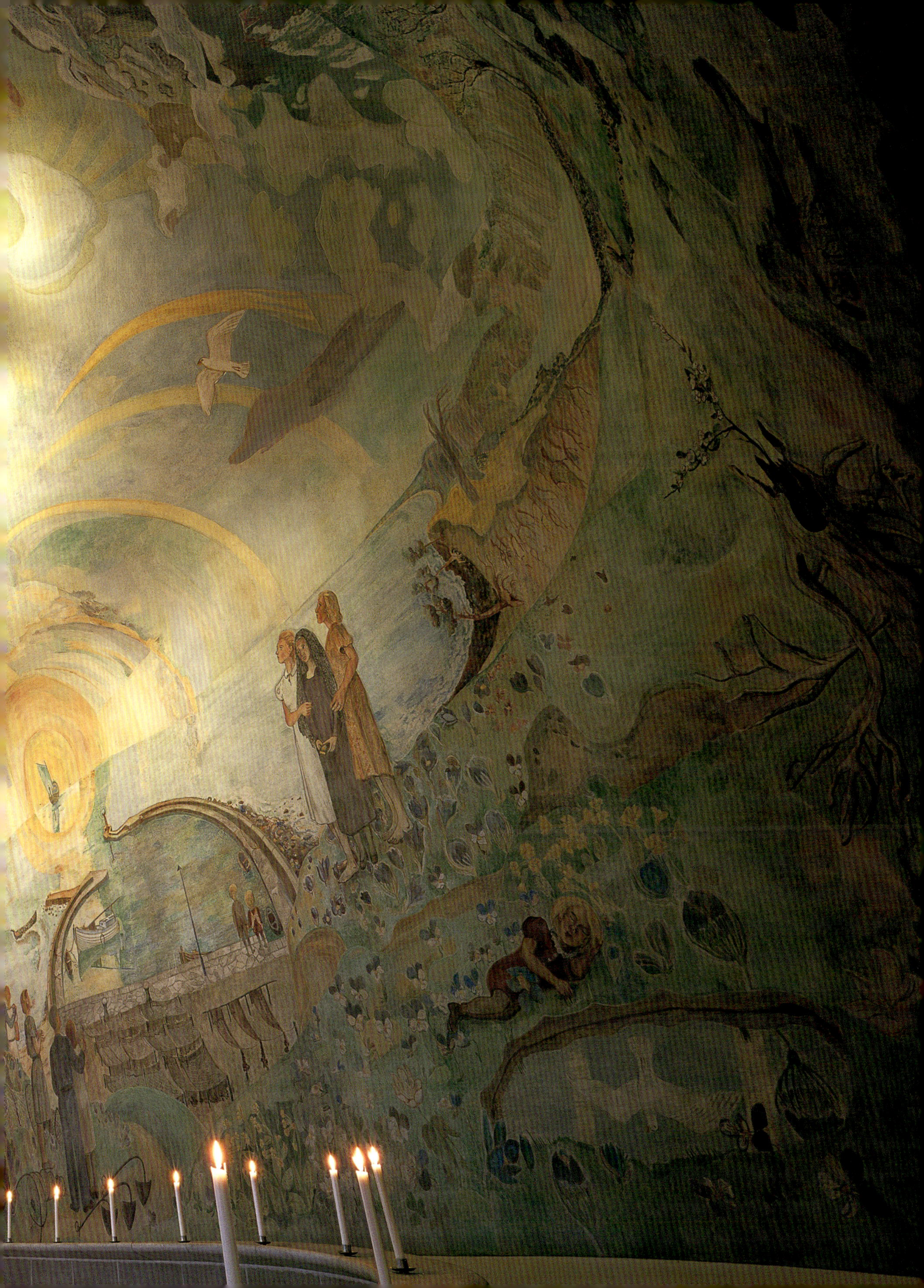

大礼拝堂の祭壇十字架と格子扉の彫刻。
家族をテーマとするブロール・ヨルト作のレリーフが格子扉に浮かぶ。

The cross on the altar of the Chapel of the Holy Cross and a sculpture on the latticework gate.
The relief, based on the theme of "family," is by Bror Hjorth.

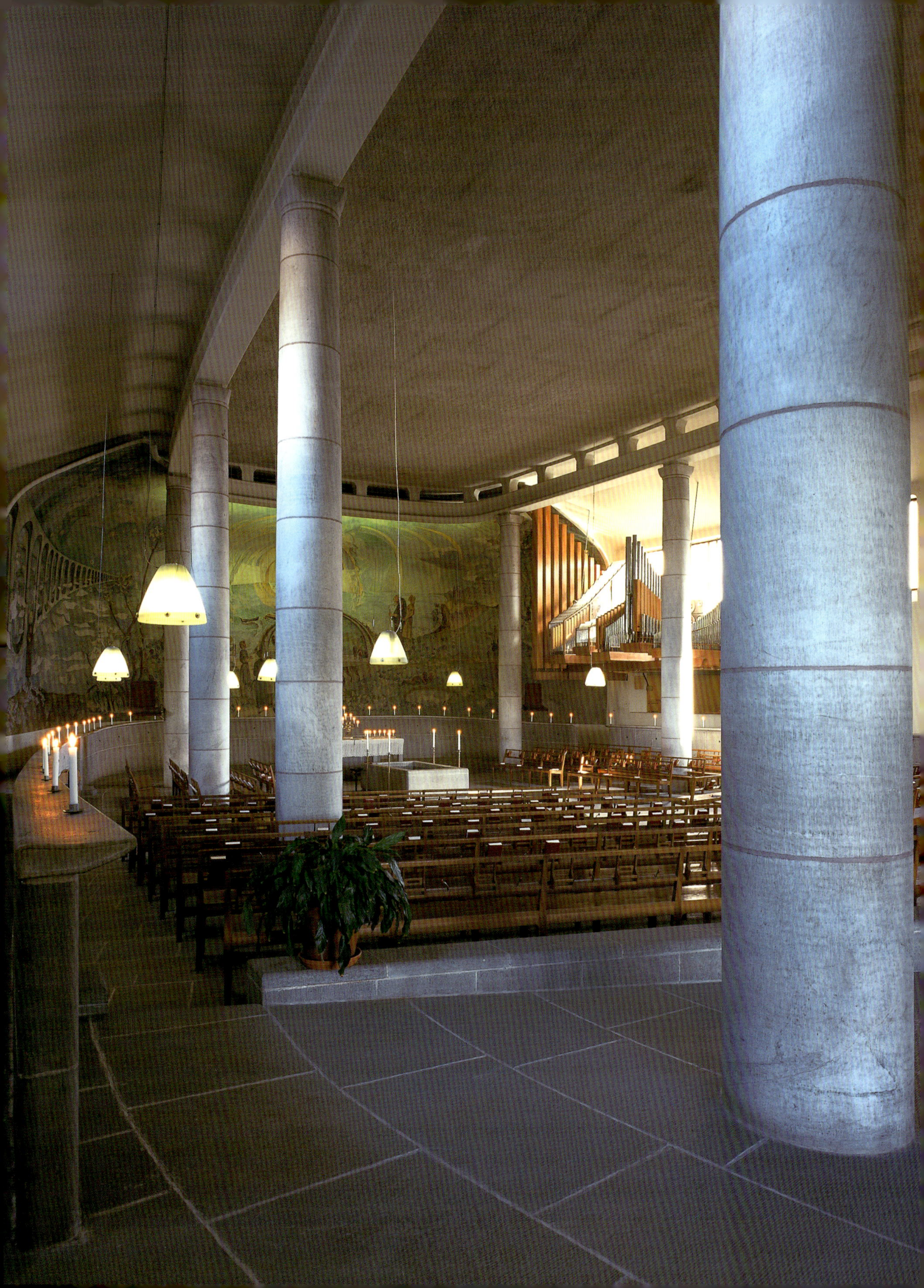

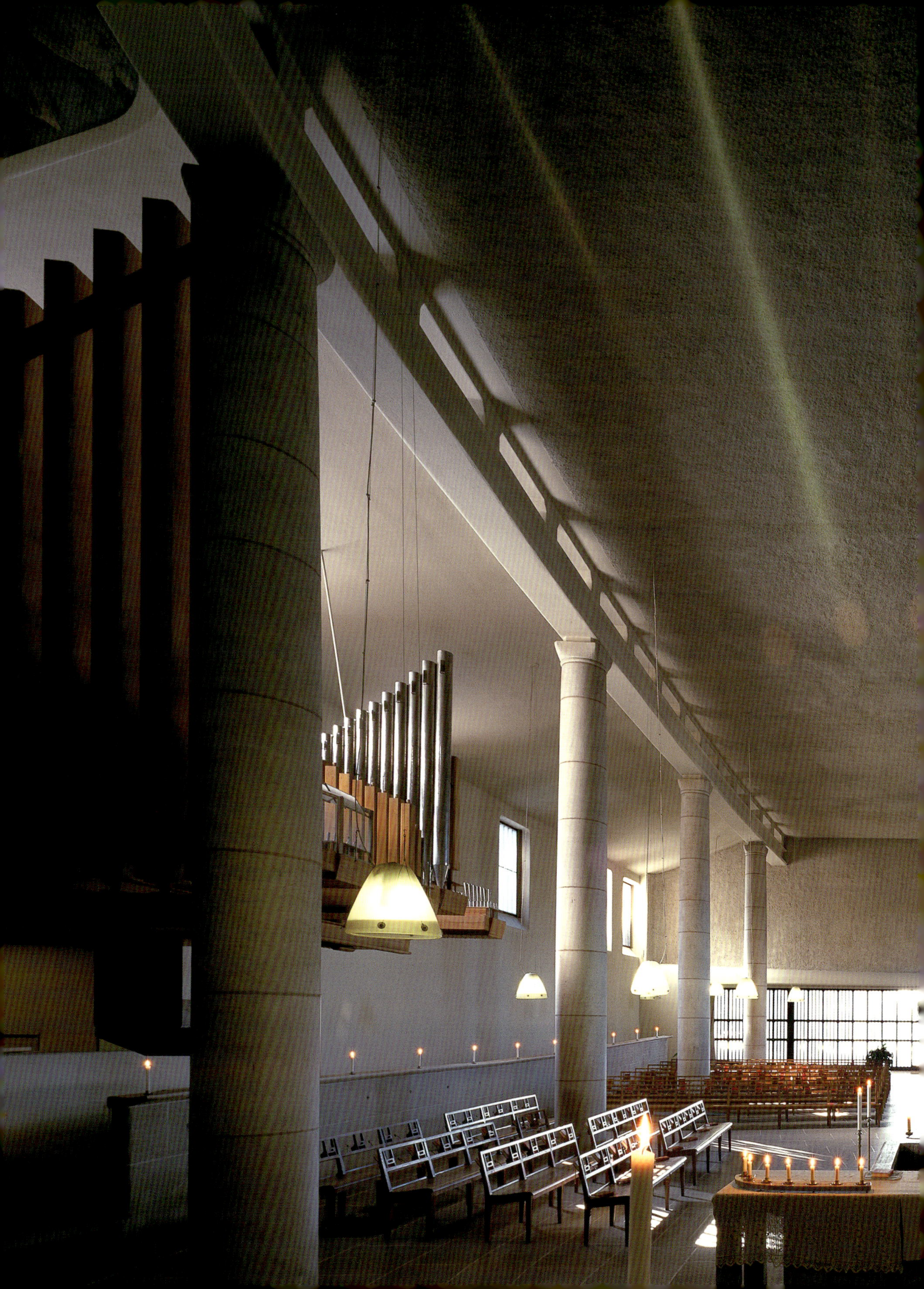

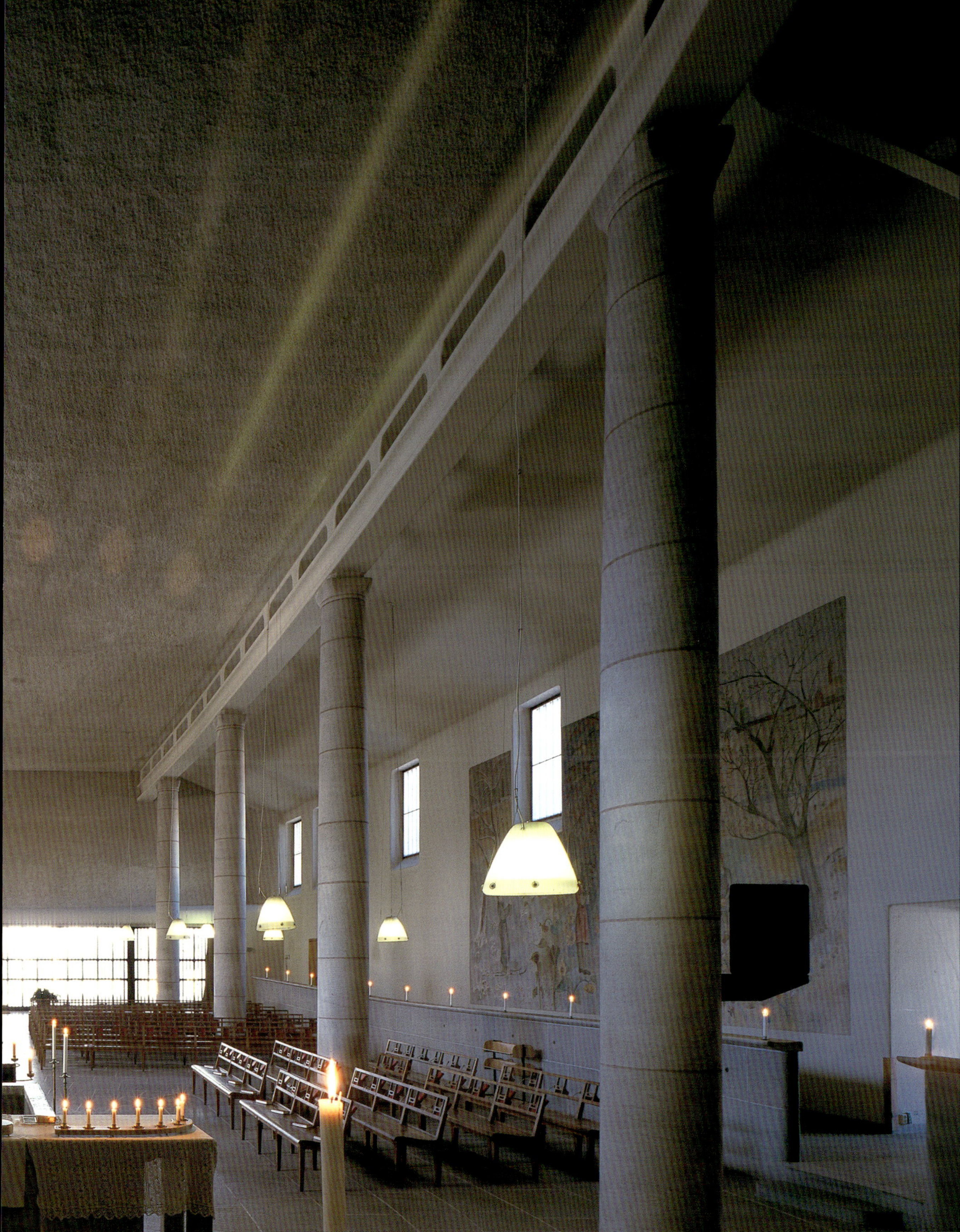

ふたつ並んだ小礼拝堂の先に大礼拝堂のロッジアが見える。敷地の高低差を利用し高いレベルに礼拝堂、裏手の低いレベルには火葬場、管理室などが集約され追悼空間との分離を実現している。

The loggias of the Chapel of the Holy Cross are visible beyond the two small chapels. By taking advantage of the difference in elevation on the lot, it was possible to separate the mourning spaces, with the chapels on a higher level, and the crematorium and administrative wing on a lower level behind them.

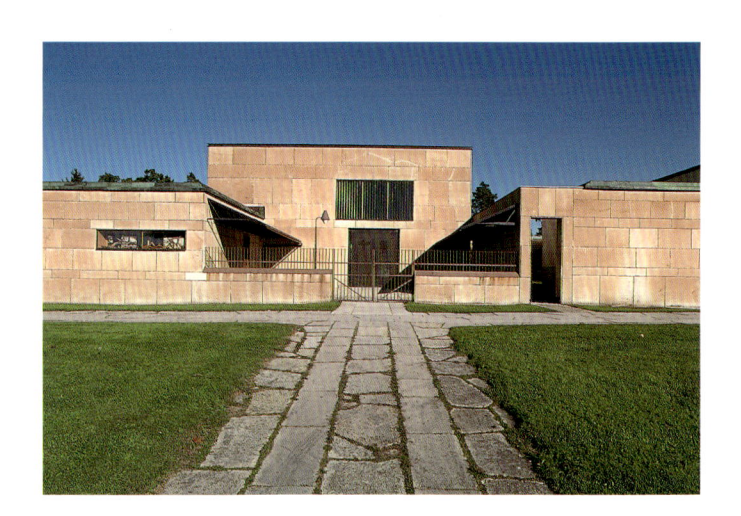

小礼拝場待合入り口庇とベンチ。大理石の薄板による軽快な庇。

The canopy and benches in the waiting area at the entrance to the Chapel of Faith. The lightness of the canopy is created by thin marble panels.

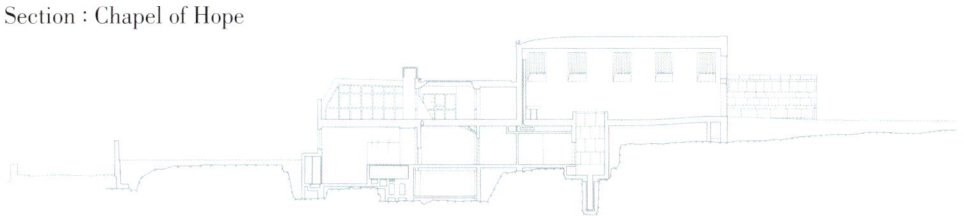

Section : Chapel of Hope

1:600

073 E.G. Asplund

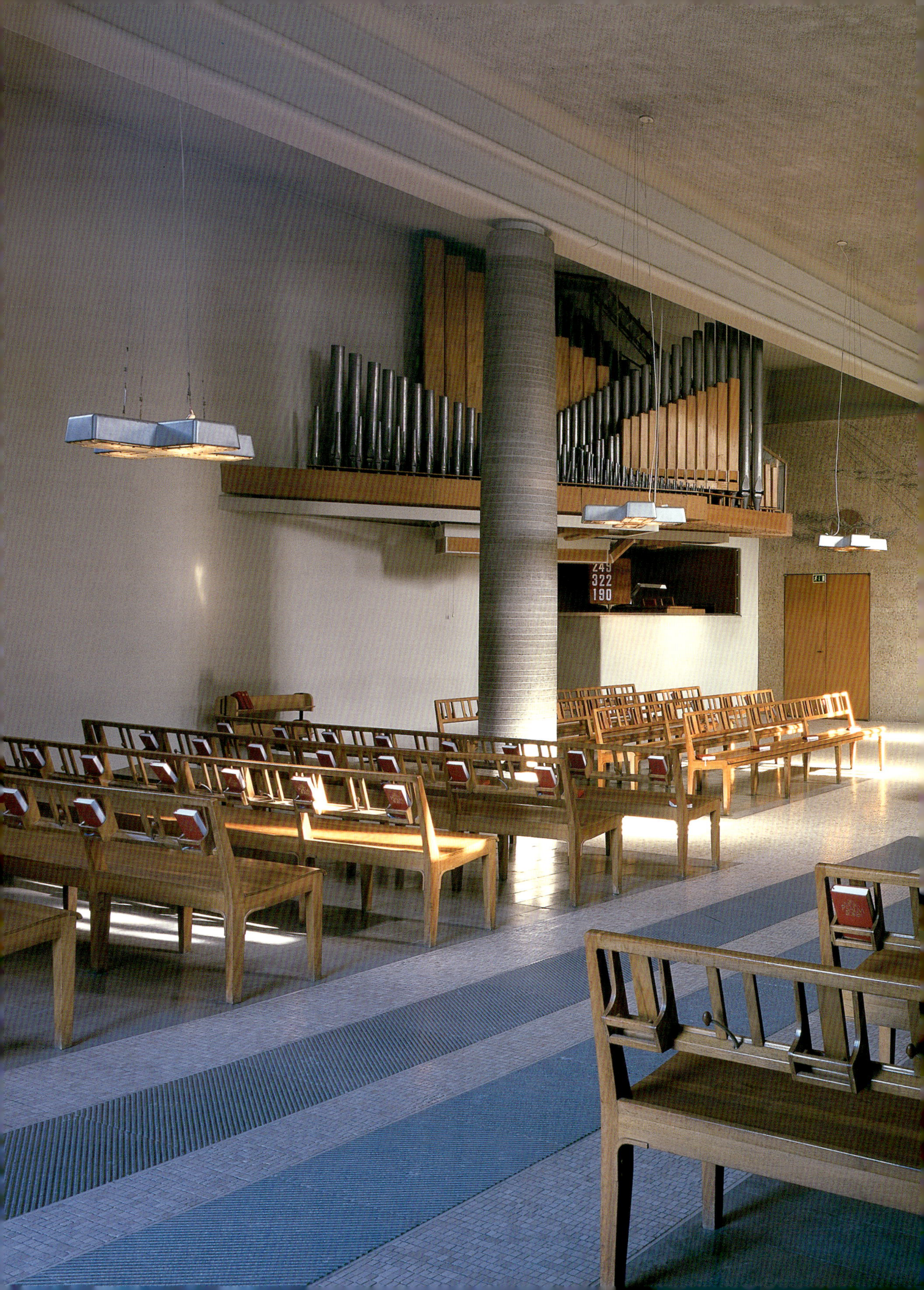
322
190

小礼拝堂（希望の礼拝堂）内観。南側の高窓にはルーバーが仕込まれ、直射光がコントロールできる。ふたつある小礼拝堂は同じ平面であるが、仕上げが異なる。ここでは正面の祭壇画がモザイク（オッテ・シェルド作）で描かれ、床にも同じ材料が使われている。

The interior of the Chapel of Hope. A louver is attached to the high windows on the south side to control the amount of direct sunlight that comes inside. The two small chapels are on the same plan, but are quite different in design. The mural at the front is a mosaic (by Otto Skold); the same sort of material used in the mosaic was also used to make the floor.

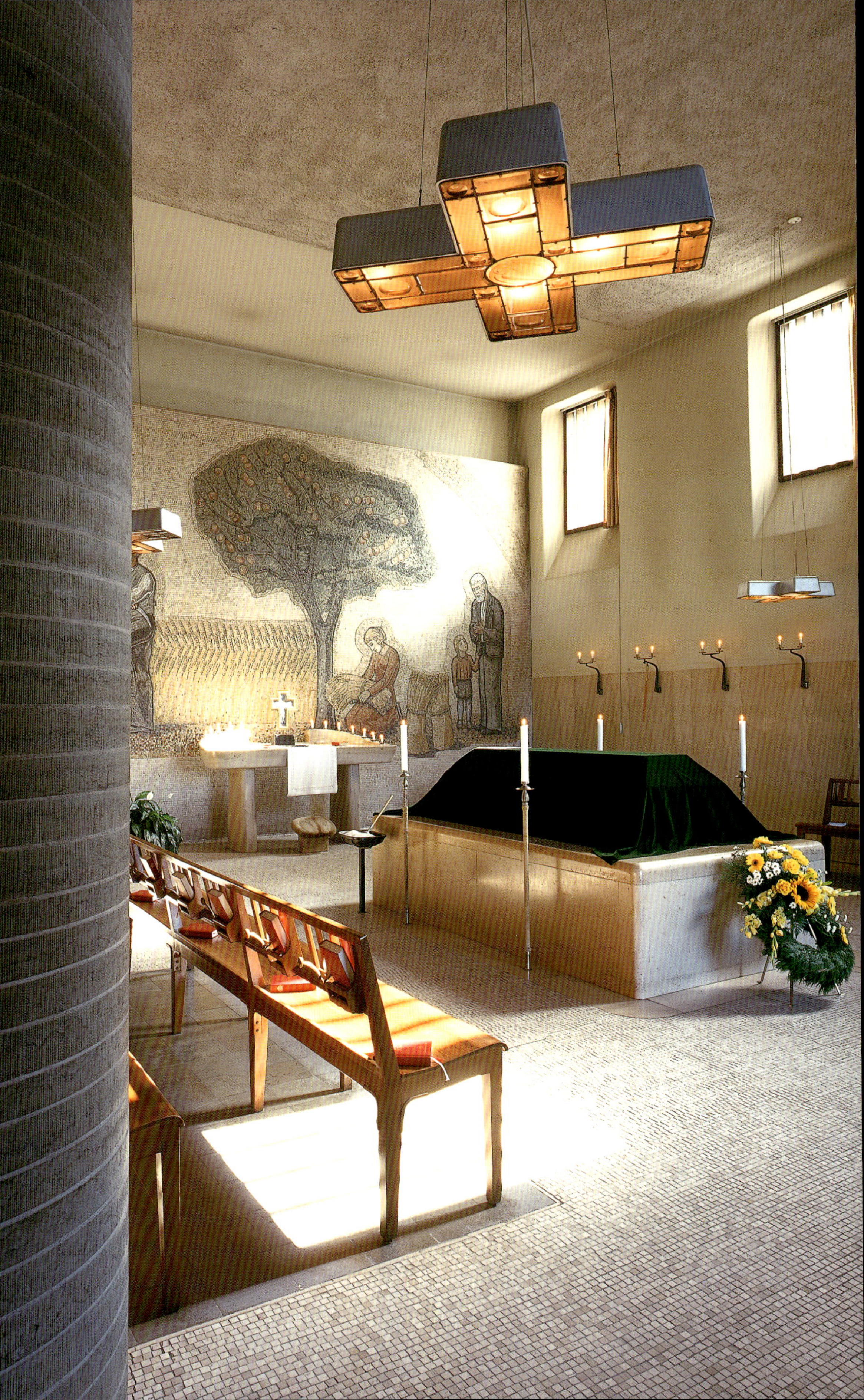

左右非対称の小礼拝堂（希望の礼拝堂）。高窓からの光に照らされた棺周り。手前石の丸柱の仕上げは、独特の味わいを感じさせる。十字形の照明器具には天使や動物のモチーフが施されている。

The asymmetry of the Chapel of Hope. Light shines down from the high windows around the coffin. The round pillar in the foreground adds a unique touch to the space. Angel and animal motifs are used to decorate the cross-shaped lighting fixture.

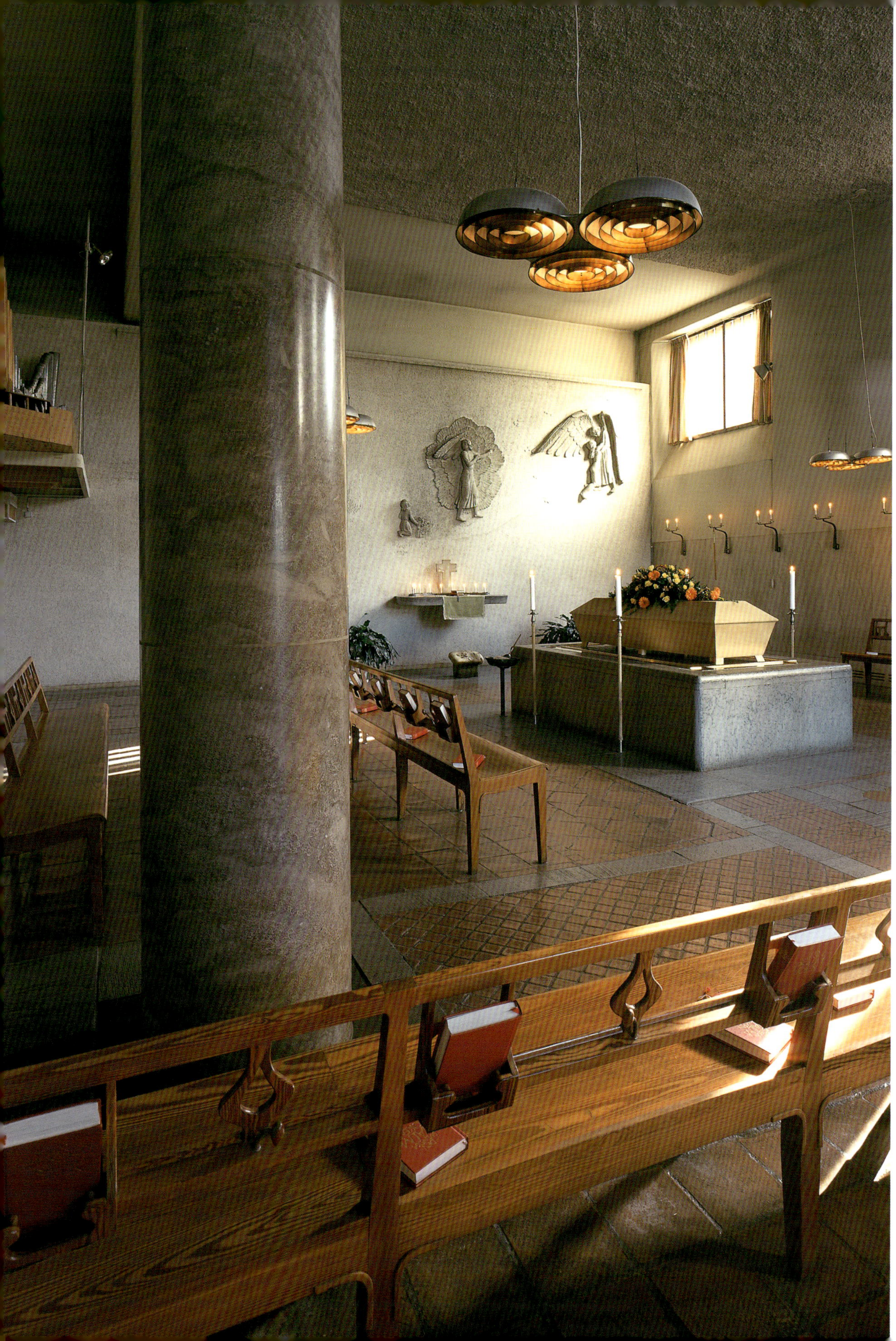

小礼拝堂（信仰の礼拝堂）内観。正面の祭壇はイーヴァル・ヨーンソンによるレリーフ画。奥の壁から手前に壁を設け、祭壇画としての自立性を高めている。床は御影石とレンガの模様張り。梁を支える丸柱は赤御影の本磨き。

An interior view of the second small chapel, the Chapel of Faith. The relief behind the altar is by Ivar Johnsson. By creating a wall in the foreground away from the back wall, the sense of independence is heightened. The floor is covered with patterns in granite and brick. The round pillars supporting the eaves are coated with a red granite finish.

E.G. Asplund

小礼拝堂待合室（上：希望の礼拝堂、左：信仰の礼拝堂）。葬儀を待つ人の心理を考慮して、天井と壁の取り合いは、アールで仕上げられ、梁・柱のH型鋼の被覆も含めて、どこにも鋭角的な仕上げが見当たらない。待合室の壁と一体化したベンチも秀逸。

The waiting room in the Chapel of Hope and Chapel of Faith. With the emotional state of the people waiting for a funeral in mind, the joints between the ceiling and walls have been designed in an "r" shape, and the eaves and the pillars have been coated with H-shaped steel, so that no sharp angles are visible. The shape of the benches, which are unified with the wall of the room, is also magnificent.

Detail of bench

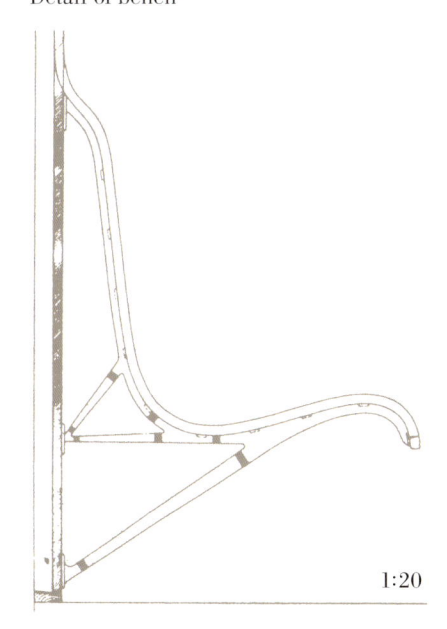

Working drawing for chair

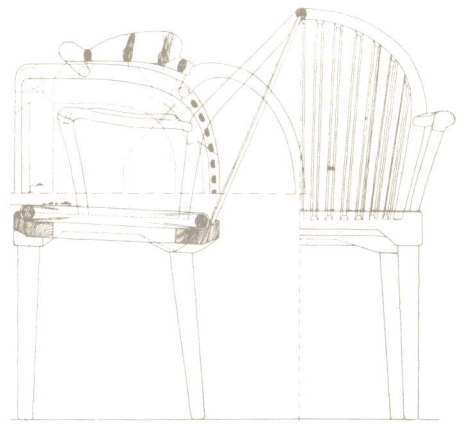

1:20

1:20

森の礼拝堂のさらに奥にある墓地管理棟。深緑色のピラミッドが4つと円錐が組み合わさった形はユーモラス。

The administrative wing is visible further beyond Woodland Chapel.
The combined form of the four, deep-green pyramids and cone provides a humorous touch to the space.

E.G. Asplund

松林に広がる墓碑と十字架。松林の樹間から射す斜めの光が森林の奥まで延び、小さな墓碑を優しく照らし出す。

Gravestones and crosses stretch throughout a grove of pines. The sunlight slants down between the trees, stretching to the back of the forest and bathing the small gravestones in gentle light.

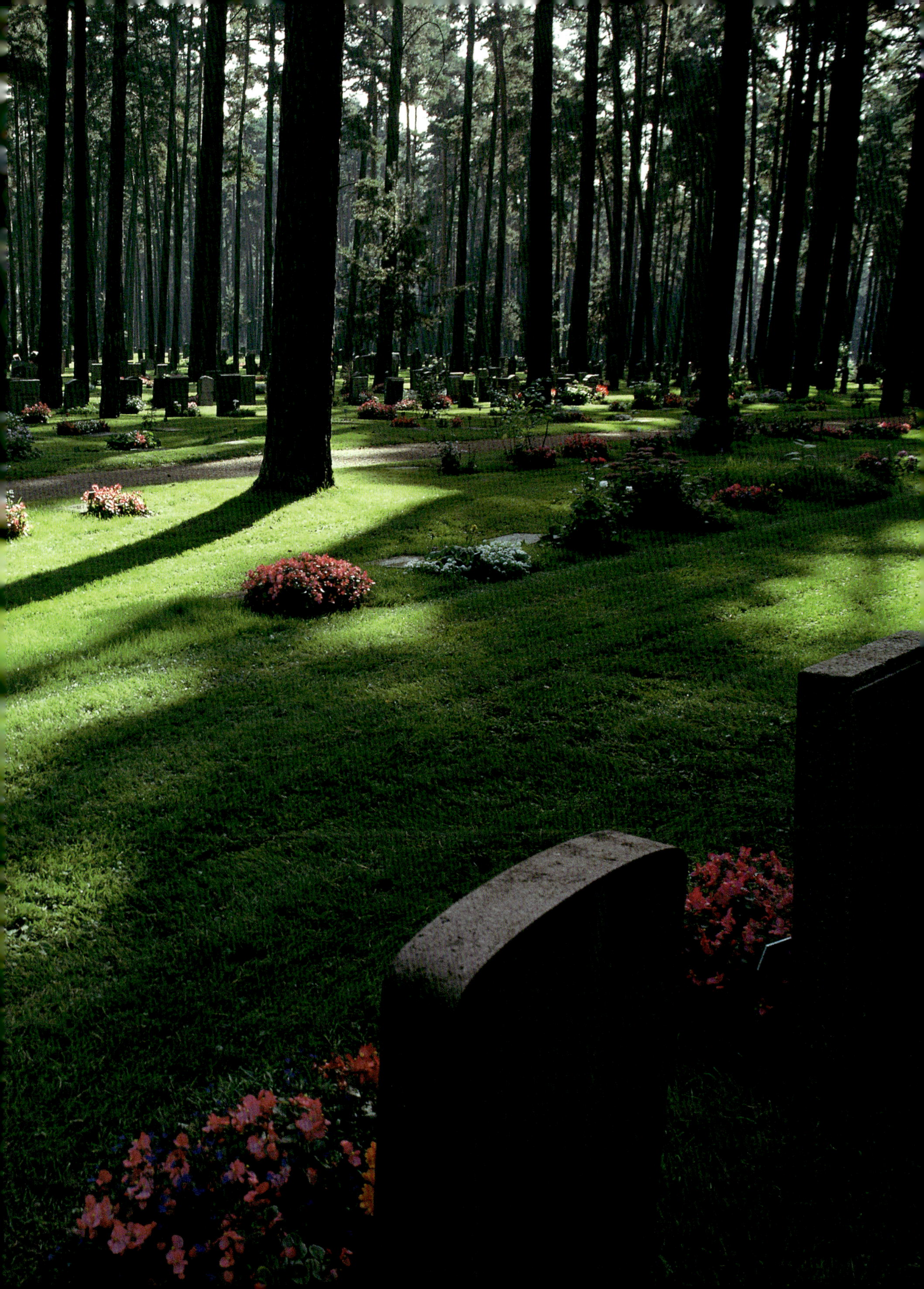

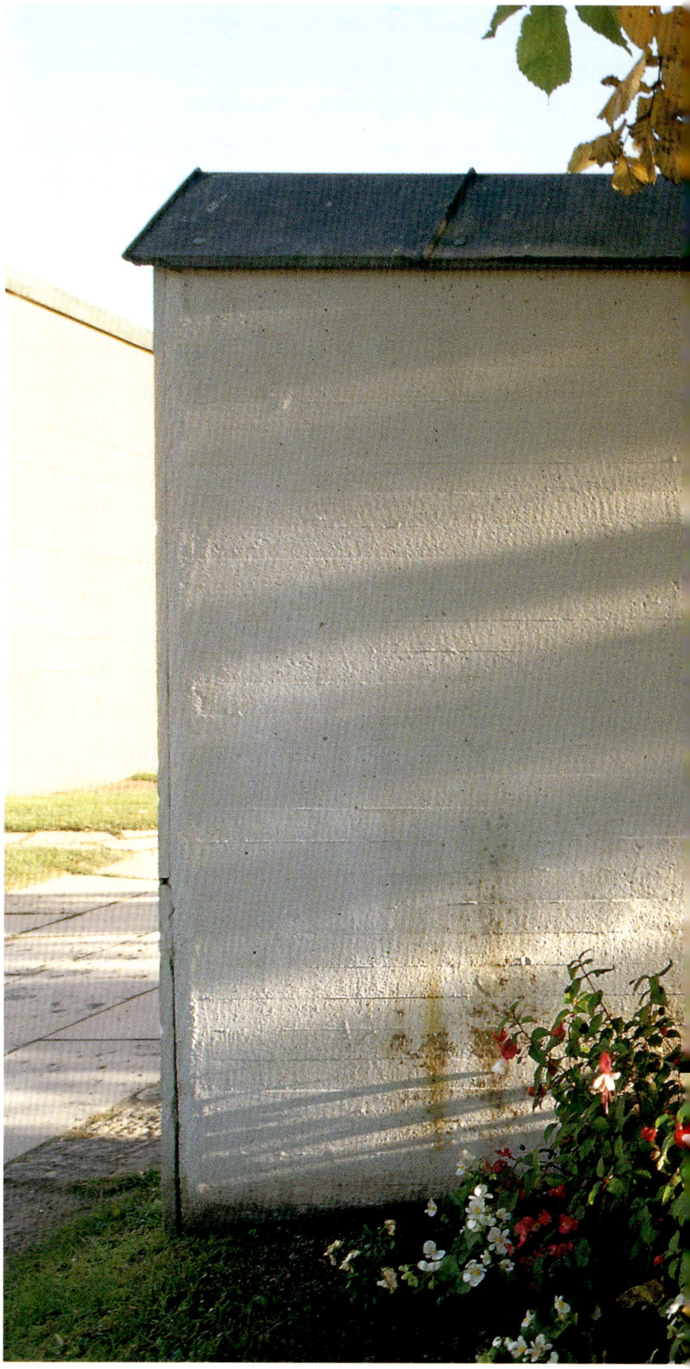

E.G. Asplund

アスプルンドの仕事場
──元所員、学生、仕事仲間に聞く

クリスティーナ・エングフォーシュ
スウェーデン国立建築博物館学芸部長

　エーリック・グンナール・アスプルンドは1940年に55歳で他界した。1985年のことなるが、当時アスプルンド生誕100周年の準備をしていた私は、建築家アスプルンドの生前を知る人びとに面会した。

　アスプルンド事務所出身者を探し出すために、まず私は彼の建築発注書に目を通した。そこには協力者たちの名前がもれなく記載されていたからである。そしてようやくアスプルンドの仕事ぶりを知るという人物一人ひとりに、直接会って話を聞くことができた。これまでのアスプルンドにまつわる文献からは、彼の素顔も仕事ぶりも伝わってこなかったのだ。アスプルンドについて知っていることがらは、ごく内輪の人びとの記憶にとどまっているだけだった。その人びともいまや80歳前後と高齢に達している。彼らは〈ブレーデンベリ・デパート〉、〈国立バクテリア研究所〉、〈イェーテボリ裁判所増築〉、〈森の火葬場〉などの代表作が生まれた1930年代当時のアスプルンドを知っていた。こうした情報は是非とも後世に残さなければならないと思った。

　もちろんこの手の調査はリスクをともなう。アスプルンドの時代はいまや遠い過去となっており、それだけに人の記憶には、後に見聞きした出来事やアスプルンド像なども紛れ込んでいる。だから、どれだけ本来の記憶をそのまま引き出せるかが問われるのである。そこで実際の出来事を中心に質問事項を組み立て、個人個人の体験を追い、研究材料として揃えることにした。そうすれば比較分析も可能になる。インタビューは事務所を率いる建築家と王立工科大学建築学科教授というふたつの彼の職業における関係者に行った。そして同時に友人、家族の目からのグンナール・アスプルンド像というものにも、私は興味をもった。

　インタビューは40人近くに及んだ。その内訳は、アスプルンド事務所の所員10名、王立工科大学の助手3名、世代差のあるアスプルンドの教え子たち20名、アスプルンドのご子息の2名、そして若干名の仕事仲間である。

　私はインタビューでの発言内容を確認、照合するために、建築家のハンス・フォグ教授の協力を得、スウェーデン建築博物館にあるアスプルンドの資料にあたった。本インタビューはスケッチ、図面と併せて『E.G. Asplund. Architect, friend and colleague』(Arkitektur Förlag, 1990)に収録されている。

● **設計事務所にて**

　アスプルンドは若者を雇った。新卒者もいれば、ストックホルムの王立工科大学にまだ在学中の学生もいたが、なかにはこの業界での経験を積んでから入所した者もいた。そのうち最年少の所員は学生ではなく、丁稚として採用されたウッレ・セッテルベリ少年であった。彼は使い走りやスケッチや図面のファイリングを任されていた。実際、アスプルンドはかなりの図面類を保管し、ファイリングに余念がなかった。アスプルンドがこれほど充実したコレクションを遺しているのには、そうしたわけがある。資料係を任された少年は模型もつくった。アスプルンドは模型制作にも熱心であった。

　この時期はストックホルム博覧会が開催され、アスプルンドの事務所も大所帯となっていた。アスプルンドは当時を振り返り、所員の仕事に目を行き届かせるのに苦労した、と語っている。一方、元所員らは口を揃えて、アスプルンドは展覧会の一部始終を仕切っていたと断言する。

　しかしストックホルム博覧会以降、事務所は縮小し所員数は6、7名を超えることはなかった。華やかな博覧会の直後しばらくは、アスプルンドは仕事に恵まれなかったのである。アスプルンドは名高い建築家であったため、依頼側も彼ならきっと高くつくだろうと躊躇した。そうでなくとも当時スウェーデン経済は低迷し、国内の着工数そのものが伸び悩んでいたのである。

　元所員のひとりに、若いドイツ人建築家ヘルベルト・コルンがいる。彼は設計実務に携わるほかに、国外からアスプルンドを訪ねてくる客の応対も引き受けた。アスプルンドはとても接客にまで手が回らなかったし、建築家はあれこれ語らず、作品自体に語らせるものだ、と考えていた。ジャーナリストたちもまた、彼のこうした考えにつきあわされることになった。

　仕事中のアスプルンドはどんな感じだったのだろうか？　彼は自分の仕事に対し、あくまで真剣に取り組み、絶対に手を抜くことがなかったという。アスプルンドはプロジェクトをまんべんなく機能で満たし、そうすることでフォルムに主たる根拠を与えていく。機能は一目瞭然でありつつも、どんな部分にも生き生きとした印象がなければならなかった。アスプルンドは決して機能主義を単なるスタイルとして片づけることがなかった。彼はどんな様式をも尊重したし、様式や建物について否定的な言い方もしなかった。所員たちには、仕事は自主的にするようにと言った。過去を振り返

るな、昔の図面を見るなと、口うるさく言ったらしい。所員たちはアスプルンドのいない隙を狙って、古い図面を見ていたようだ。

　アスプルンドが所員たちの傍らを離れることは少なく、おかげで勤務時間中の所内はしんと静まり返っていたという。アスプルンドの事務所では、後から紙を重ねて線をなぞれるよう、薄手のタイプ用紙にスケッチを起こしていた。アスプルンドはこれらのスケッチを手元に集め、作業内容を完全に掌握していた。所員たちは、アスプルンドの意図を引き出すために働いていたようなものだと言う。アスプルンドは作業中、ひとことも話さずに、自分の世界に閉じこもり、ひたすら集中していた。

　ディテールを重視する点は、いかにもアスプルンドらしい仕事の進め方である。かたちが決まるまでの道程は長かった。教鞭を執る立場でも、やはり彼はディテールにこだわった。学生たちはどんなディテールも省いてはいけないと教えられた。いっさいが図面に描き込まれていなければ、建築家の目が行き届かなくなってしまうからだと。

　アスプルンドは建築の問題ひとつひとつを、さながら科学者のまなざしで分析した。スケッチにかかる前に、彼はこんな問いかけをする。「はて、この状況ならどんな窓がしっくりくるだろうか。」たとえばほかの作品の図面を流用するなど、彼に言わせればもってのほかであった。ストックホルムの〈森の墓地〉内の〈信仰の礼拝堂〉の設計で彼は床のれんが敷きのために徹底的にれんがのスタディを行なう。ここではれんがを焼く間にどれだけ収縮するかが問題となった。彼はデータが揃った時点で、収縮率を7％と見積り、ようやくれんがのパターンを決め、つづいてれんがの数を確認し、それから図面に落とし込むのであった。しかし実際、燃焼時の収縮率は5パーセント、ことによると3パーセントに過ぎず、アスプルンドは肩を落とした。これにはなす術もなく、また一から始めるよりほかなかった。このデザインを下敷きに輪郭を削って微調整すればいいとの発想は、彼にはまったくない。当時の所員スヴェン・シェールは、経費の心配はいらないからと、れんがのパターンを一から起こすよう指示を受けた。

　所員たちは、事務所の経営が決して安泰ではないことを察していた。彼らの作業はアスプルンドが納得するまで延々と続けられるのが常であったし、結局、提出期限ぎりぎりまで粘って図面を

仕上げることも珍しくなかった。〈森の火葬場〉の提出図面がそのことを物語っている。アスプルンドはここで特殊な手法を採用、というより2種類の図面を合成した。その一番の目的は、建物がどのような印象になるのかをリアリスティックに見せることにあった。そこで彼は、通常の立面図の上にパースをかけたようなものを作成する。視覚的な奥行きを出すためである。また所員には火葬場の周囲に草を描き込むよう、それも写実的に、と指示を出す。「そのために製図台の前に何日も座り続けるはめになった。」とレナルト・ベリヴァールは当時を振り返る。「そうして草の一本一本を描き込んでいったのです。アスプルンドがそれだけの経費を許すということに感心もしたし、ありがたくも思いました。」ちなみに当時のスウェーデンでは、建築家の設計料は時間ベースではなく、建築費に対する固定料率で決められていたのである。

　一度、アスプルンドが米国旅行に出かけ、事務所を数週間留守にしたことがある。事務所は〈イェーテボリ裁判所増築〉の仕事を抱えて忙しく、所員たちは彼の留守中にも増築棟のファサードのスケッチを描き進めるよう言い渡されていた。うちのふたり、オーケ・ポルネとニルス・リセーンは19世紀に建てられた隣の裁判所の様式に倣ってファサードを描くよう指示され、かたやトーレ・アールセンは近代的なファサードを描くことになっていた。ポルネとリセーンは、近代的な建築に心惹かれていたので、所長の指示に落胆する。だがアスプルンドの狙いは、ふた通りの案をつくることでその違いを比較することにあった。はたして帰国したアスプルンドは、近代案を採用する。結局、裁判所増築棟は近代的なファサードで建てられらた。

　1930年のストックホルム博覧会で若い建築家たちが学んだのは、建物の構造は建物のかたちに表れていなければならないとする教訓である。それだけに、元所員レナルト・ベリヴァールにとって〈森の火葬場〉は衝撃的であった。鉄の構造が外観から把握できないのである。彼は自分で何枚かのスケッチをしたとき、背後の鉄の構造が目に見えるようにした。すると驚いたことに、アスプルンドはただ微笑んでこう言ったのだ。「かたちと構造が一致しなければならないといっても、そんなものは話半分に聞いておきなさい。」

　所員らに言わせると、アスプルンドは大の技術家であったが、そのぶん意識も高く、野心もあり、物怖じしない性格ゆえに、リスクも冒した。ストックホルムの〈ブレーデンベリ・デパート〉に使われた

外壁もその一例である。ここにはスウェーデンではまだ先例の少なかったイタリア産トラヴァーティンのパネルが使われたが、やはりこれでは雨も多く寒さの厳しいスウェーデンの気候には耐えきれず、外壁をやり替えるはめになった。アスプルンドは間口がわずか7メートルしかない細長い敷地を相手に、有効面積を極力広くとろうと、厚みの薄い材料を物色したのである。カーテンウォールの初期の例でもあった。

　アスプルンドは構造家スティグ・エデーンと組むこともあった。エデーンはエンジニアとしては建築に対する興味も共感も人一倍強かったし、それに頭も切れ、発想も柔軟であった。エデーンはアスプルンドの考えを汲み取り、それを構造物に具現化していった。エデーンの回顧録には〈森の火葬場〉では、ごく早い段階からプロジェクトに引き込まれた、といったエピソードなど、アスプルンドとの貴重な共同作業が書き綴られている。エデーンは王立工科大学でも何年かアスプルンドの助手を務めている。ある日、学生を引き連れてストックホルム近郊ソルナにあの機能主義建築〈国立バクテリア研究所〉の見学に繰り出したこともあった。エデーンには、アスプルンドの注文どおりに階段をつくる仕事があった。「アスプルンドは、こんなふうに階段をつくれるはずだ、もちろん強度も確保して、と言うのですが、おかげで私は何度も図面を描き直すはめになりました。おまけに階段の費用がやたらと高くついてしまったものだから、これではとても機能主義と呼べる代物じゃありませんよ。」

　新規のプロジェクトに取りかかると、アスプルンドは将来その建物を利用することになる人びとの活動を調査した。建物のヴォリュームや材料、部屋の面積や形状などをはじき出す前に、彼はそうした活動を図式化した。物理的な事柄を数値化することよりも先に、人間の活動を分析することから始めるのが彼の流儀である。大学教授でもある彼は、この手順を踏めば複数の部屋をとりまとめることができるとして、助手や学生を困惑させた。と言うのは、それがどんな建物に応用されるかについて、まったく言及しないのだ。アスプルンドとしては、とりあえず人びとの活動を図式化する練習を学生にさせたかったのである。

　仕事中のアスプルンドは猛烈な集中力を発揮し、それだけに邪魔が入るとたちまち不機嫌になった。誰かが鉛筆を削るほんの些細な音さえ、彼を苛立たせ、雷が落ちた。だから所内は日頃

から沈黙に包まれていた。それでも仕事が一段落つくと、アスプルンドはまるで人が変わったように、陽気で温厚な側面を見せた。「うちの事務所にとっては珍しくないことでしたが、コンペに参加していたときなど、場の空気はぐっと和らぎました。コンペ提出のためにアスプルンドが連夜机に向かってパースに色付けをしていたときなど、あの彼が口笛を吹いたり、突然大声で歌い出したり、ということもありましたね。」これはヤン・ヴァーリンデルの弁である。

● 王立工科大学の教授

アスプルンドは1931年に王立工科大学の教授に就任し、その生涯を閉じる1940年10月までこの職にあった。建築学科の課程は4年あり、うち前半の2年は住宅建築なるものにあてられ、技術や材料に関する基礎が教えられた。3年生、4年生は本格的に建築学を専攻し、その主任をアスプルンドが務めた。

1930年代初頭のスウェーデンでは建設件数そのものが少なく、ストックホルム博覧会を手がけたこの有名建築家でさえなかなか仕事にありつけなかった。アスプルンドはこの時期に離婚し、再婚する。扶養家族はふたつに増えた。教職の収入は民間の建築家の収入よりも安定していた。そうした公務に就くことによって、当然、教職という社会的立場と現業的立場との線引きもしなければならなかった。

教え子たちへのインタビューでは、講義をする姿、設計批評をする姿、国内外の建築視察旅行を引率する姿の3つの場面のアスプルンドが語られた。

教え子のなかにはハラルド・ミェーベリやラーシュ・オーケルンドのように、アスプルンドの講義のノートを今でも大切に保管している者もいる。なるほど、彼の講義は堅苦しく、隙がなく、厳粛なものであった。内容は建築設計や建築家の仕事をとりまく状況だとか、建築法規や依頼主とのつきあい方にも及んでいる。彼は住宅の間取りについても丁寧に解説し、各部屋の広さをどのように割り振るかを講じた。光の動き、人間の動きは、床、壁、納戸、ベッド、ストーブの配置に劣らず重要であった。さまざまな建築作品が写真で紹介され、学生たちの目は釘付けになった。当時はまだビジュアルな資料が不足しており、多くの教師は写真の代わりに文献リストの紹介で済ませていた。

講義内容に関しては、元学生らの証言は一致しているが、講義内容への個々の評価には開きがみられる。講義が退屈で、建築家になるのに役に立たなかったと述べる者もいる。特に高校を出てそのまま進学した若い学生に多い。反対に、アスプルンドの講義は素晴らしかった、役立った、彼の話を一言も聞き漏らすまいとした、と言う元学生もいる。こちらは幾年かの実務経験を経て大学に戻ったやや年長の学生に多い。

　アスプルンドが設計演習に出した課題は、ときに彼自身の仕事と重なっていた。鉄道駅、サマーハウス、学生寮など。アスプルンドの講義に対する意見は元学生らの間で分かれるが、逆に学生たちの作品に対してアスプルンドが行なった批評については、学生から異口同音の答えが返ってくる。彼の批評は的確であった、と誰もが言う。その講評は細部までよく行き届いており、公平で、学生の励みになった。彼は学生のスケッチをめったなことでは切り捨てたりせず、むしろそのなかから良い点を見つけ出し、それを伸ばそうとした。またそれらを最終解答というようにはとらえず、その先も作業を続けるべきプロジェクトとして扱った。学生が自分の描いたファサードの良し悪しを知ろうとしたら、この講評は期待外れであったろう。アスプルンドはそのようなコメントはしなかったから。ただ、ファサードには室内のようすが映し出されなければならない、と注意することはままあった。人間がその場その場でどのように動くかを考えなさい、家具が通路を塞ぐことがないように、と口を酸っぱくして言った。かように非実用的な案には厳しかった。そして学生が空想の翼を羽ばたかせたときには褒めたし、なにより学生が独自に考えたり独創的であることを大いに歓迎した。元学生のひとり、クルト・ストレーレナルトによると、「先生は私たちが建築家の仕事に関心をもつよう尻を叩いてくれたし、夢中にさせてくれました。」

　アスプルンドが学生を連れて自作などの見学に出かけた話も、彼のまた別の魅力を伝えている。元学生のヴェリ・パーテラとエーリック・スタルクにとって、師との見学旅行は強く記憶に刻まれることとなった。アスプルンドは学生を相手に、自分が受注内容をどのように分析したか、それに対しどのような解答に行き着いたか、設計中にどんな問題に突き当たったかなどを解説した。また自分自身はどこに納得がいっていないかを明かすなど、自作への批判的な態度も見せた。

　〈森の火葬場〉を訪れた折に、アスプルンドは語った。ここでは人間の死がふたつの側面、すな

わち儀式的な側面と技術的な側面をもっている、と。さらに、火葬場の技術的な部分にいかに威厳を添えるかがデザイン上の課題であった、と続けた。〈聖十字礼拝堂〉については、柱と天井の取合いにアスプルンドは不満を残していた。学生の崇拝の的だった〈イェーテボリ裁判所〉にしても、アスプルンドに言わせれば窓の幅が狭すぎた。彼は視界の角にやっと入るくらいに一隻のボートが川を流れてくるのを指差し、イェーテボリにはせっかくの川の景観があるのに、このプロポーションの窓ではそれを生かせない、とこぼした。いわく、スケッチも描いたし、パースも立面も描いたし、スタディも繰り返した、それでようやくこれならいける、というところまで行き着いたのに、実際に建物ができて使われてみると、それがうまく行かなかったことに気づいた。彼は建物の仕上がりにおおむね満足のようすであったが、その表情からは、作品に対する関心がかつてほどはないことがうかがえた。それでもフォルムに対するこだわりだけは、いつまでも引きずったようだ。

1930年代当時の建築学科には女子学生は数えるほどしかいなかった。その貴重なひとり、イングリッド・エングヴァール＝ウッデンベリによると、男子学生と女子学生の分け隔てをしなかったこともアスプルンドの良さであった。当時のアカデミックな世界には、まだ男女平等の概念がもち込まれていなかった。講義の時間、男子学生は女子学生を遠巻きにして座り、彼女たちとの距離を置いた。教師らは彼女たちを弱者扱いするか、さもなければまるで腫れ物に触るかのようにご機嫌をとった。アスプルンドはそのどちらでもなかった、とイングリッドは話す。

元所員たちにインタビューを行なったときには、たとえアスプルンドの人間性なり思想なり仕事なりに関して各人各様に特徴を挙げたにせよ、彼らの発言に明確な類似や一致がみられた。それにひきかえ、元学生たちの話は一見するとてんでばらばらであった。それでもしばらくすると、根底ではひとつのパターンを描いていることに気づいた。すると、どの発言にも納得がいったし、最終的にはアスプルンドの仕事の仕方と教え方とが一本の線でつながった。

◉依頼主や仕事仲間とのつきあい

アスプルンドがひとりの建築家として示した責任感には、彼と依頼主との関係が如実に反映されている。プログラムにしろ予算にしろ、また期限にしろ、彼は心して受け止めた。図面は期限内に仕上げたし、着工後は決して変更を入れなかった。彼はいったん契約を交わしたらそのと

おりに遂行したが、それでも彼自身の正解にたどり着くための努力を惜しまなかった。必要とあれば、相手を説得した。〈イェーテボリ裁判所増築〉のときは、建設直後にアスプルンドと依頼主らは激しい議論を戦わせた。依頼主側は後日、そのときの彼の言い分にあまりに説得力があったので、こちらが折れた、と弁解している。

　アスプルンドの仕事仲間といえば、やはりあのアルヴァ・アールトである。アールトは彼の親友でもあった。アスプルンドはアールトの13歳年長であったが、ふたりは1920年代初めに出会っている。このときアールトはアスプルンド事務所の扉を叩き、雇用を申し入れるのだが、あいにく断られる。1920年代末にふたりは再会し、親しくなった。1930年代、彼らの親交は深まる。旧所員らによると、アールトはたびたび事務所に顔を出したようだ。

●尊敬と共感

　アスプルンドから得た経験をひとことで言ってほしいと旧所員たちに訊くと、皆口々に、自分たちが一人前の建築家になるのにアスプルンドの影響は絶大なものだった、と返してきた。アスプルンドは彼らにこう諭した。建築はヒューマンでなければならない、そして人のため、人の感情のため、そして機能のために、君たちは尽力しなければならない、と。

　以上、旧所員や学生とのインタビューを行なってきたわけだが、これらのインタビューに登場するアスプルンドの人物像は、ひとつに収束しない。各人が、アスプルンドという人間をさまざまな角度から見ているのだ。的確さ、粘り強さ、注意深さ、職業上の責任感などは彼の重要な側面だが、思いやりや人間愛もまた忘れてはいけない側面である。

　アスプルンドの仕事を見ていると、どうやら彼にはいくつもの才能を同時に操る能力があったらしい。そうした能力をそなえた人物は、そう多くはない。

　アスプルンドは人間の活動の場を創造する、いわばクリエーターである。自分がひとりの人間として蓄積してきた経験の厚みから、それらを創造しているのではないか。だからこそ彼の建物には深い普遍的な論理、すなわち万人に理解される論理が働いているのである。

Asplund at Work
—Interviews with Assistants, Students and Colleagues—

Christina Engfors
Head of Department of
Architectural Education,
Swedish Museum of Architecture

Erik Gunnar Asplund died in 1940 at the age of 55. In 1985, during the preparations for a celebration of the centenary of Asplund's birth, I met people who had recollections of Asplund as an architect.

In order to find out who had worked at the architect's office, I went through Asplund's written presentations of his building commissions where his collaborators are properly named.

Eventually, I had the opportunity to interview in a systematic way the people who had personal memories and experiences of Asplund's way of working, experiences that until then were absent from the Asplund literature.

This kind of Asplund-knowledge was only to be found in the memories of a small group of people who were around 80 years old. They had worked with him in the 1930s when important buildings like the Bredenberg Department Store, the State Bacteriological Laboratory, the Göteborg Law Courts Extension and the Woodland Crematorium were built. It was of great interest to secure this knowledge for the future.

There are of course risks with this kind of research. The Asplund era happened a long time ago and the memories are mixed with later events and later descriptions about him. It was important to find a method that brought out the memories as intact as possible. Therefore, the structure of the questions was concentrated on real events to get hold of the personal experience and a research material that made comparisons possible. The interviews dealt with Asplund's different tasks - the architect in his office, the professor of architecture at the Royal Institute of Technology. Gunnar Asplund as understood by colleagues, friends and family members interested me as well.

I interviewed almost 40 people; i.e., around ten assistants from Asplund's office, three assistants from the Royal Institute of Technology, about 20 students who met Asplund through the years, two of his children and a small number of colleagues.

To confirm what was said in the interviews and to control the statements that were made, I looked thoroughly through the Asplund collection at the Swedish Museum of Architecture together with the architect and professor Hans Fog. We found sketches and drawings that people had worked with and talked about in the interviews.

The interviews accompanied by sketches, drawings and photos were published in *E.G. Asplund. Architect, friend and colleague.* (Arkitektur Förlag, 1990).

At the Architect's Office

Asplund chose very young assistants. They had just graduated from or were still studying at the architectural department at the Royal Institute of Technology in Stockholm. Some of them had earlier training in building technology.

The youngest member of Asplund's office staff, however, was not a student but a youngster employed as an errand boy as early as 1928. As an errand boy at the office, Olle Zetterberg was also entrusted with the filing of sketches and drawings. It is a fact that Asplund kept much of his drawing material and had a great interest in filing, and that is the reason why the collection he left is as complete as it is. The errand boy who became an archivist also became a modelmaker. Asplund took great interest in modelmaking.

This happened at the time of the Stockholm Exhibition and Asplund's office was big. Later, Asplund said that he found it trying and difficult to oversee and survey the office work. The assistants all claim that Asplund controlled every nail in the exhibition. But after that, the office was never larger than six or seven people.

During the years immediately after the big exhibition, Asplund had rather few and rather small commissions. Asplund was famous and the commissioners thought that perhaps he was very expensive. But Sweden suffered from an economic depression and on the whole not much was built.

Among his assistants, Asplund had a young German architect, Herbert Korn, who apart from architectural work took care of Asplund's visitors from abroad. Asplund had very little time for visitors, and was of the opinion that the works should speak and not the architect. That was a view that the journalists had to put up with as well.

What was characteristic of Asplund at work?, I asked the assistants. They answered that Asplund had a serious and careful approach to what he did. He penetrated the function of the project extremely thoroughly to find the important basis for the form. Function was obvious, but everything had to give a living impression. Asplund never talked about functionalism as a style. He respected all styles and never mentioned a style or a building in disparaging terms. He encouraged the assistants to work independently. They were told not to look back and he urgently requested they not browse through the old drawings, which they did when he was away.

Asplund very often sat beside the assistants and they all worked in deep silence. When they were sketching they often used thin typewriting paper that afterwards was stacked up. Asplund collected these papers. He had a firm grip on the work, and the assistants said that they were only helping him develop his intentions. While he worked, he did not say a word. He turned inwards and concentrated.

The importance of the details is a distinctive feature in Asplund's working methods. There was a long searching process before Asplund was satisfied with a shape. As a professor, he also was emphatic about details. The students were told not to omit a single detail in the drawings. Everything should be there and nothing left out of the architect's control.

Asplund analyzed every architectural problem in an almost scientific way. Before he began sketching, he asked questions like: What kind of window is right in this special situation? He never accepted, for example, the use of a window drawing twice. When he worked on the brick floor at the Chapel of Faith at the Woodland Cemetery in Stockholm, he initiated a thorough study of bricks. An important question to answer was: How much would the stones diminish during the burning process? When he had gotten all the answers, he designed the brick pattern, counted the stones and had all of them marked on the drawing. Then something terrible happened. The burning process did not make the stones diminish by 7% but by 5 or 3% and Asplund nearly collapsed. There was nothing to do but to start it all over again. Apparently, it never occurred to Asplund that he could use the design and deform the outer edges. The assistant, Sven Kjerr, was told to draw the whole pattern once more without considering the costs.

The assistants assumed that Asplund's office economy couldn't have been very good since he always worked until he was content with the result, and that often was the same moment when the drawings had to be delivered. The drawing presentation of Woodland Crematorium is one example of this. Here Asplund used a special technique or rather combined two techniques. It was essential that the viewer should get a realistic impression of the building to be. Therefore, he added a false perspective to the traditional drawing of the facade. He wanted to achieve a visual depth. He told his assistants to draw the grass around the crematorium in a realistic way. "I sat there for several days," said Lennart Bergvall, "and pointed out every blade of grass. I was impressed and delighted that Asplund accepted these costs." At that time, the architects in Sweden were paid not per hour but per settled rate.

Once Asplund left the office for some weeks and went on a tour to the U.S. The office was busy working on the Göteborg Law Courts Extension and the assistants were told, while he was away, to go on sketching the extension facade. Two of them, Åke Porne and Nils Rissén, were to sketch in a style that was similar to the old 19th century courthouse and one of them, Tore Ahlsén, was told to sketch a modern facade. The first two were very disappointed since they too wanted to work on a modern-looking building. But for Asplund, it was important to see the alternatives and compare the differences. After he got back, he chose the modern facade, and that is finally how the courthouse extension was built.

A lesson the young architects had learned from the Stockholm Exhibition of 1930 was that the building construction should be visible in the shape. Therefore, Bergvall was shocked when he worked on Woodland Crematorium and found out that the iron construction was not visible. On his own he made some sketches where the iron construction behind could be seen, but to his great astonishment Asplund just smiled and said: "That there should be a correspondence between the shape and the construction is a saying one must take with a grain of salt."

The assistants at the office claimed that Asplund was a very interested and clever building technician, but like the concerned, ambitious and audacious person he was, he took risks. The facade material of Bredenberg's Department Store in Stockholm is an example of this. The panels of travertine, an Italian stone that had not been used much in Sweden before, yielded to the cold and rainy climate and had to be replaced. The fact is that Asplund had to work with an extremely narrow site with only a width of seven meters. He wanted to realize a useful space that was as large as possible and looked for a very thin material. This was an early example of the curtain wall.

Asplund collaborated with a structural engineer, Stig Ödeen, on the project. He was an engineer with a great interest in and feeling for architecture, a brilliant and open-minded man. He understood Asplund's ideas and developed them into constructions. In his memoirs, Ödeen writes about his rich collaboration with Asplund. An illustration of this is when at a very early stage he was drawn into the project of Woodland Crematorium. For some years Ödeen was also Asplund's assistant at the Royal Institute of Techology. One day they went on an excursion to the State Bacteriological Laboratory in Solna near Stockholm, which is considered a functionalist building. Ödeen said that he had the job of constructing the staircase in a way that followed Asplund's wishes. "Asplund believed that it is possible to make a staircase look like this and at the same time achieve the strength. I had to draw it over and over again until I succeeded. Furthermore, the staircase is awfully expensive, so don't call it functionalism!"

At the start of a new project, Asplund studied the activity of the people who were going to use the building in the future. Before he calculated the volumes, materials, space areas and figures, he made a scheme of activity. Thus, he started by analyzing human activity, not by quantifying physical matter. As a professor, he presented this working method for combining the different rooms and it puzzled both assistants and students, as he did not mention what building it was for. He wanted the students just to practice and sketch an anonymous communication schedule.

Asplund at work was utterly concentrated and therefore got very irritated by disturbances. Even small intrusions like someone sharpening a pencil could annoy him and cause him to rebuke the offender. Thus, silence usually reigned at the office. But when Asplund relaxed from work, he completely changed and showed the world the happy, kind and warm sides he was also gifted with. These sides could break through even at work. "When the office took part in competitions, which was rather frequent, the atmosphere was much more easygoing. It happened that when he sat during the nights colouring perspectives, Asplund would start whistling and even burst out into song," Jan Wallinder told me.

Professor at the Royal Institute of Technology

Asplund was appointed professor at the Royal Institute of Technology in 1931 and remained there until his death in October 1940. The architecture program was four years long. The two first years were concerned with what was called house-building and gave the students a technical and material foundation. The third and fourth years were dedicated to architecture and Asplund was the head of that department.

Not much was built in Sweden at the beginning of the 1930s, the commissions were few even for the famous architect of the Stockholm Exhibition. Asplund divorced his wife around this time and remarried. From now on, he had two families to support. The income of a professor was more secure than that of a private practicing architect. Certainly, such an official position also signified a social and professional distinction.

My interviews with Asplund's former students were divided into three different parts: Asplund as a lecturer, as a critic and as a leader of excursions in Sweden and abroad.

Some of his former students, like Harald Mjöberg and Lars Åkerlund, had kept their notebooks from Asplund's lectures. Apparently, the lectures were formal, thorough and serious. He talked about the conditions for architectural design and for an architects work. He lectured about the legislation concerning building and its relation to the commissioners. He presented house plans and taught them how to make dimensions for different rooms. Light and human movements were as important as the measurements of floors, walls, closets, beds, and stoves. He gave the students photos of various architectural works. These were highly appreciated since there was a shortage of literature and many professors replaced pictures with lists of references.

As for the contents of the lectures, the students were in agreement, but when it came to personal estimation of the contents they disagreed. There were those who found the lectures dull and unhelpful, especially those who were very young and came directly from high school. But there were those as well who said that Asplund's lectures were brilliant and useful and that they did not want to miss a word of them. These students were often a little older than the others and had spent some years in architectural or building practice.

The projects that Asplund gave the students to sketch as exercises were sometimes the same as his own commissions: railway stations, summer houses, students hostels. If the students' opinions about Asplund's lectures varied, the opposite was true of his criticism of their exercises. The assertion that his criticism was excellent was unanimous. His judgements were thorough, fair and encouraging. Almost never did he reject sketches. Rather, he was looking for what was positive and developable. He did not regard them as final solutions but as projects to continue working on. The student who wanted to know whether he had made a good or a bad facade was disappointed, since Asplund never commented in that way, though he often said that the facade should mirror the inside. How people move in different places was something he returned to, including whether the furniture blocked the pathway, and there was always criticism of unpractical solutions. He appreciated it when the students used fantasies and above all he encouraged independent and original thinking. As one of them, Curt Strehlenert, said: "He stimulated our interest in the architect's work and made us dedicated."

The excursions that Asplund made with his students, especially to his own buildings, expose other sides of his personality. For some of them, Veli Paatela and Erik Stark among others, these excursions have engraved themselves on their memories. Asplund explained how he analyzed his commission, which solution he had chosen and why, and talked about the difficulties he had to face during the process. He also pointed out things he was not satisfied with, thus revealing a critical attitude to his own work.

At Woodland Crematorium, Asplund explained that death here has two sides, one ceremonious and one technical, and that it had been essential for him to design the technical department of the crematorium with dignity. In the Chapel of the Holy Cross, Asplund was not content with the connection of the pillars and the ceiling. At the Göteborg Law Courts, which the students all admired very much, Asplund said that the windows were made too narrow. He pointed at a boat which had hardly come into view on the stream outside and said that the window shape did not sufficiently consider the Göteborg townscape. He said that he had made sketches, perspectives, sections and experiments, and at last had thought that it was going to be all right, but now that it was built, it was not a success. On the whole, he seemed content with the result, but you could see from the look on his face that the project did not really interest him anymore. The problem of form, however, continued to occupy his mind even when the work was finished and the building completed.

In the 1930s, there were very few female students of architecture. One of them, Ingrid Engvall - Uddenberg, told me that one thing that she had appreciated about Asplund was that he made no distinction between male and female students. At this time, equality between the sexes was not introduced in the academic world. During the lectures, the boys sat at a safe distance from the girls in a wide circle around them. The professors treated the girls in either a patronizing or an excessively polite almost courting way. Asplund, however, did not belong to this type, she said.

The answers that the assistants in the office gave in their interviews had a clear resemblance and correspondence, even if they stressed different traits in Asplund's personality, thinking and working. What the students told me first seemed completely disparate. After some time, an underlying pattern was discovered, the statements became understandable and finally, the correspondence between Asplund's working and teaching methods appeared.

Relations with Commissioners and Colleagues

The responsibility Asplund showed as an architect certainly reflected his relations to his commissioners. He carefully considered a project, the budget and the time allotted. He delivered drawings on time and never changed anything during the building process. He kept the agreements that were made, but he struggled for the solutions he believed in. He could be very convincing. The commissioners in Göteborg defended themselves by saying that Asplund's arguments were very convincing during the intense debate that followed the erection of the Law Courts Extension.

Of all of Asplund's colleagues, Alvar Aalto, who was his close friend was the best known. Asplund was 13 years older than Aalto and their acquantance began in the early 1920s when the young Aalto knocked at Asplund's door and asked for work but was rejected. At the end of the decade, they met again and got to know each other. Throughout the 1930s their friendship deepened. Asplund's assistants said that Aalto often visited the office.

Respect and Empathy

When Asplund's assistants were asked to sum up their experiences of him, they all answered that he had had a great influence on their development as architects. Asplund told them that architecture should be human and that man and his feelings and functions should lead their efforts.

The picture of Asplund at work as it appears from the interviews with assistants and students is complex. They pointed out different sides of Asplund's personality. Accuracy, persistence, carefulness, and professional responsibility were mentioned as very important traits, and so were sympathy and humanity.

Asplund's working method seems to have been a combination of a variety of abilities at the same time. This capacity is rare.

Asplund was a creator of rooms for human activities. He created from the depth of his experience as a human being. Therefore, his buildings have a deep universal logic that can be understood by everyone.

References:
Christina Engfors: *E G Asplund. Arkitekt, vän och kollega* (Arkitektur Förlag, 1990).
Christina Engfors: *E G Asplund. Architect, friend and colleague* (Arkitektur Förlag, 1990).

カールスハムンの中学校 1912-18 カールスハムン
Secondary School at Karlshamn, Karlshamn

　1912年にスウェーデン南東部の港町カールスハムンで、新しい中学校の設計コンペが行われた。I.G. クラーソン、E.ラーレルステッド、A.ノルドフェルドによる審査委員会は、64の応募案からアスプルンドの案を1等に選んだ。アスプルンドはすでに住宅の習作を3棟建てていたが、メディアに設計活動が紹介されたという意味で、これが実質上のデビュー作である。

　審査結果を発表する当時の雑誌には「たいへん優れた平面であり、また自国のモティーフをベースにきわめて美しい構成の建築にした。」という審査評が紹介されている。ここでいう「自国のモティーフ」が、当時主流であったナショナル・ロマンティシズムの表現を意味することは明らかである。応募案の説明文には「地元産のレンガ」をプッツ（スタッコ）で仕上げる、と書かれており、アスプルンドが使用材料の面でも地域に独自の表現を意図したことがわかる。

　この作品は、「クララ・スクール」で師事したエストベリの「エステルマルムの高校」（1910年）と、多くの類似点が認められる。ただし、エストベリがファサードをシンメトリーに構成したのに対し、アスプルンドは破風の位置を中央からずらし、その左右で窓の形態に変化をつけた。師匠ゆずりのナショナル・ロマンティシズムは、アスプルンドのなかで完全に消化され、より近代的でリラックスした味つけがされている。

In 1912, a design competition was held to build a new junior high school in the town of Karlshamn in southeastern Swedish. The judging panel of I.G. Clason, E. Lallerstedt and A. Nordfeld selected Asplund's design as the winning proposal out of 64 entries. Asplund had already built three private residences, but in terms of having his work covered in the media, the school design was his real debut.

In a magazine article announcing the results of the competition, the judges were reported to have said, "The planes are very excellent and the great structural beauty of the architecture is rooted in homeland motifs." The "homeland motifs" here clearly refer to aspects of National Romanticism, which at the time was flourishing. And since Asplund mentions his plan to use "locally-produced brick" with a stucco finish in the explanatory note he included with his proposal, it is evident that he also intended to make use of materials that were unique to the region.

In this work, it is possible to find many similarities with Östermalm High School (1910) by Ragnar Östberg, who Asplund had studied under at Klara School. But whereas Östberg designed his facade to be symmetrical, Asplund shifted the gables away from the center, and made use of different shaped windows on either side. In his school, Asplund had completely digested and seasoned the National Romanticism he had learned from his teacher with something more modern and relaxed.

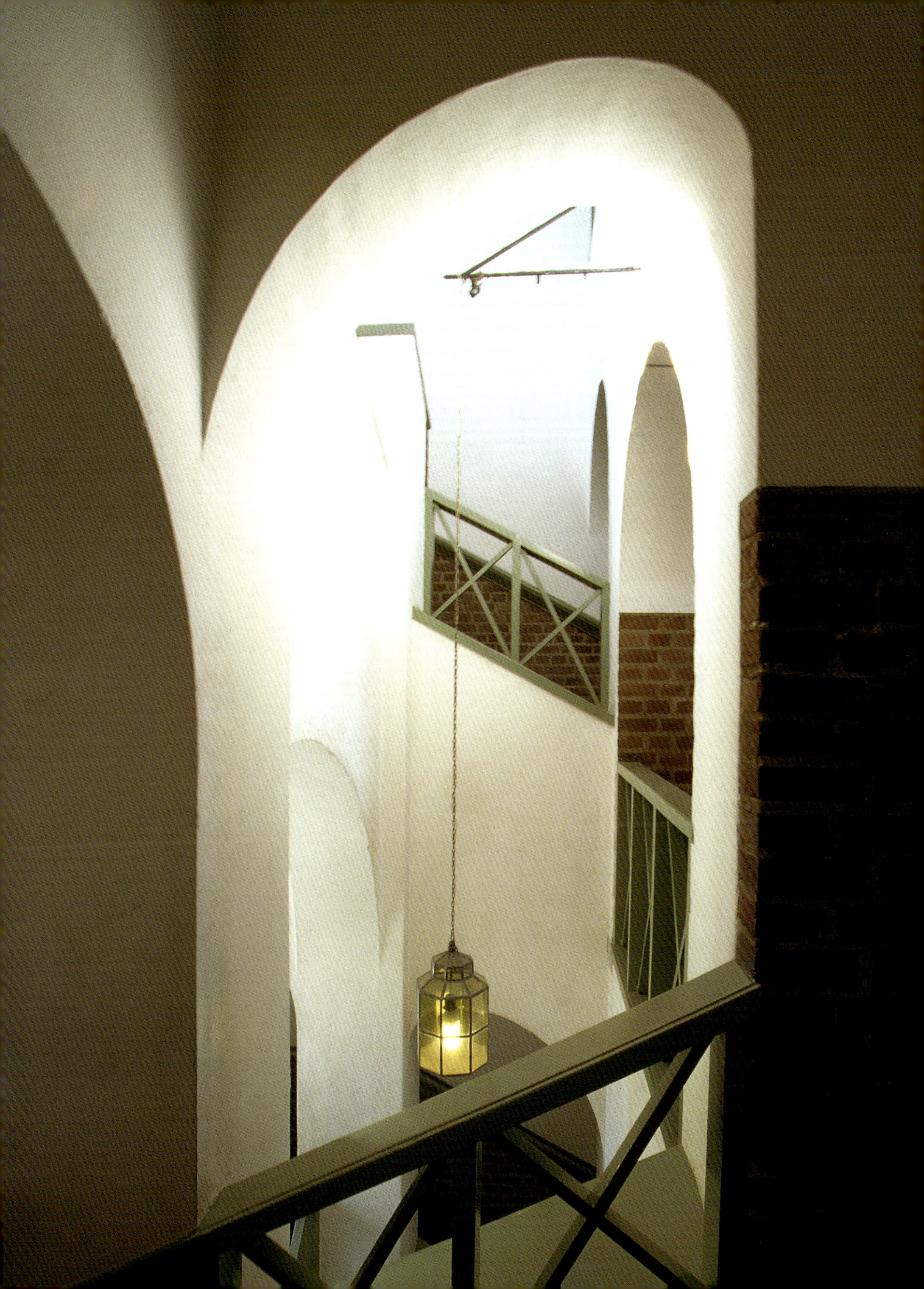

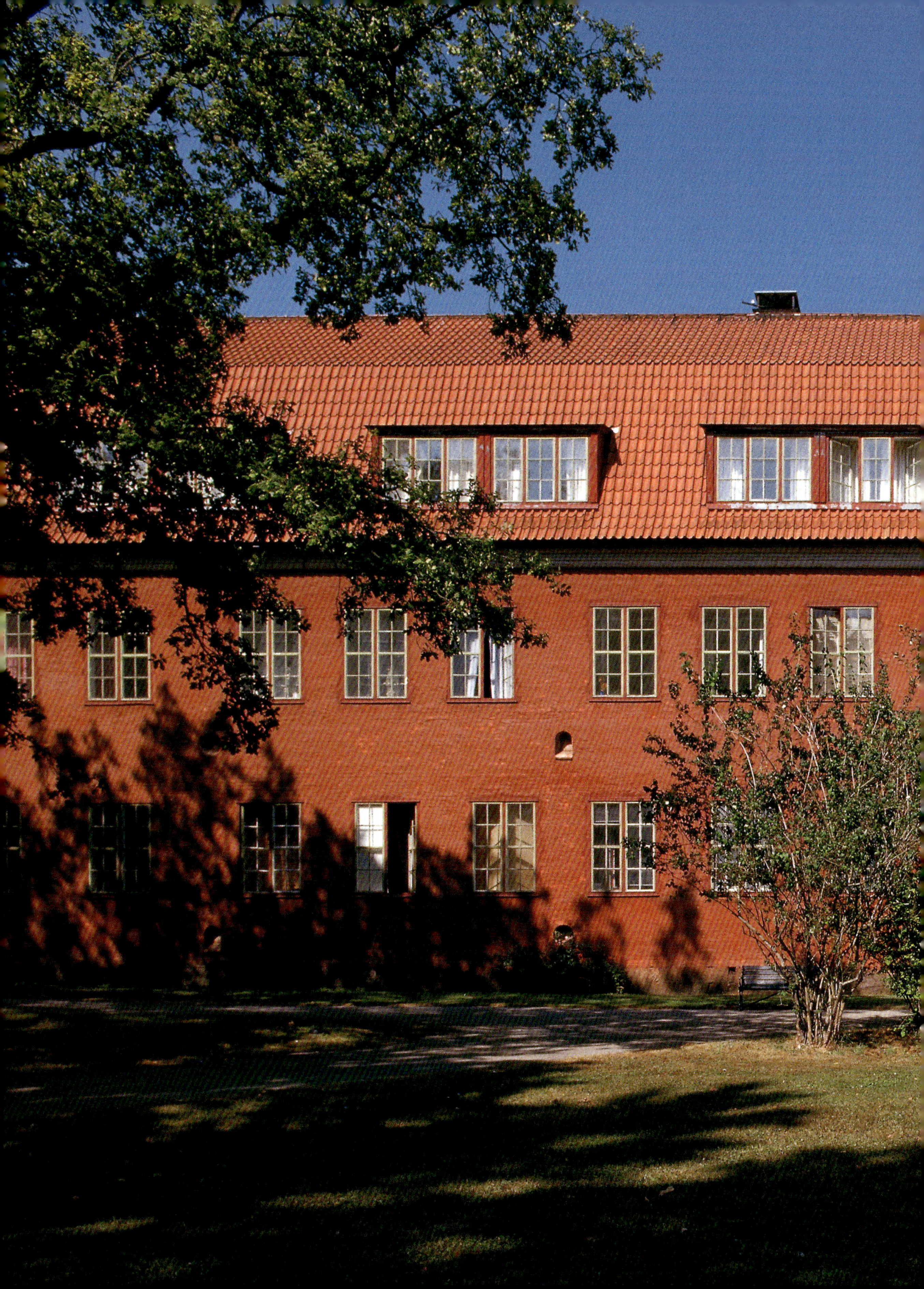

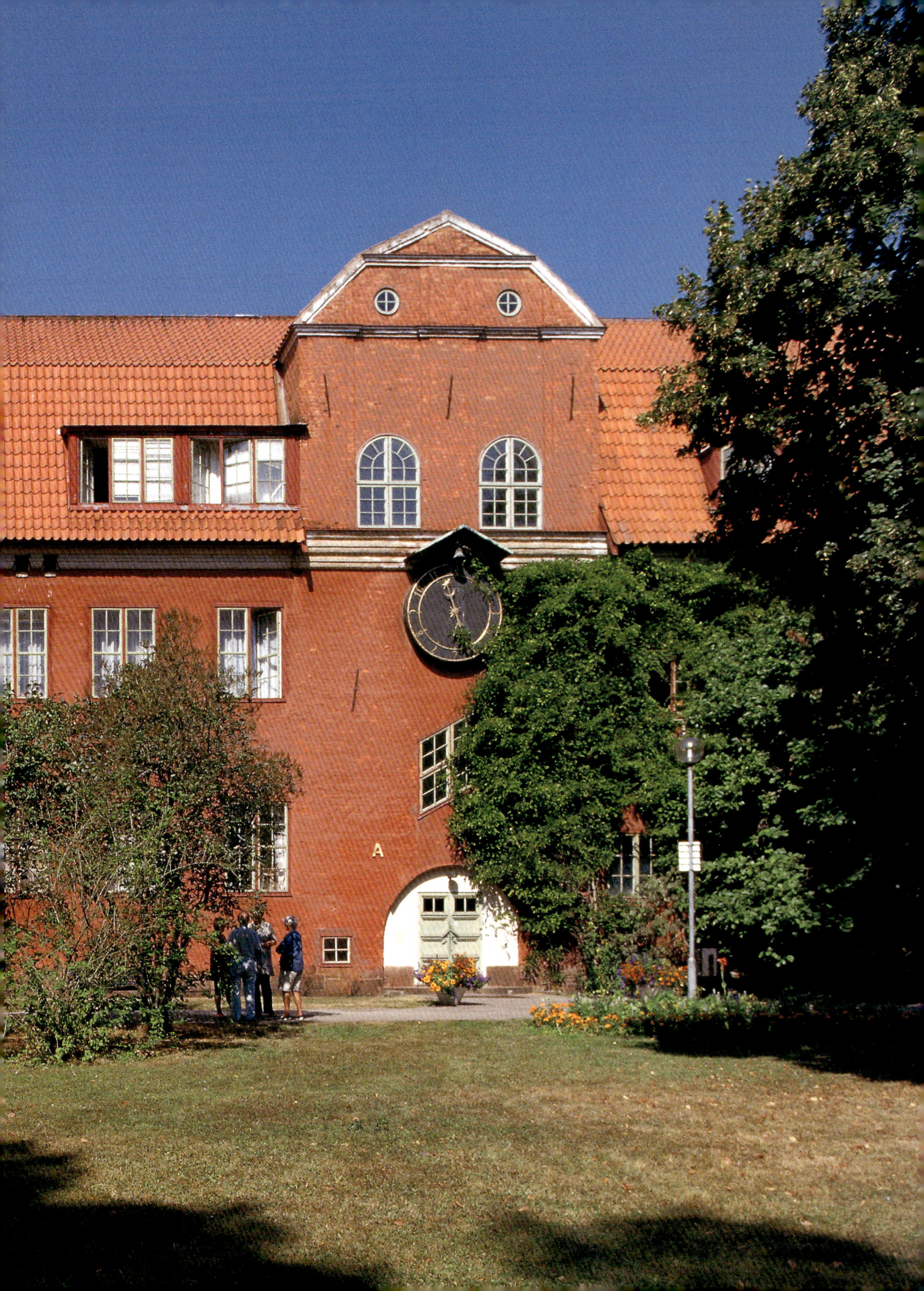
A

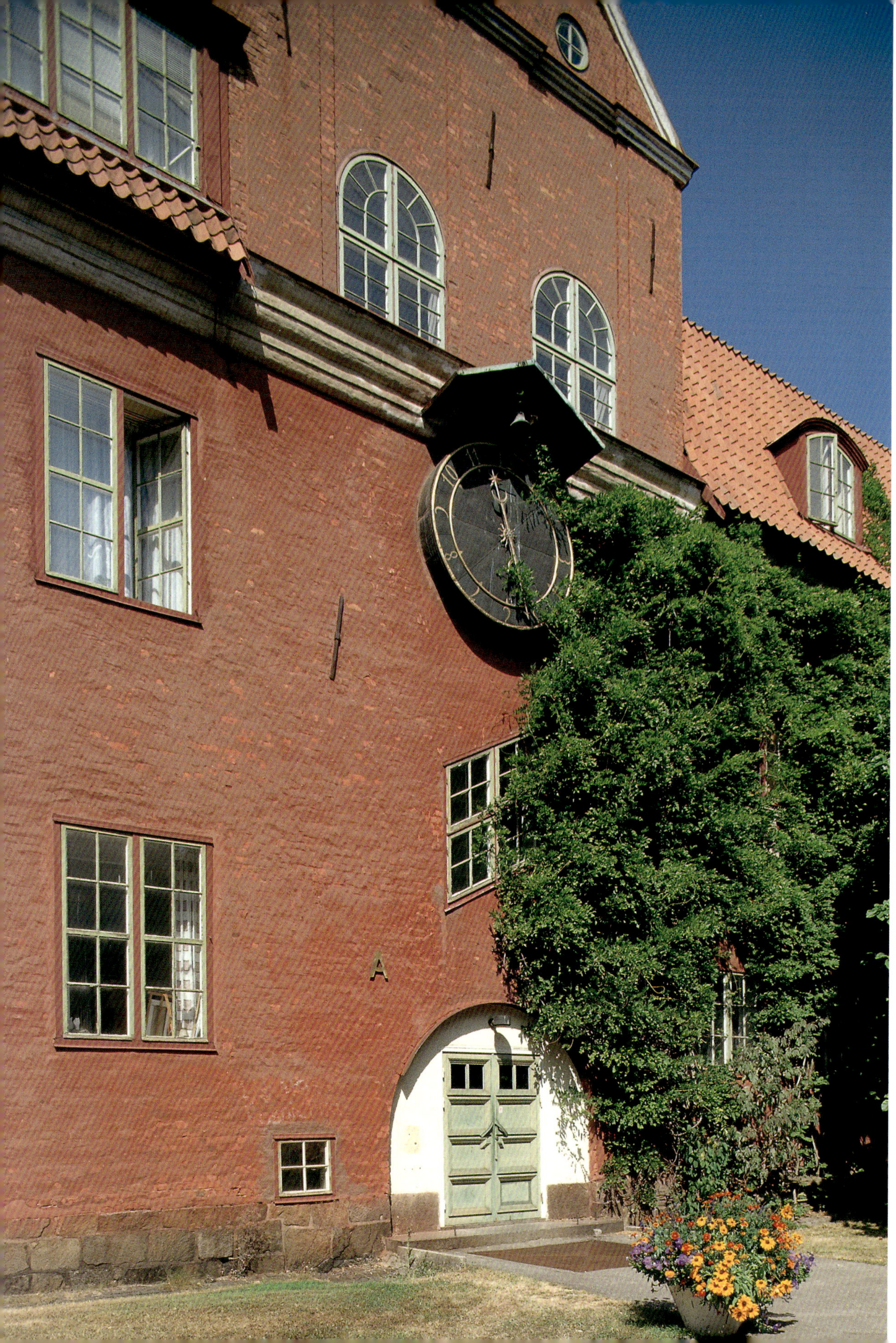

れんがの外壁をくり抜いた正面入り口。
アーチ状の白壁に矩形の扉が収まる。

The main entrance stands within a carved-out section of the brick exterior. The rectangular doors are set in an arched, white wall.

ファサードには、円(時計)、菱型(階段窓)、アーチ、矩形など、多様な形状が組み合わされている。外壁のれんがは伝統的なプッツ(スタッコ)で仕上げられている。

The facade combines a variety of shapes including a circle (the clock), diamond (staircase window), arches and rectangles. The brick on the exterior wall is finished with a traditional type of stucco.

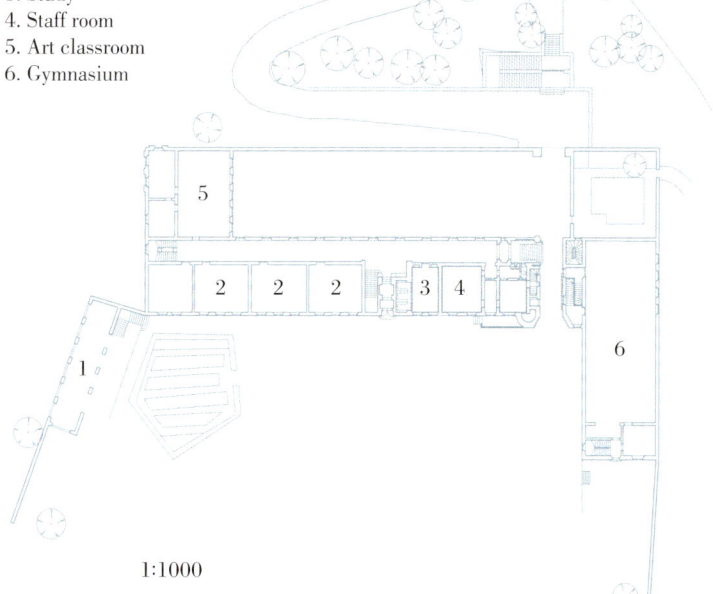

船底天井と縦長アーチ窓による最上階講堂。妻面壁のレリーフ状柱列と幕板のデザインは古典主義様式でまとめられている。

The top-floor auditorium features a curved ceiling and arched, oblong windows, and the classical style of the space is completed with column reliefs and modesty panels.

First-floor plan
1. Rest house
2. Classroom
3. Study
4. Staff room
5. Art classroom
6. Gymnasium

1:1000

台形状の天井をもつ廊下。ゆったりとした廊下に、窓から柔らかい光が差し込む。

A corridor with a trapezoidal ceiling. Light softly streams through the windows into the spacious hallway.

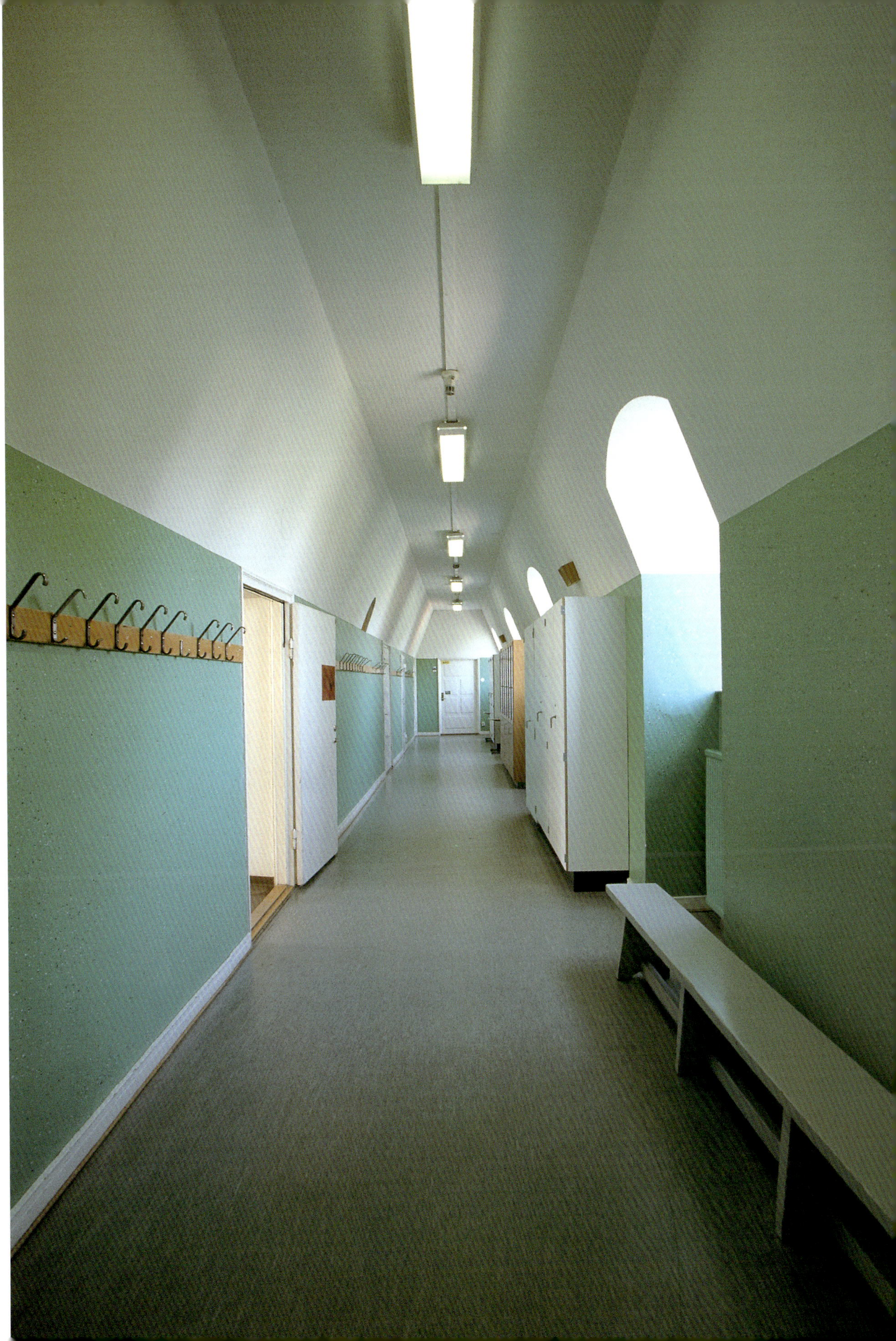

スネルマン邸 1917-18 ユーシュホルム
Villa Snellman, Djursholm

アスプルンドが設計した住宅は数少なく、いずれも伝統的な民家をベースにした素朴な小品である。施主が裕福な銀行家であったスネルマン邸の規模は、例外といえよう。壁面は、開口部とクラシックな装飾の配置だけで構成しようと試みている。2階の円形平面の居間に合わせてそこだけ立面の小窓を変えたり、1階の窓が翼部の軸の振れによりギュッと引っ張られて2階の窓の位置とずれたり、と立面の単調さを避ける工夫が見られる。

敷地はストックホルム郊外の高級住宅地ユーシュホルムの、わずかな傾斜地の林のなかにある。前面道路に対して「顔」に見える妻側が向き、L字型に囲まれた玄関の正面へとアプローチで導かれる。施主一家が住む2階建ての母屋と、厨房・洗濯室・使用人室が集められた翼部とが、微妙な角度に接続される。別棟にしたのはお互いに適度な距離感を保つ意図だろうが、直角よりわずかに内側に角度がつけられたのは、使用人室から玄関の方に自然に注意が向く効果を計算したのだろう。

パースのついた有名な2階の廊下は、このスケールでは距離感覚を大きく乱されるほどの効果には至っていない。初期案の段階で、すでに使用人のための階段が描かれていたから、それを残したまま廊下を長く見せようとスタディするうちに思いついたのだろう。この住宅ではわずかな隙間を生み出しては、収納をいたるところに確保している。生活の利便性を限界まで配慮すると同時に、アスプルンドがある種のゲーム感覚で住宅設計を楽しんだ証拠といえよう。

Asplund didn't create many residences, but all of them are simple, small-scale works based on traditional house design. The scale of Villa Snellman, which was owned by a wealthy banker, however, is exceptional. Merely in terms of their openings and the positioning of their classical decorations, the wall surfaces in the house are experiments in composition. And only in the second-floor living room did Asplund use a small, half-circle window for the elevation surface to match the circular plane. Due to the wing's staggered axis, the first-floor windows are positioned slightly off-center from the firm, taut windows on the second floor. Asplund used this device to avoid a monotonous elevation surface.

The lot, a slightly sloping plot of land in a grove, is located in an exclusive residential area in a suburb of Stockholm called Djursholm. The gable side, resembling a "face," points toward the road and an approach leads to the front entrance in the L-shaped enclosure. The second floor of the main building, where the client's family lived, and the wing, which contains the kitchen, laundry room and servants' room, are connected at a subtle angle. The wing was intentionally designed to maintain an appropriate distance from the main house, but Asplund's reason for making the angle between them slightly less than 90 degrees was probably a calculated attempt to make the servants to keep an eye on the front door from their room.

At this scale, the second-floor hallway, with its distinctive perspective, doesn't heighten one's sense of distance or confusion. In the early stages, a staircase for the servants had been planned, and in making sketches, Asplund seems to have decided to leave the staircase as it was and give the hallway a longer appearance. All the small niches in the house are meant to ensure sufficient storage space. This is proof both of Asplund's concern for daily convenience and his unique, playful style of house design.

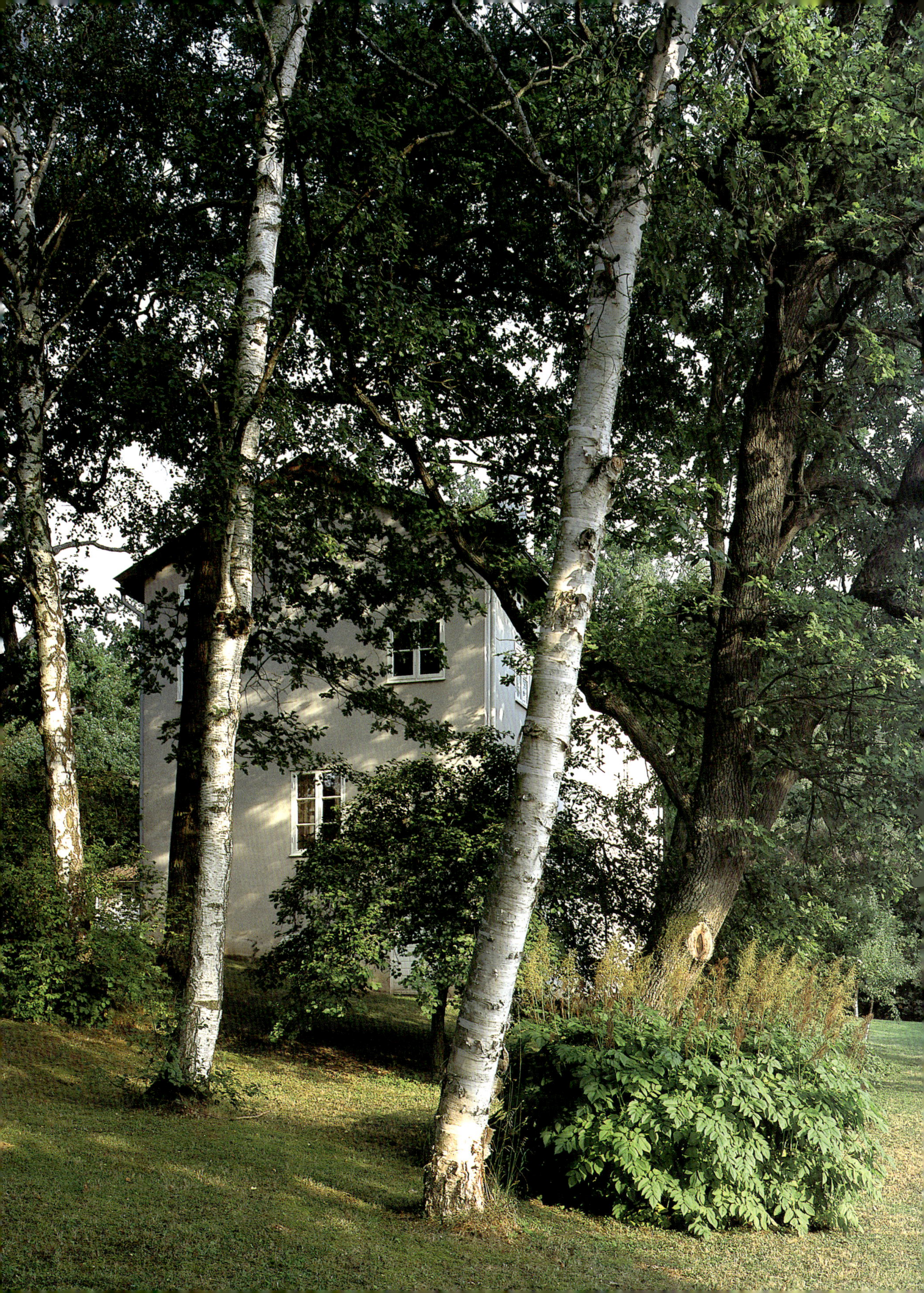

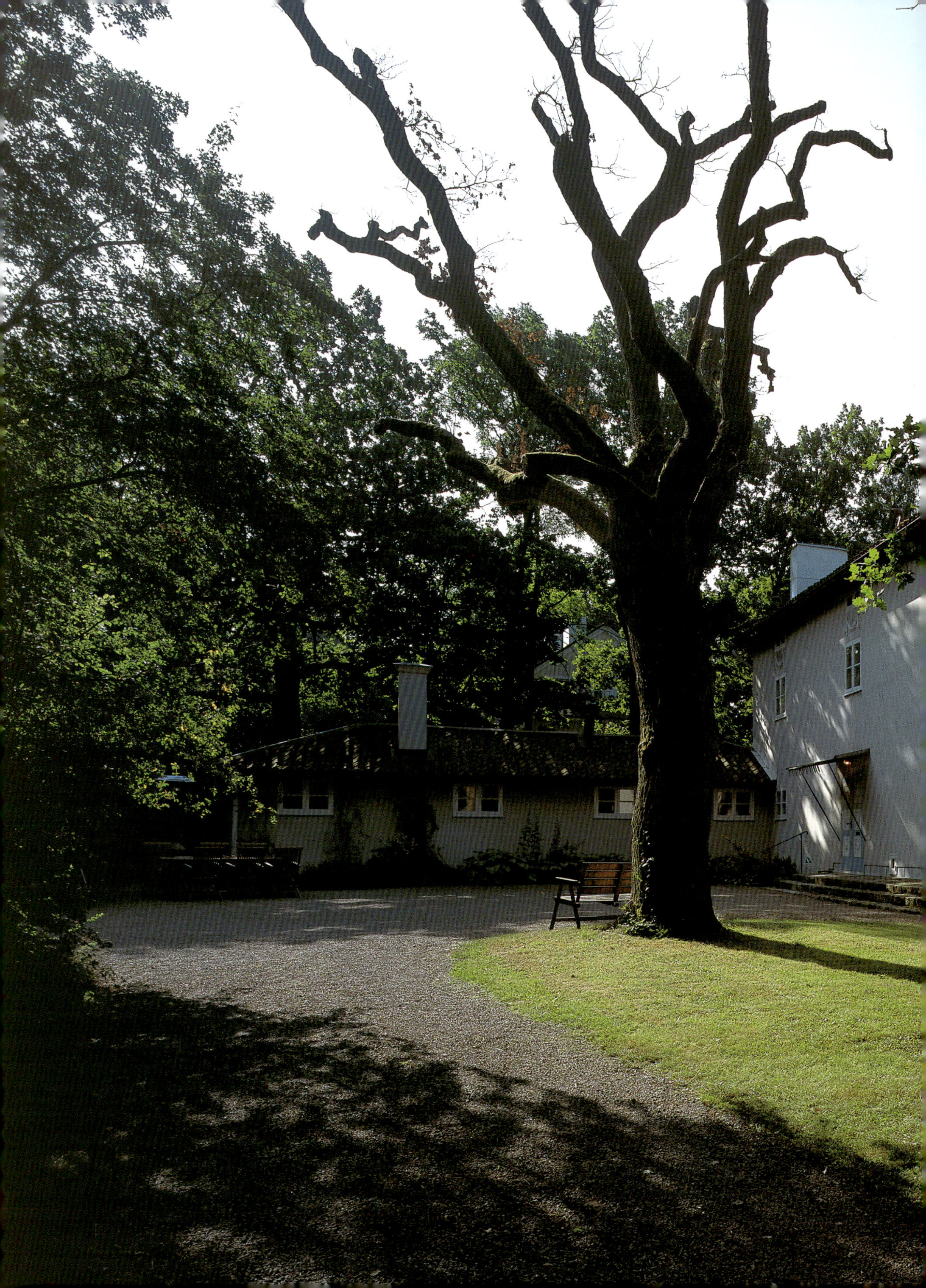

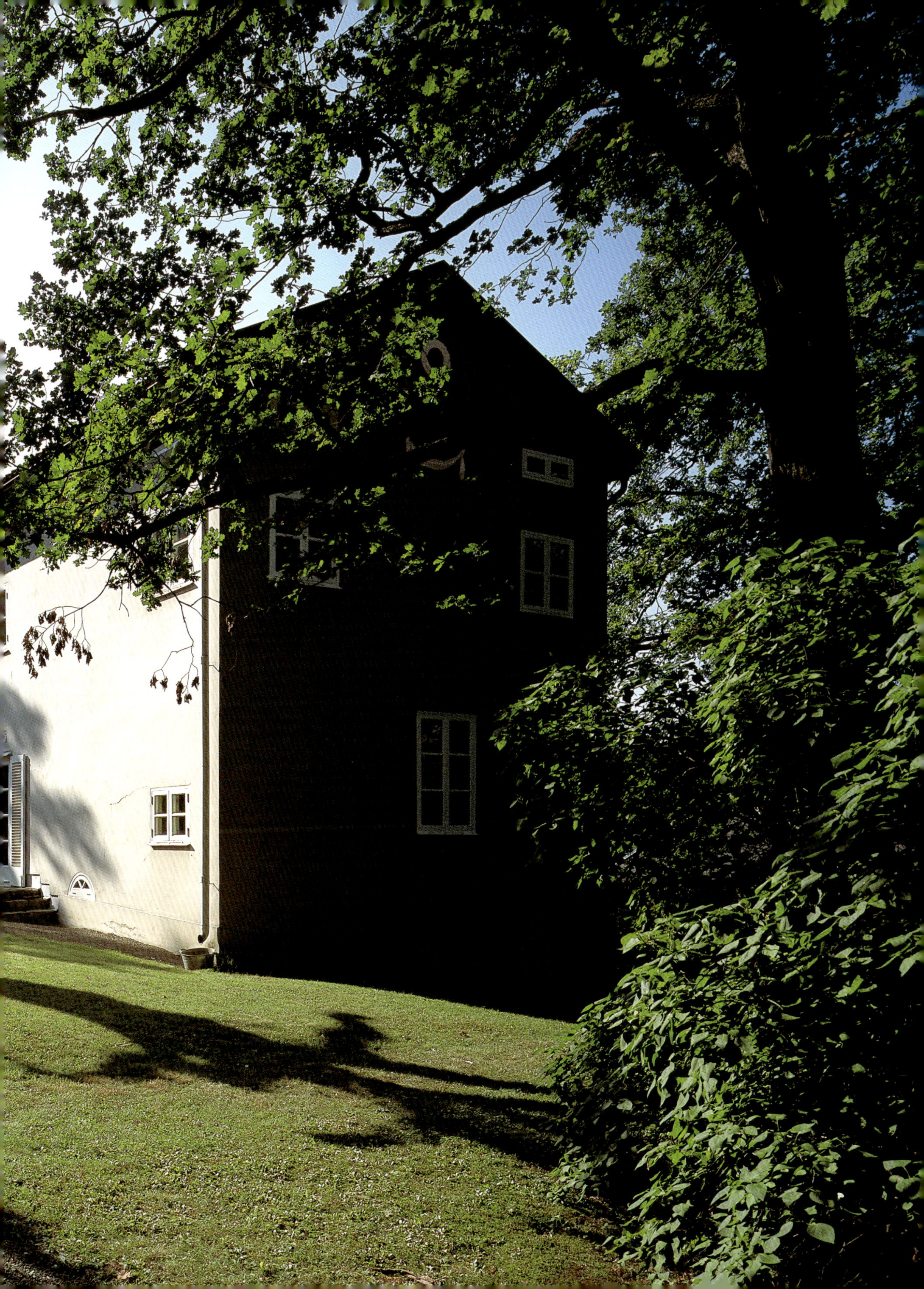

1階と2階の窓の位置が微妙にずれている。両開き扉はホールへの出入り口。軒下に見える横長窓は、屋根裏部屋の採光用。

The first- and second-floor windows are subtly out of sync with each other. The double doors act as entrances to the hall. The long horizontal windows that are visible under the eaves on the second floor provide natural lighting for an attic room.

南側全景。南側に向かって敷地が傾斜しているため、南面は北面に比べて天地が大きい。2階の円弧の飾り窓がある部屋が家族団欒用の楕円ホール。

A full view of the building's south side. As the lot slopes toward the south, the south side appears larger than the north. The room behind the circular window on the second floor is an ellipsoid hall for family gatherings.

North elevation

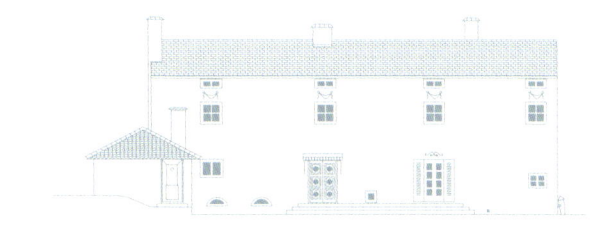

South elevation

1:400

First-floor plan

1. Hall
2. Living room
3. Dining room
4. Guest room
5. Kitchen
6. Servant's room
7. Laundry room
8. Bedroom
9. Elliptical room

Second-floor plan

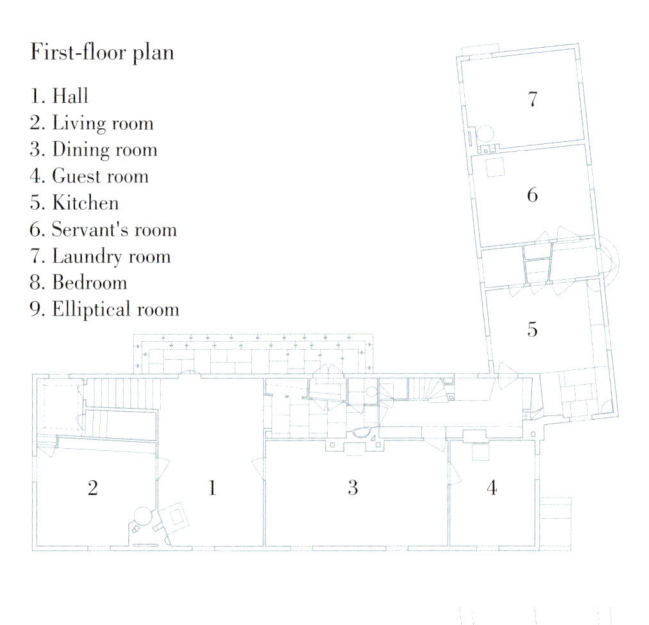

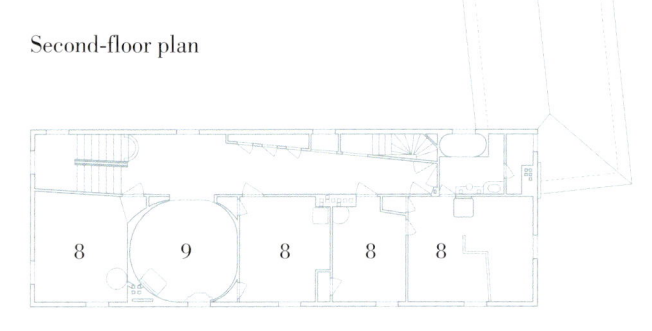

1:300

西側母屋と付属棟。母屋の西立面は顔のように見える位置に窓が設けられているが、ここでも1階の窓の位置が微妙に右にずれている。玄関前は、晴天の日には家族団欒のスペースとなる。

The west facade of the main house with the attached wing in the background. On the west elevation of the main house, there is a window resembling a human face, but here too the first-floor window is slightly off-center. In good weather, the area in front of the entrance is used for family gatherings.

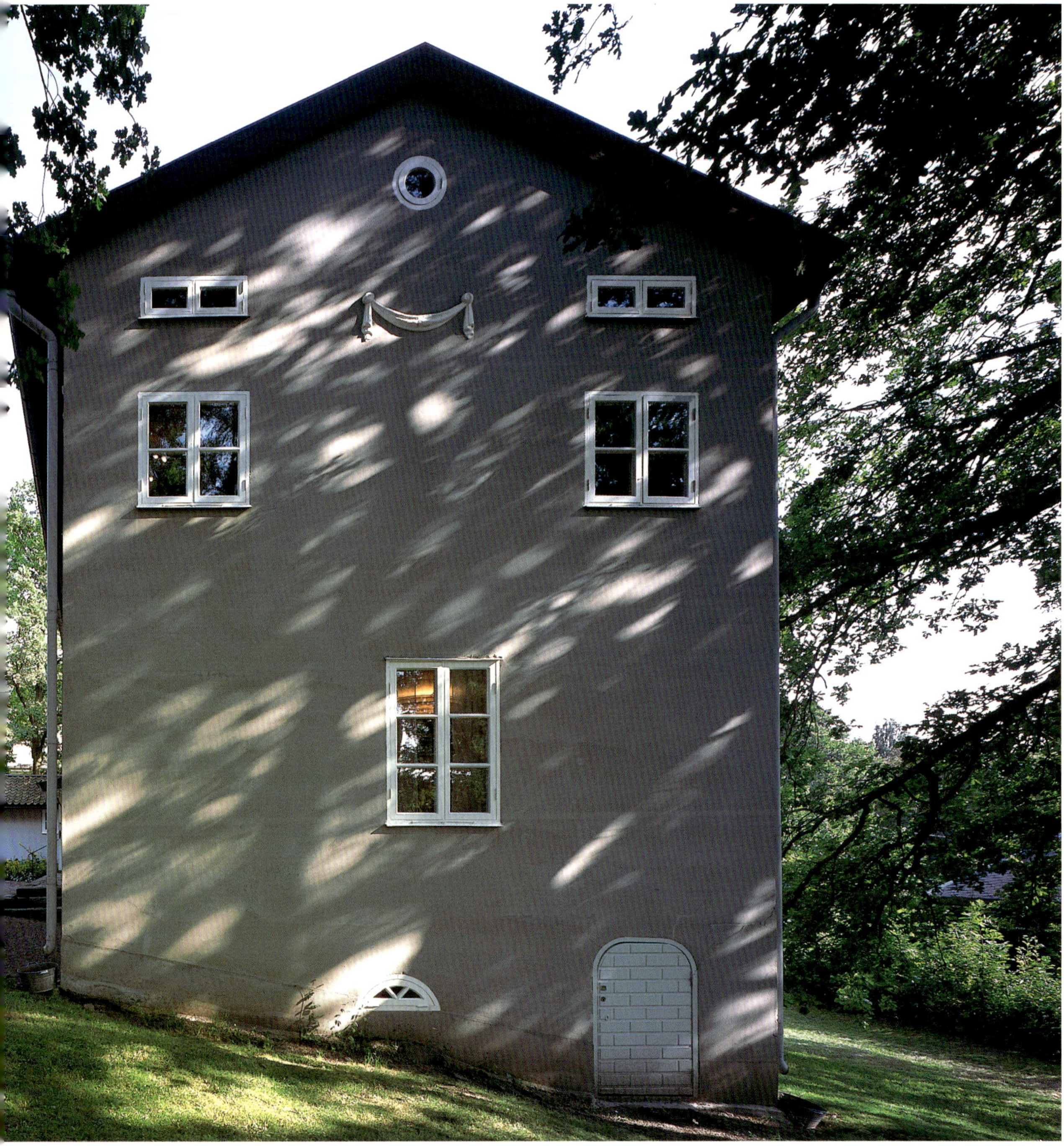

ゲスト用のひさしのある玄関(手前)と、家族用の出入り口(奥)。
異なる機能をもつふたつの出入り口が共通の基壇に並ぶ。

The canopied guest entrance (foreground) and the family entrance (background). The two entrances, though they serve different functions, are located on a common podium.

ゲスト用玄関扉の詳細。祝祭的な装飾を施した庇と、
水色の扉枠と白い装飾幕板が美しい。

Detail of the guest-entrance door. The festively decorated canopy, the light-blue door frame and the white, ornamented poling boards make a beautiful combination.

一面に砂利が敷きつめられた北側全景。

A full view of the north facade of the building with gravel lining the ground.

1階ホール、左は食堂。板張りの天井には植物文様が描かれている。各部屋にはデザインが異なる陶器製暖炉が配されている。この部屋から直接北側の前庭に出ることができる。

The first floor hall with the dining room on the left. A plant motif is painted on the planked ceiling. In every room, there is a ceramic fireplace, each with a different design. The forecourt on the house's north side can be reached directly from this room.

1階ホールより食堂を通して客間を見る。
食堂の壁紙は絵の具で彩色したもの。

The guest room is visible beyond the dining room from the first-floor hall. The wallpaper in the dining room is decorated with colored paint.

2階廊下は奥に行くにつれ幅が狭くなっている。遠近法による視覚トリックが使われている。

As the second-floor hallway leads further toward the back, the passage seems to grow narrower. This is a visual illusion created by the laws of perspective.

2階楕円ホール。天井は一段高くなっている。暖炉を囲む板張りの壁はどこかいびつに丸く、胎内空間のようである。家族がくつろげる安らぎの空間。

The ellipsoid hall on the second floor. The ceiling is markedly higher here, and the occasionally warped and wood-paneled walls enclosing the fireplace give the round space a womblike quality. The room provides a homey, relaxed space for the family.

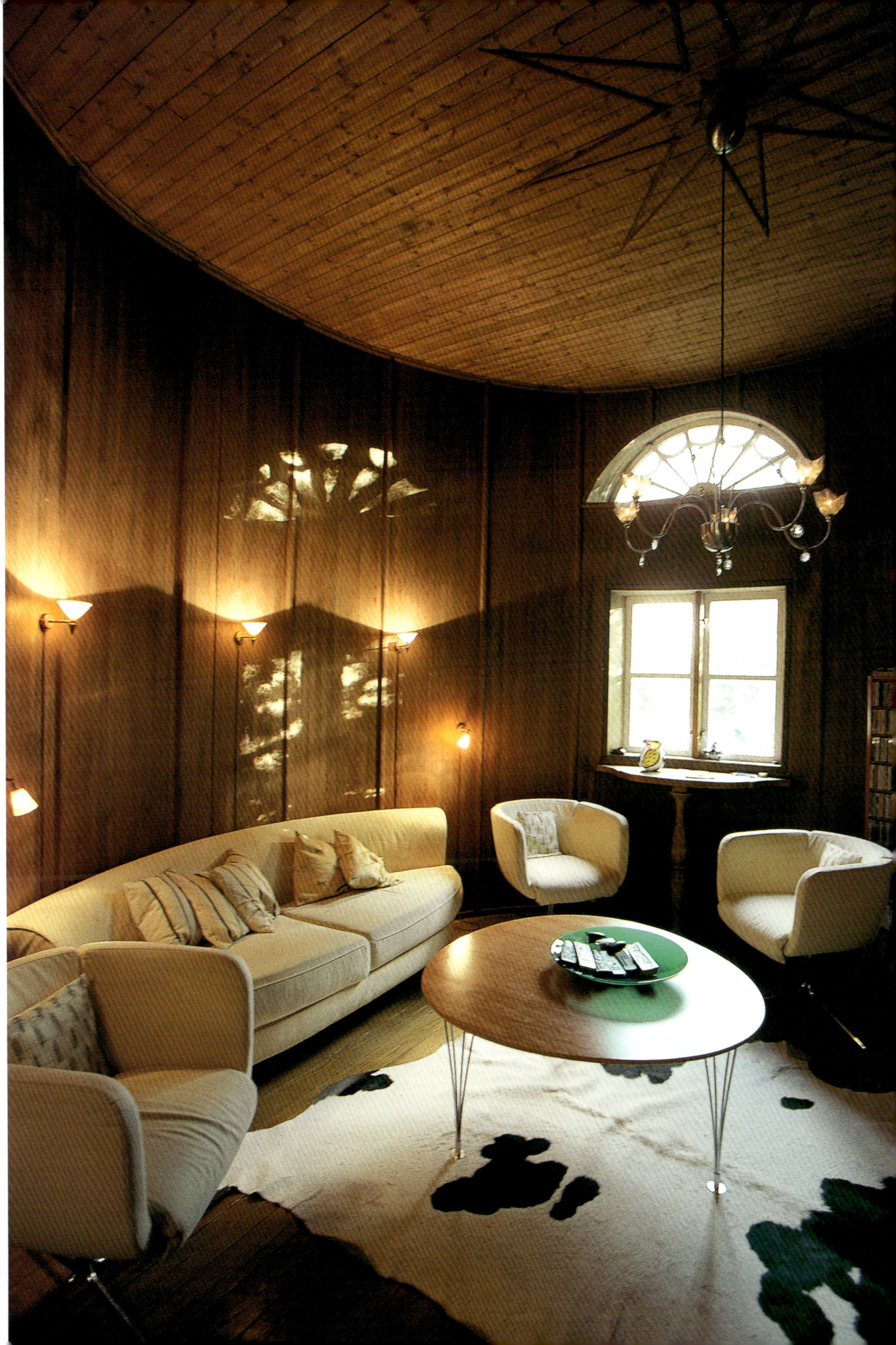

2階から配膳台のようすが見えるよう階段境壁に丸窓が穿たれている。突き当たりの壁には作りつけのサイドボード、その左がキッチン。あらゆる隙間が収納スペースとして有効に利用されている。それはまるで船舶のようだ。

To make the service table visible from the second floor, a round window was cut into the boundary wall of the staircase. To the left of the sideboard, which is built into the wall at the end of the room, is the kitchen. Equipped with a variety of empty spaces, the room can be used to good effect. It has the appearance of a ship.

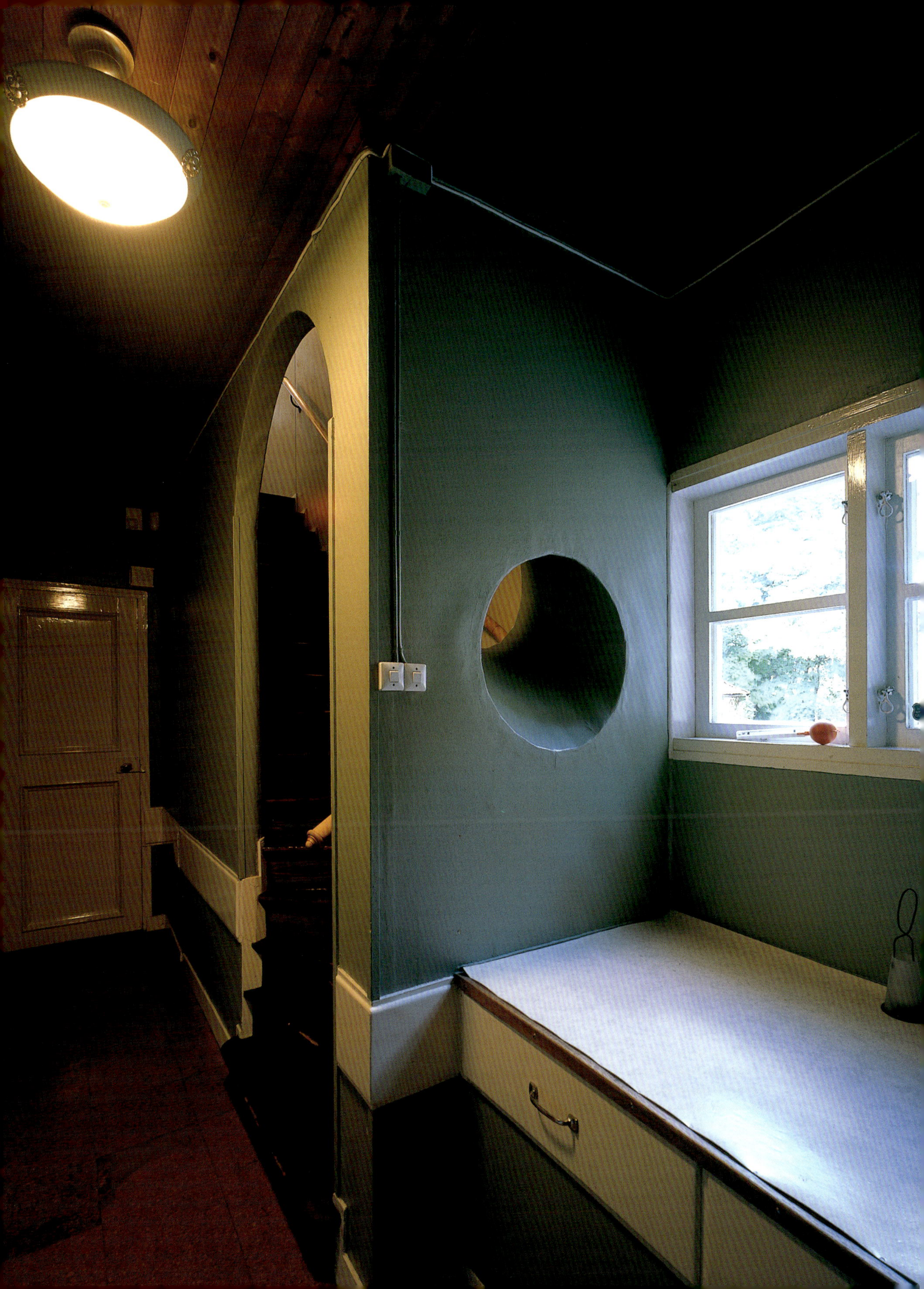

リステール州裁判所　1917−21　セルヴェスボリ
Lister County Courthouse, Sölvesborg

　スウェーデン南東部の町セルヴェスボリの駅から、まっすぐ延びる大通りの突き当たりにこの建物が見える。アスプルンドにしてはめずらしくファサードをシンメトリーにデザインしたのは、強い軸線を感じさせる敷地の条件ゆえであろう。実際、プランを見ると、駅からのまっすぐな力が建物にぶつかって、円形平面の法廷が後ろに飛び出したかのような構成となっている。飛び出した勢いによって、玄関ホール側の壁や床の目地までが斜めに広がったような動きのある平面の表現である。階段室の配置も、円柱形の法廷にぶつかった力を左右に受け流すような印象の個性が与えられている。ふつうなら最も権威あるデザインにすべき法廷の内部は、窓の配置により微妙にシンメトリーが崩されている。アスプルンドらしい、どこかユーモラスで近代的な感覚である。

　ファサードは、マッキム、ミード＆ホワイトの「ロウ邸」を連想させる。裏側の立面はイレギュラー・シンメトリー*、側面ではア・シンメトリーとするなど、立面の構成原理を各面で意図的に変えたようだ。この建物が建つスウェーデン南部地方は、デンマークの文化圏に近接することから、ハーフティンバーの民家が多く見られる。背面のデザインは、ナショナル・ロマンティシズムの潮流がすでに去ったあとではあるが、クラシシズムのなかに地域色を表現しようと試みた結果であろう。

*イレギュラー・シンメトリー：基本的には全体をシンメトリーに構成するが、部分的な要素であえて左右の変化をつける構成手法のこと。

Asplund's courthouse stands at the end of an avenue that runs straight from the train station in Sölvesborg, a town in southeastern Sweden. The reason for the symmetrical design of the facade, a rarity for Asplund, is related to the shape of the lot and its strong axis line. In looking at the design plan, a powerful line actually seems to run straight from the station and crash into the building, causing the circular plane of the courthouse to jut out in back. And due to the momentum of this jutting section, the planes of everything from the walls in the entrance hall to the floor joints appear to be slanting. The position of the staircase also creates the impression that it is attempting to deflect the energy that is pushing up against the building.

In the interior of the courthouse, which would normally be designed to express a maximum of authority, the sense of symmetry is subtly destroyed by the positioning of the windows. This creates a vaguely humorous, modern impression that is characteristic of Asplund's work.

The facade recalls McKim, Mead and White's W.G. Low House. And because the back plane of the building has an irregular symmetry* and the sides are asymmetrical, the structural principle for the elevation surfaces seems to have been intentionally altered for each of them. In the area of southern Sweden where the building stands, due to the proximity of Danish culture, there are many half-timbered homes. Though Asplund's design for the back of the building was made after the popularity of National Romanticism had already faded, the result can be seen as an attempt to express regional color in a classical mode.

*Irregular symmetry: A structural approach using sectional elements to alter the left and right sides of what is fundamentally an entirely symmetrical structure.

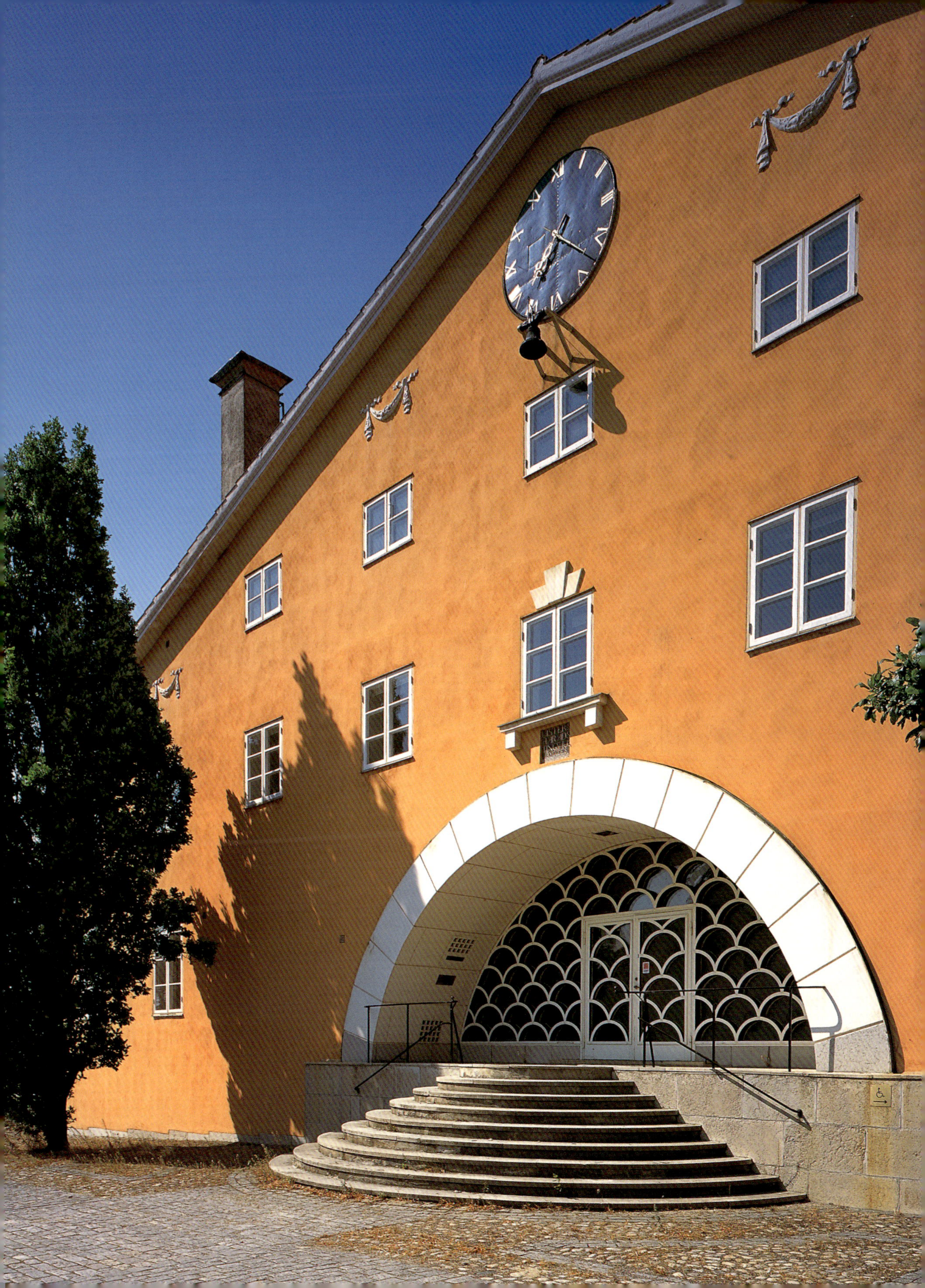

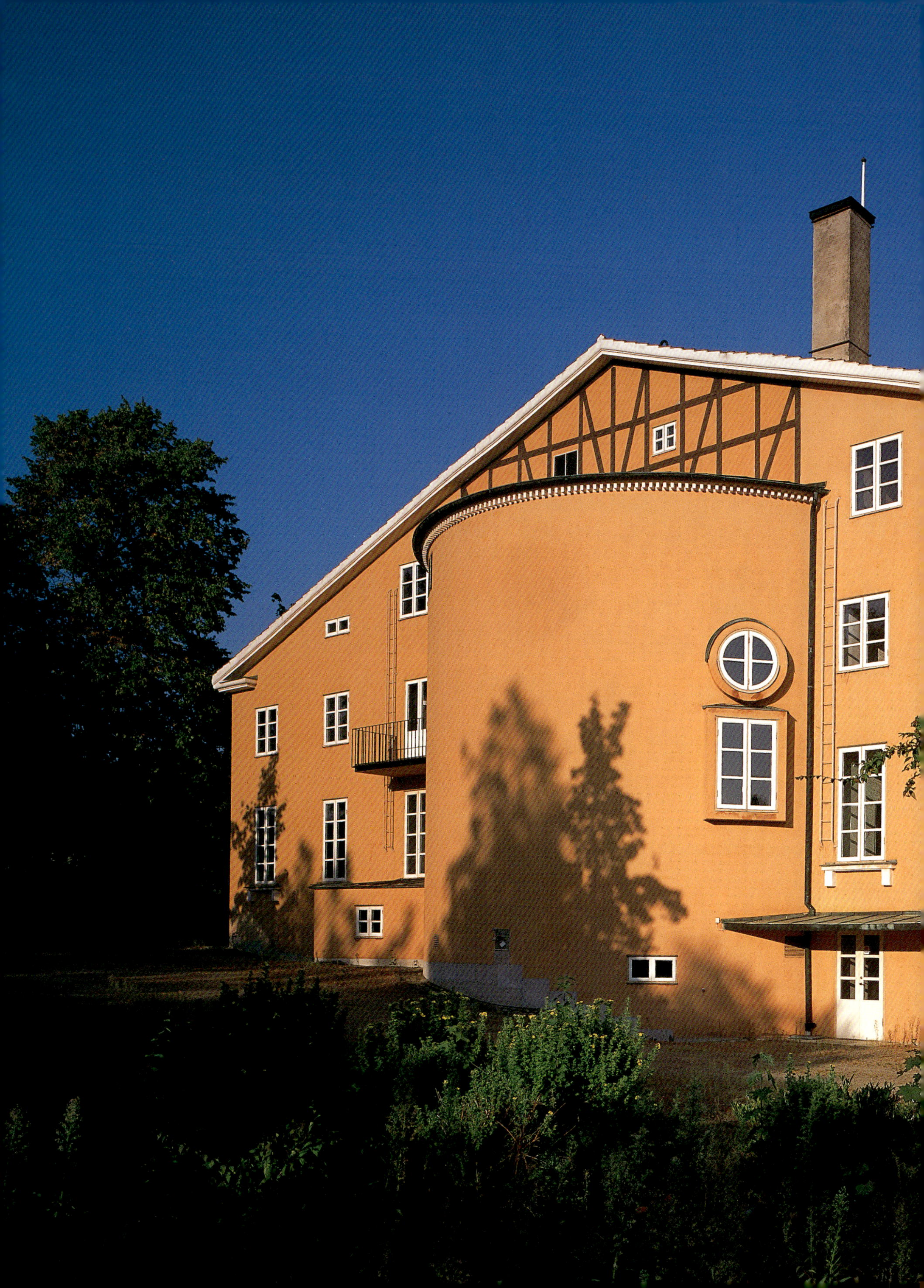

夕日に染まる西面。厳格な様式からの解放を求めるかのように左右非対称となっている。円筒形に膨らんだ外壁がユーモラス。ハーフティンバーは伝統的民家の建築工法を引用。正面の厳格な様式性とは対照的に、裏面はバナキュラーな香りにあふれている。

The west side of the building in the setting sun. The asymmetry of the design seems to be trying to liberate the building from its austerity. The swollen cylindrical shape of the exterior wall provides a touch of humor. The half-timbering makes reference to the construction methods used in traditional houses. In contrast to the austere appearance of the entrance, the back of the building is imbued with a vernacular flavor.

東正面。基壇に至る外部階段は半円形の積層デザイン。桁行き方向に対し、妻面が極端に広い大屋根による構成は、スケール感の喪失と引き替えに、記念性の獲得に成功している。

The east entrance. The external staircase leading to the podium has a layered, semicircular design. In terms of ridge direction, the traverse wall creates a commemorative air to replace the loss of scale that is produced by the extremely wide, large roof.

Second-floor plan

First-floor plan

1:300

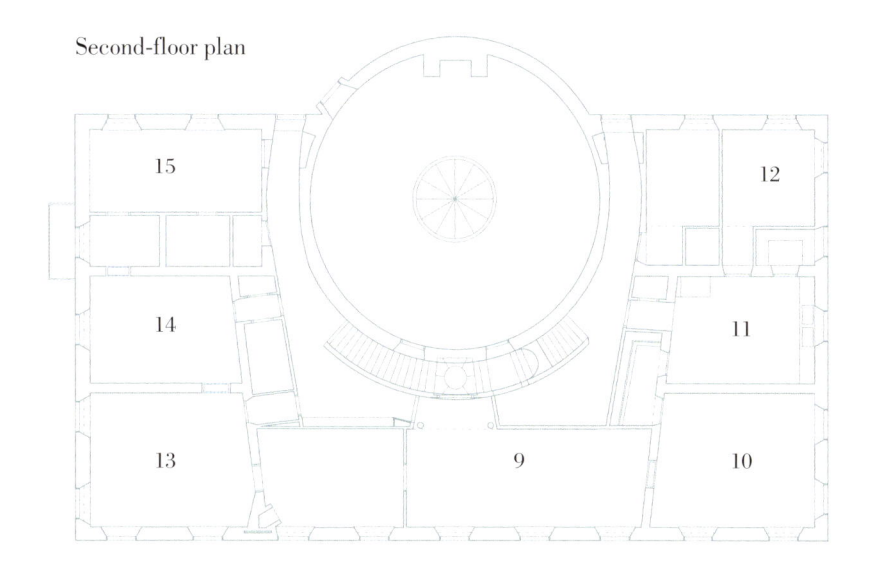

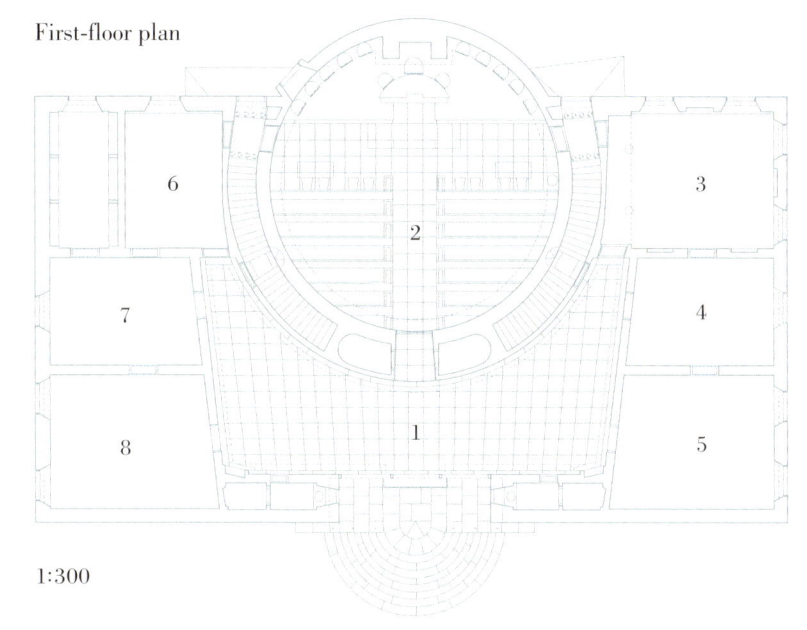

1. Entrance hall
2. Courtroom
3. Meeting room
4. Defense attorney's room
5. Prosecuting attorney's room
6. Judge's chambers
7. Clerk's chambers
8. Reception area
9. Salon
10. Dining room
11. Kitchen
12. Servant's room
13. Living room
14. Bedroom
15. Bedroom

E.G. ASPLUND

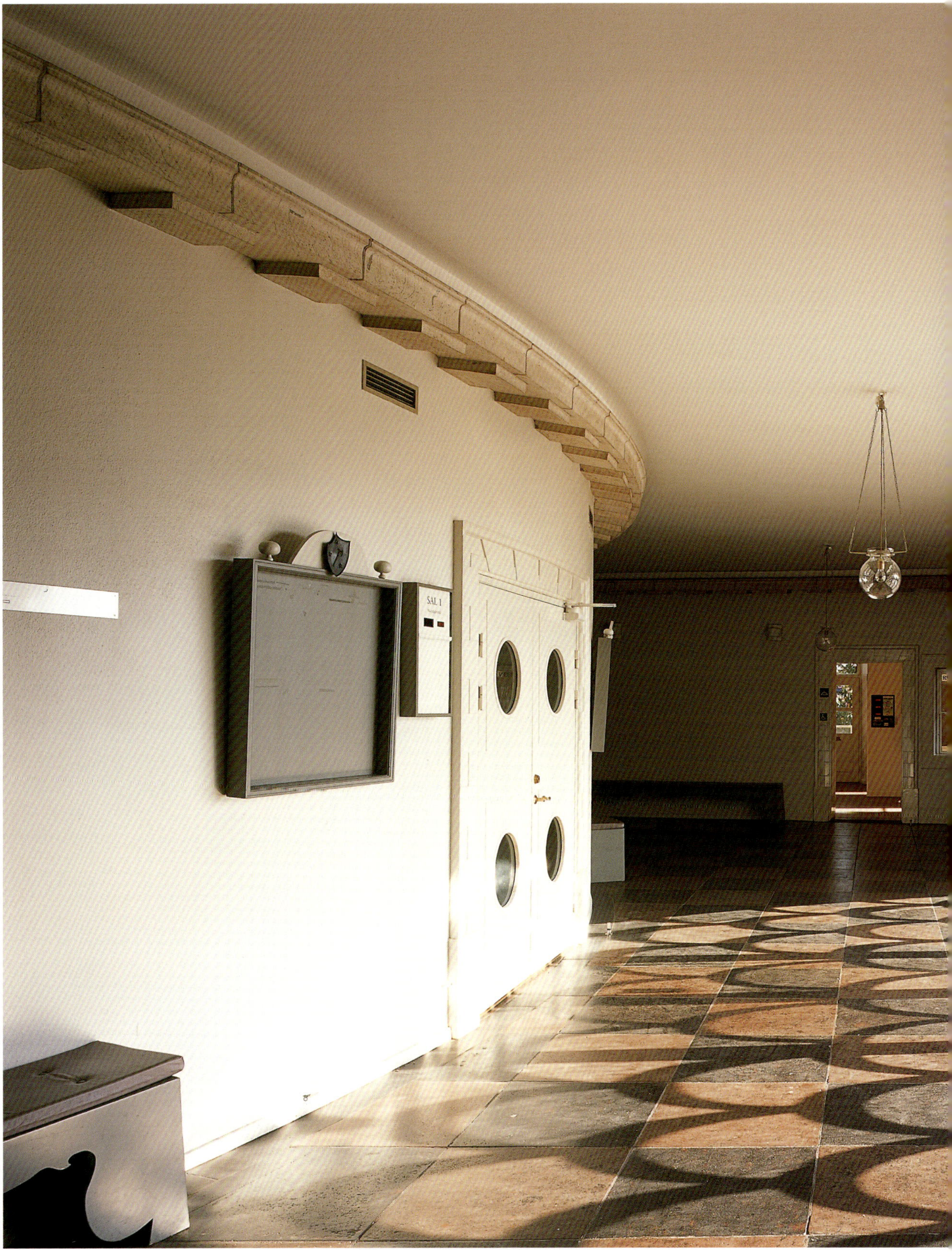
SAL 1

エントランスと法廷ロビー。アーチから差し込む光が御影石床面に優雅な百合のパターンを描き出し、待合の人々の心を癒す。左側の円周壁の扉が法廷への入り口。

The entrance and courtroom lobby. The light that shines through the arch creates an elegant lily-shaped pattern on the granite floor, easing the minds of those waiting inside. The door to the left in the circular wall is to the courtroom.

エントランスホール内部から見たアーチ。
The arch as seen from within the entrance hall.

外部階段とエントランスアーチ。平面と立面で繰り返される円弧の重層。アイアンワークの手摺が外部階段から基壇までをシンプルにつないでいる。

The exterior staircase and entrance arch. The layering of circular arcs is repeated in flat and elevated surfaces. A simple ironwork handrail leads up the stairs to the podium.

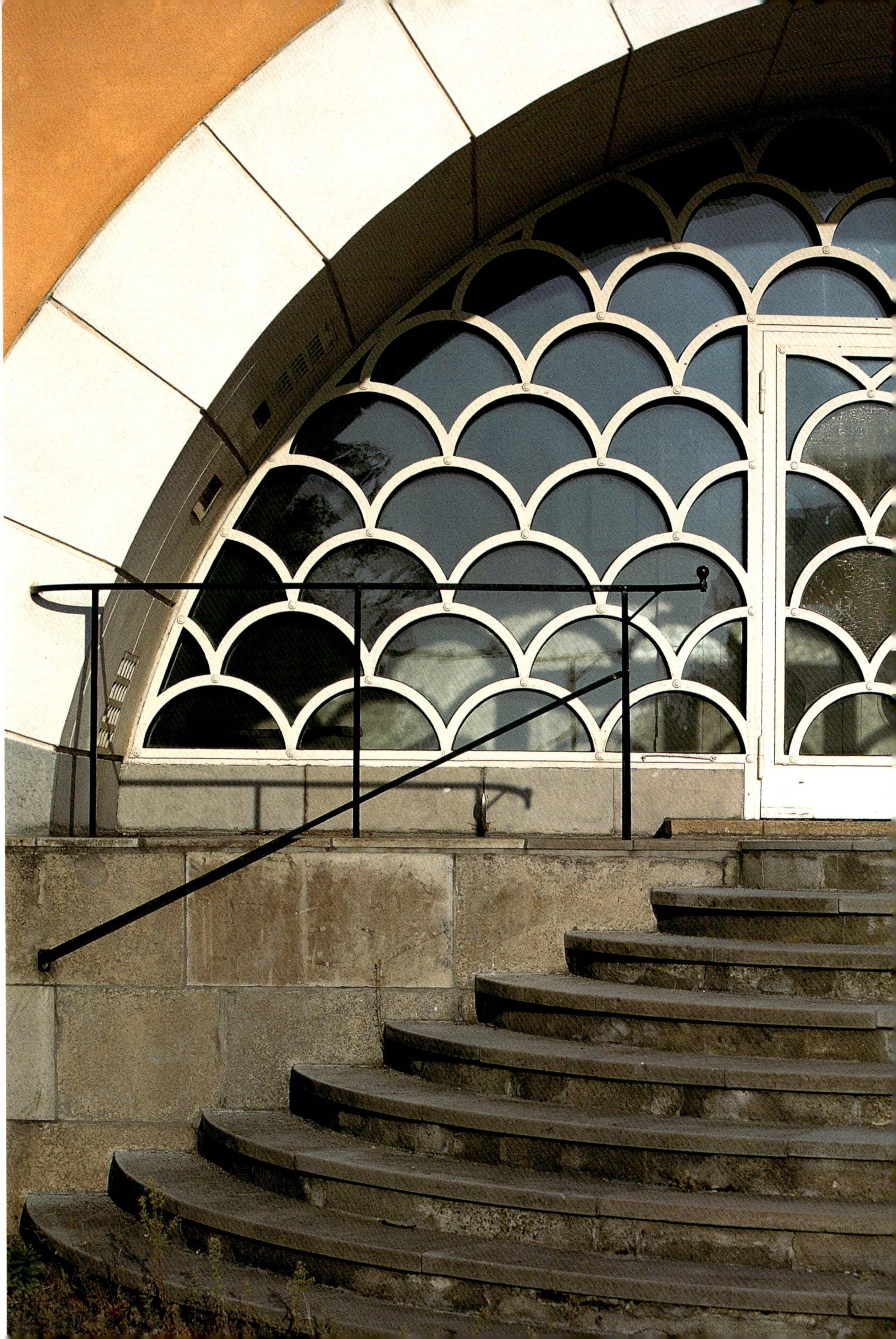

中央にトップライトをもつ円形の法廷。正面奥が裁判長席。午後になると円形と四角の窓から法廷内に光が差し込む。

A circular courtroom with a skylight in the center. The seat straight ahead in the rear is for the judge. In the afternoon, sunlight floods the court from the square and circular windows.

裁判長席より傍聴席を見る。法廷の2分の1は傍聴席が占める。

The public gallery as seen from the judge's seat. The seats in the public gallery occupy half of the courtroom.

傍聴席の側面を飾るユーモラスなふくらみをもった装飾。

The side of the seats in the public gallery are decorated with a curious bump.

141 E.G. ASPLUND

「ポリスマン」の愛称をもつ法廷内の時計。
The clock in the courtroom is endearingly known as "Policeman."

法廷外周には判事居住階へ至る階段がある。
3階判事居住階にあるチューリップ柱と呼ばれる木製の装飾柱。

Around the perimeter of the courtroom is a staircase leading to the judge's chambers. The decorative wooden pillars on the third-floor judge's chambers are called "tulip pillars."

法廷奥の会議室。西側の窓から、斜光が部屋の奥まで延び、会議室全体が柔らかい光に包まれる。グレーの2本の円柱が、空間に格調を与えている。

The conference room in the rear of the courtroom. Oblique rays of light stream as far as the back of the room, bathing the entire space in soft light. The two cylindrical columns, painted grey, add a sense of nobility to the space.

スカンディア・シネマ　1922–23　ストックホルム

Skandia Cinema, Stockholm

アスプルンドは、この映画館を設計していたとき、秋の夕暮れと黄色く色づいた葉を想っていたという。イメージの出発点になった夕暮れとは、イタリア旅行のときタオルミナで体験した、カーニバルの夕べの記憶であろう。「祝祭の雰囲気と映画の華麗な幻想の世界を、親しみのこもった温かい感じ」にデザインするよう施主から依頼されたアスプルンドは、強烈な印象を受けたあの夜を真っ先に思い浮かべたにちがいない。星空の下での忘れられない体験は、インディゴブルーに塗られたヴォールト天井と、星のように散りばめられた照明、月を模した拡声器によって再現された。商業建築ゆえに改装がくり返されたため、この照明は現在失われている。1991年から、当初の状態に戻すべく修復工事がたびたび行われているので、その進展に期待したい。

館内およびロビーは、赤を基調とした華やかな仕上げになっている。ポンペイ風の唐草模様や神話の神々を描いたビロードの刺繡、古代遺跡をモティーフにした石膏レリーフ、すべてデザインが異なるバルコニー席への扉などに、建築家の若き日の旅の記憶が刻まれている。当時は毎晩2度の上映があった。833の座席が満席になり、クロークが全開となると、55人もの係員が働いたという。

スクリーンの両脇には、アダムとイヴの立像が左右に置かれていた。階段室の手摺は蛇をかたどり、階下のふたりに接近しつつある。彼らが楽園を追われる日は近い。設計意図を想像する楽しさも、アスプルンド建築の魅力のひとつである。楽園はなにを象徴しているのだろうか。そういえば建築家は、自分の肖像を館内に残している。

When Asplund was designing this movie theatre, he was thinking about the autumn twilight and yellow-colored leaves. The twilight in question was Asplund's memory of an evening carnival he had seen in Taormina during a trip to Italy.

Hired by his client to design something with "a familiar warmth and the air of a festival and the gorgeous fantasy world of the cinema," Asplund must have immediately recalled the intense impression that night made on him. He reproduced that unforgettable experience under a starry sky by creating a vaulted ceiling painted indigo blue with lights that studded the space like stars and a speaker that looked like the moon. Due to the commercial nature of the building, and repeated renovations, the lights are no longer extant. In 1991, however, a restoration project to return the theatre to its original condition was begun; and one can only hope for the best.

The interior as well as the lobby are fitted out in a gorgeous red finish. Everything from the velvet embroidery covered with Pompeii-style arabesques and depictions of mythological gods, the gypsum relief depicting ancient ruins and the doors to the balcony seats, each of which has a different design, is stamped with memories from the architect's youthful travels.

At the time it opened, the theatre had two film showings every night, all 833 seats would be filled, and up to 55 workers were on duty in the cloakroom. On either side of the screen were statues of Adam and Eve. The staircase handrails, in the shape of a snake, also seem to be related to the couple downstairs - the day when they would be chased out of Paradise was nearing. One of Asplund's great charms is trying to imagine why he designed certain things. For example, what does Paradise symbolize here? Incidentally, the architect even made a portrait of himself for the building.

BALKONG
VÄNSTER

劇場への入り口が並ぶ下階回廊。当初は舞台両袖にあった黄金のアダムとイブ像は現在回廊に置かれている。劇場を囲う漆喰壁にはクラシックなレリーフが彫り込まれ、ブラケットの薄明かりに照らし出される。壁と暗い天井とはスリットを設けて縁を切り、暗黒の夜空を象徴している。

In the corridor of the lower floor is a row of entrances to the theatre. The golden statues of Adam and Eve, which originally stood on either wing of the stage, are now in the corridor. On the plaster wall around the theatre are carved, classical-style reliefs, which are dimly illuminated with bracket lighting. Slits and cut edges in the walls and dark ceiling symbolize the darkness of the night sky.

PARKETT
HÖGER

階段室両側壁にはめ込まれた丸鏡は合わせ鏡となっており無限の像を結ぶ。映画館という異次元空間にユーモラスな遊び心が随所に組み込まれている。

Round mirrors are inlaid in both walls along the staircase to create an image of infinity. A funny, playful spirit is present everywhere in the theatre, a space which exists in another dimension.

Electric wall-fittings (1922-23)

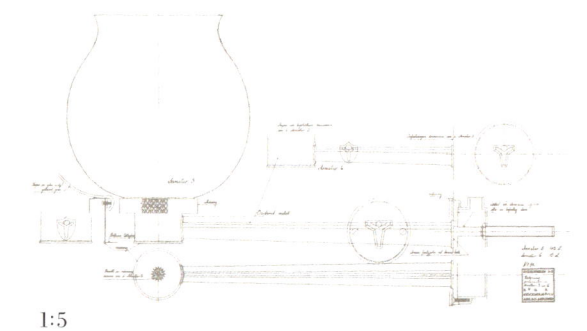

1:5

竣工当時は乳白色のグローブによるやわらかい光が壁面のレリーフを照らしていた。

At the time construction was completed, soft light from translucent-white globes illuminated the wall reliefs.

下階から上階への階段には幻想的な天井画が描かれている。

Fantastic pictures are painted on the ceiling above the staircase leading from the lower to the upper floor.

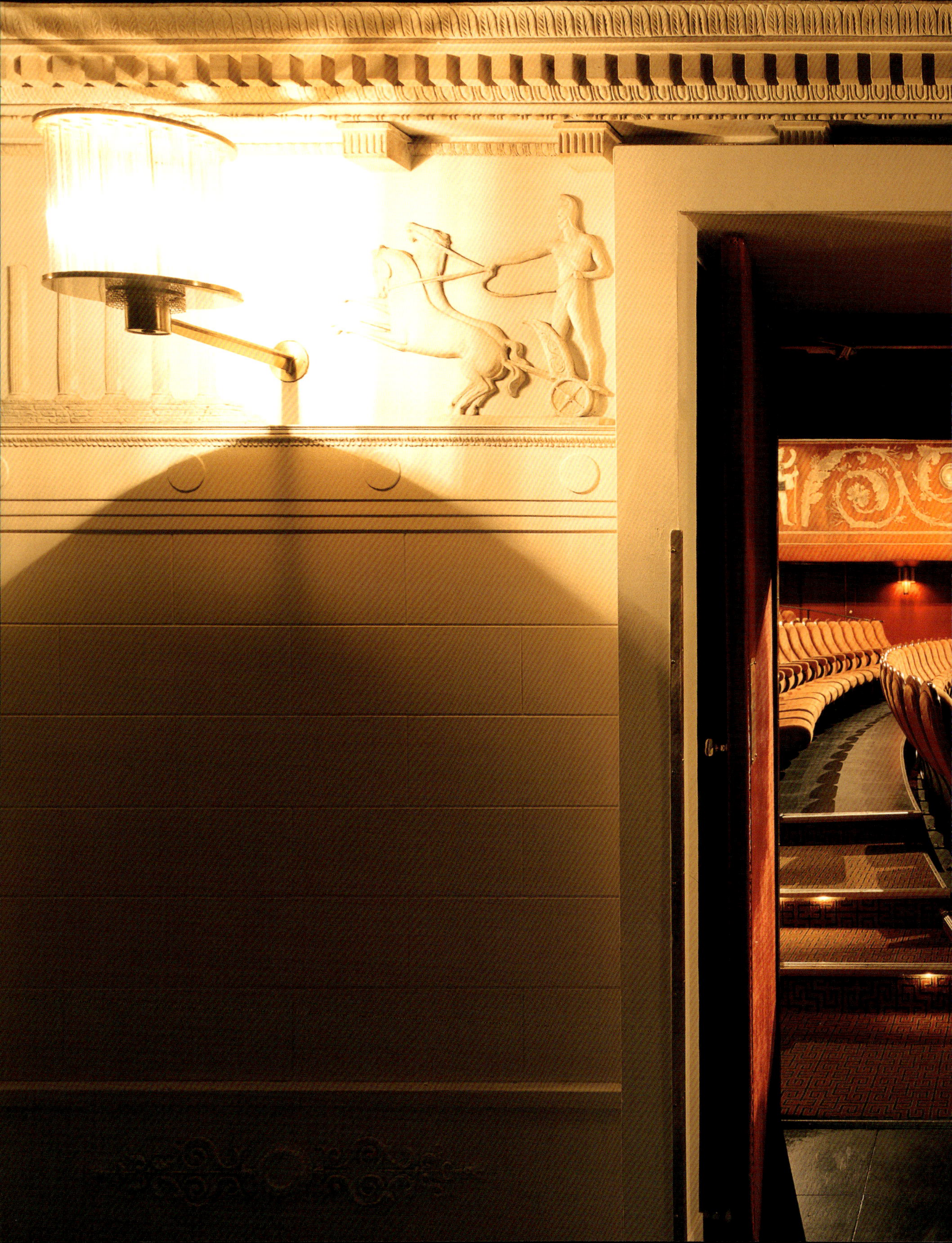

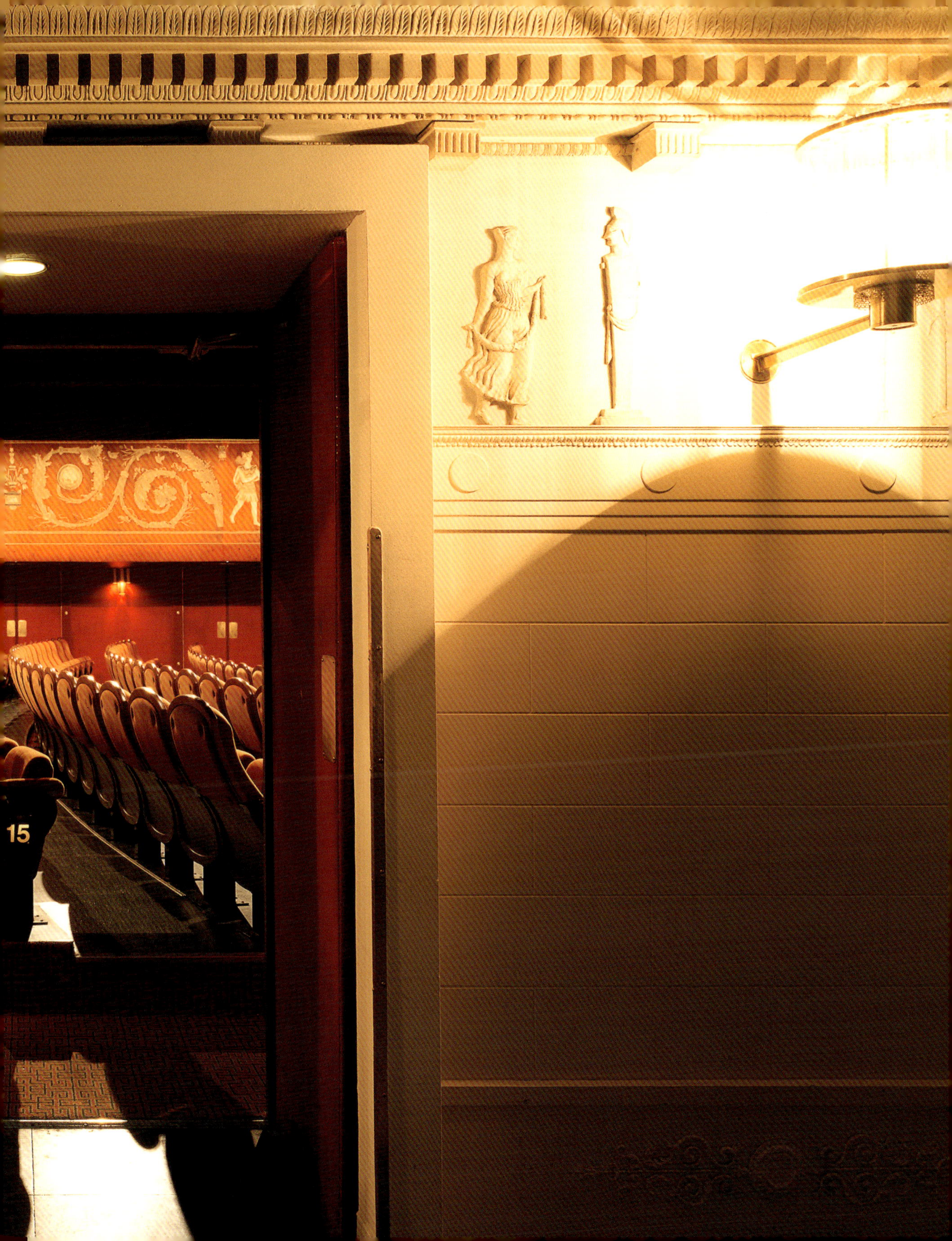
15

竣工当時の劇場内の様子。当時はスクリーン前にアダムとイブの像が配されていた。夜空の星をイメージしたと思われる照明が印象的。

The interior as it looked when construction was completed (facing the screen). At the time, statues of Adam and Eve flanked the screen. The lights, which are said to have been inspired by stars in the night sky, are an impressive touch.

Lower-floor plan

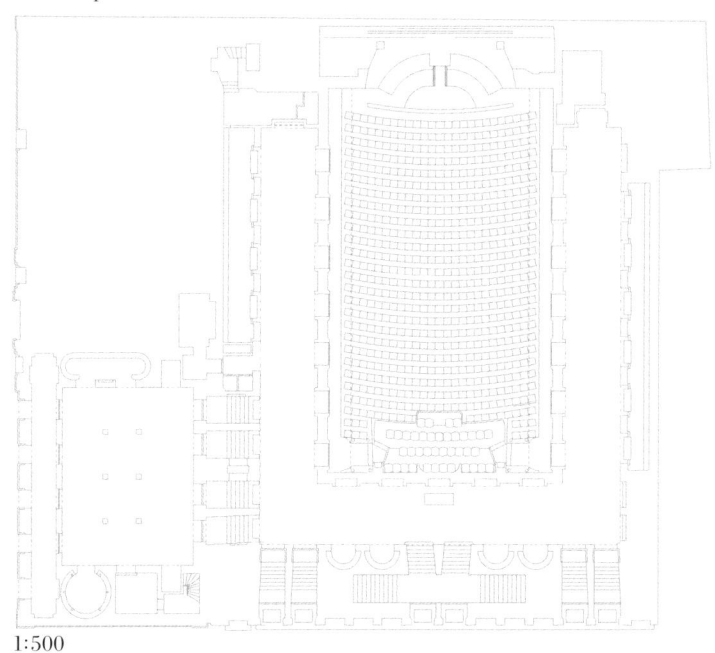

Upper-floor plan

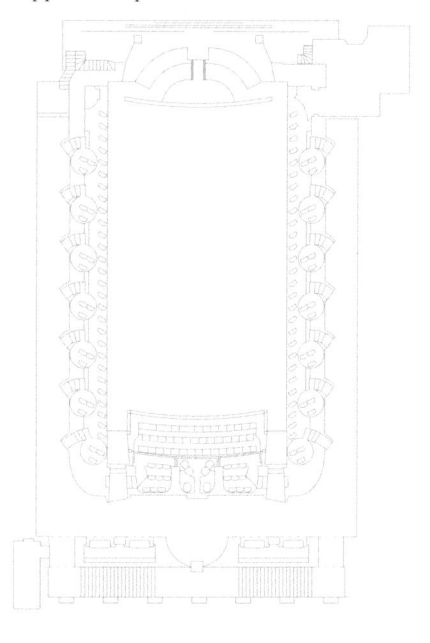

1:500

152 E.G. Asplund

映写室側を見る。2階客席を支える柱には細いコリント式オーダーが使われていた。
A view of the interior (facing the projection booth). The columns that support the second-floor seating area make use of detailed Corinthian order.

Section through hall (1922-23)

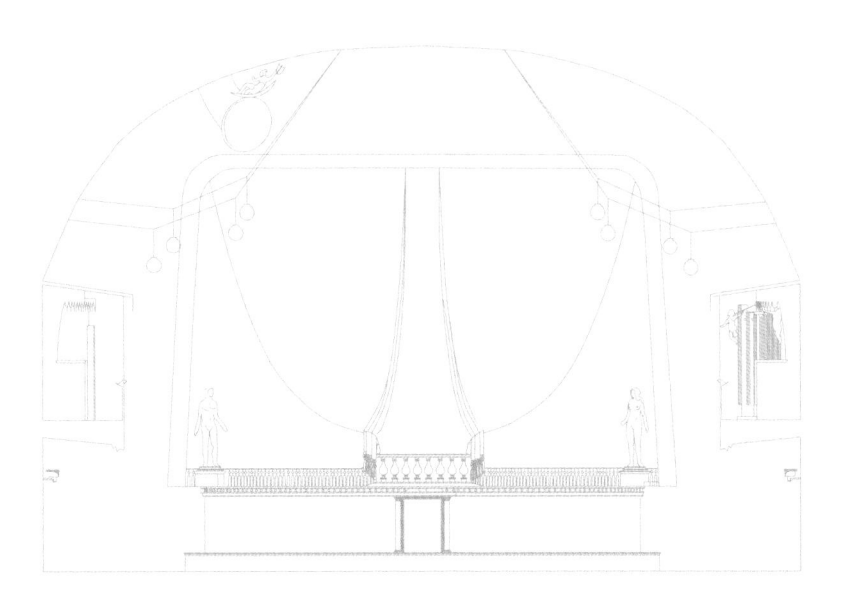

1:150

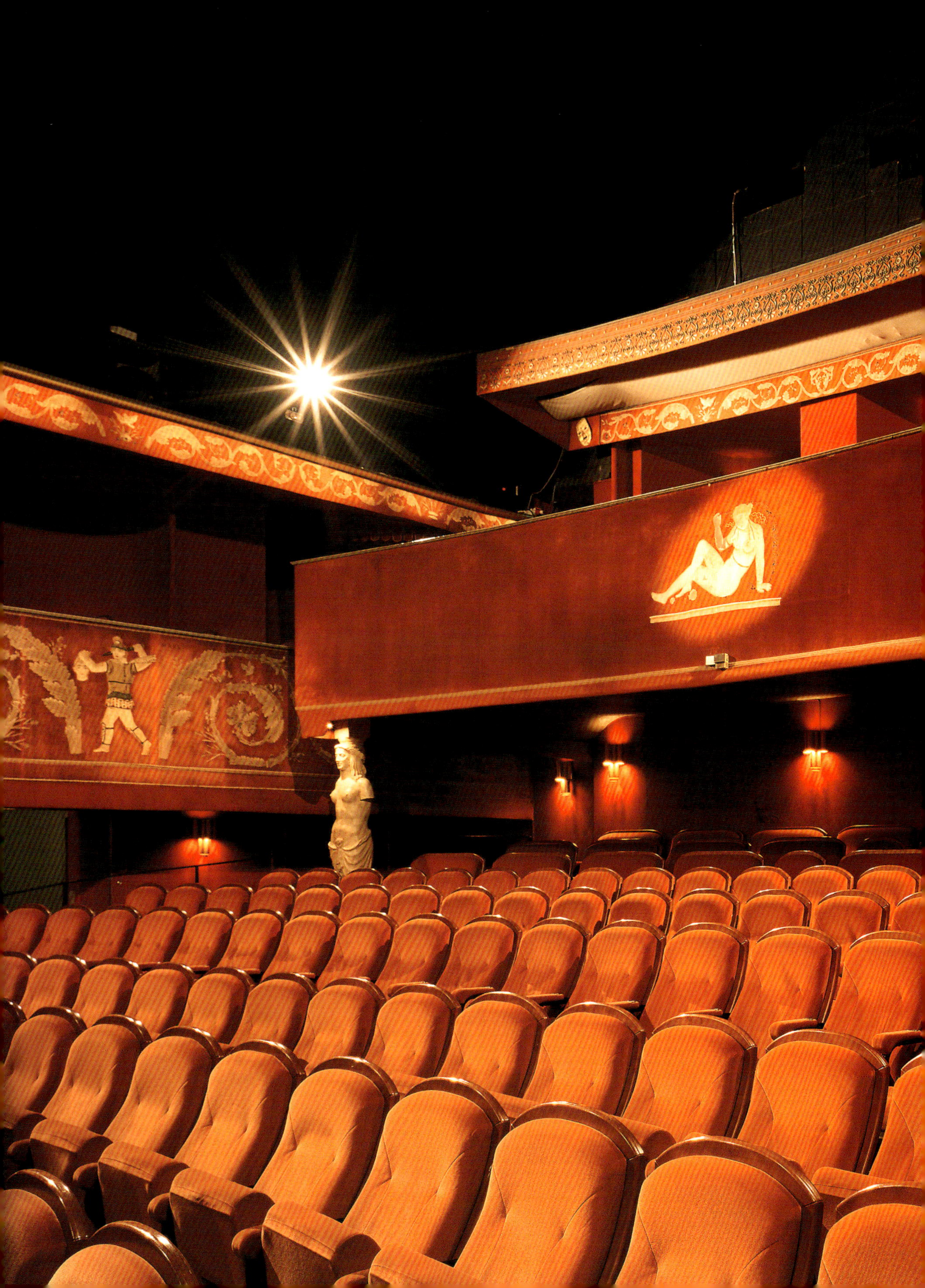

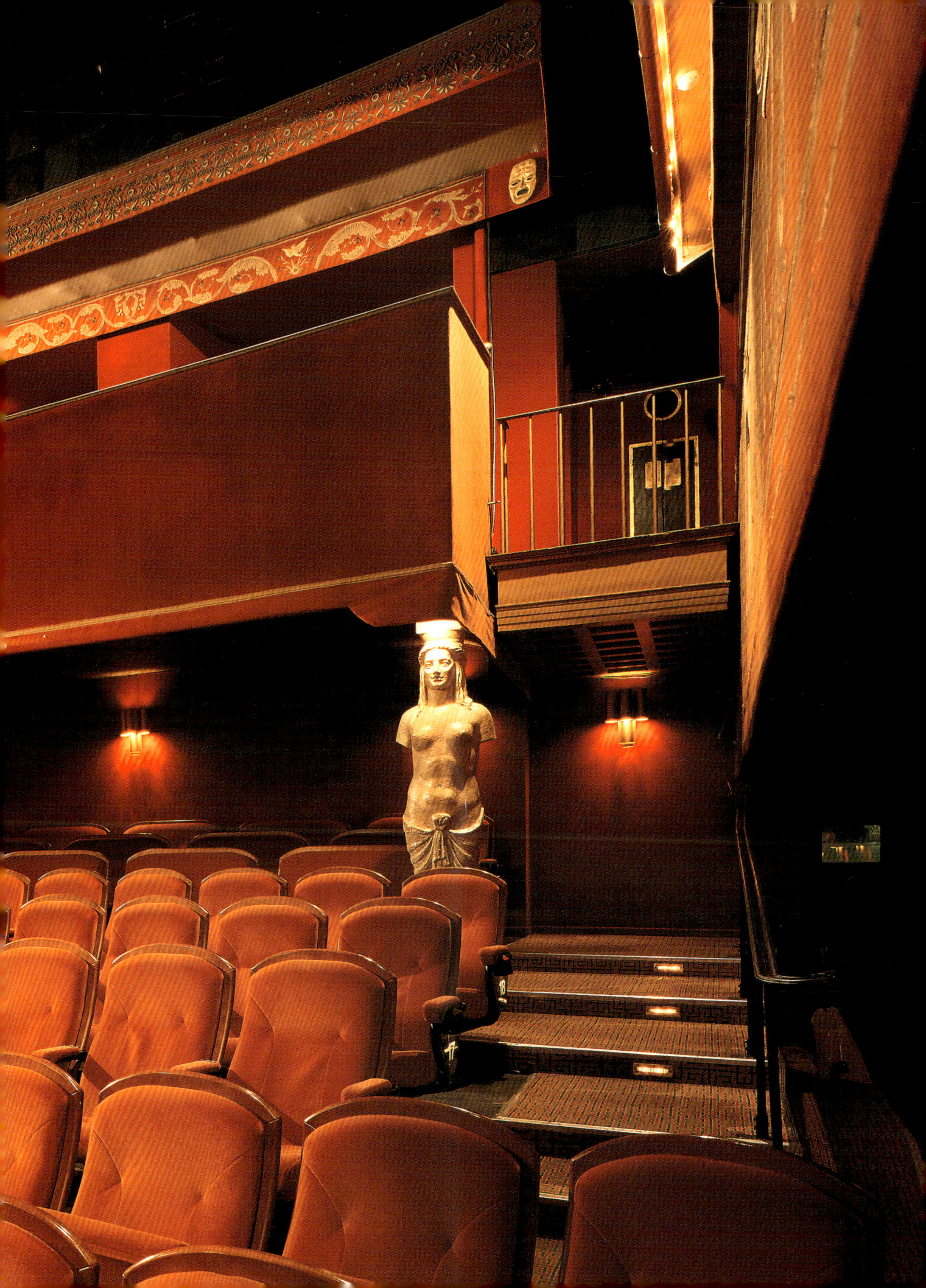

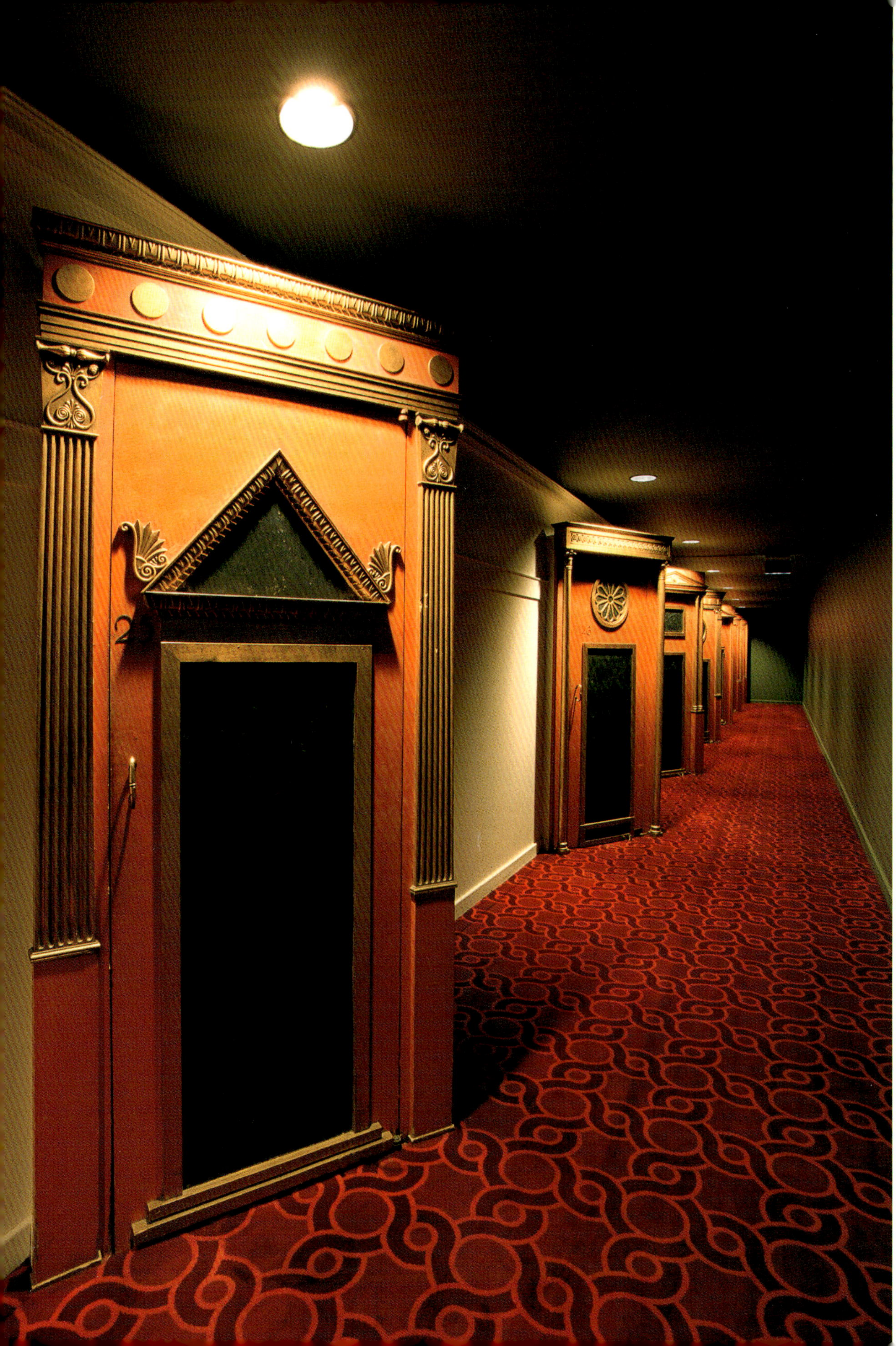

上階回廊に並ぶさまざまなデザインの扉。黒く塗られたひとまわり小さい扉は夢の国への入り口か？ 扉はすべて斜めに飛び出しており観客を誘導する。開館当初は、各扉の前にドアーボーイが立ち、観客を迎え入れたそうだ。

The variously designed doors that line the right side of a corridor on the upper floor. Are the black painted doors, which are designed to be a size smaller than their frames, meant to be the entryway to a land of dreams? All of the doors jut out at an angle, inviting the audience inside. At the time the theatre opened, ushers were positioned outside each of them to welcome people.

劇場内はイタリアで見た夜空の下でのカーニバルが発想の原点となっている。劇場の天井はインディゴブルーに塗られ、夜空を印象付ける。

Asplund's idea for the interior originated in a carnival he saw under the night sky in Italy. The ceiling of the theatre is painted indigo blue to create the impression of a night sky.

劇場天井付近の月と天女のオブジェ。当初は拡声器として使われていた。

An objet d'art depicting the moon and an angel hangs down near the ceiling. It was originally used as a loudspeaker.

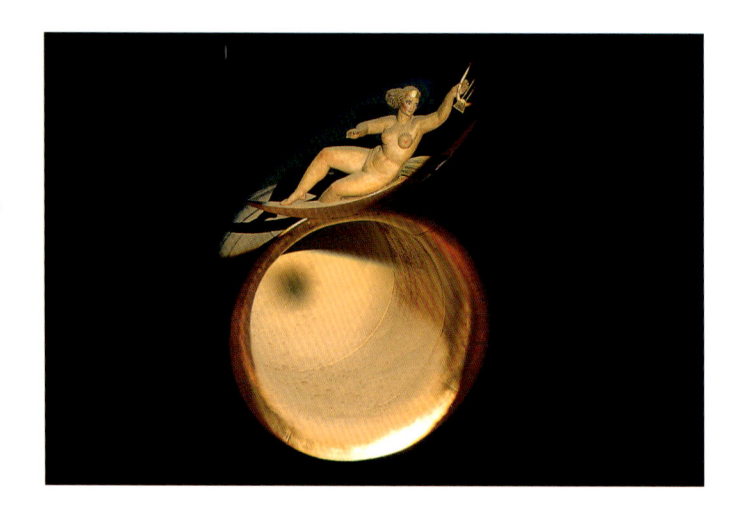

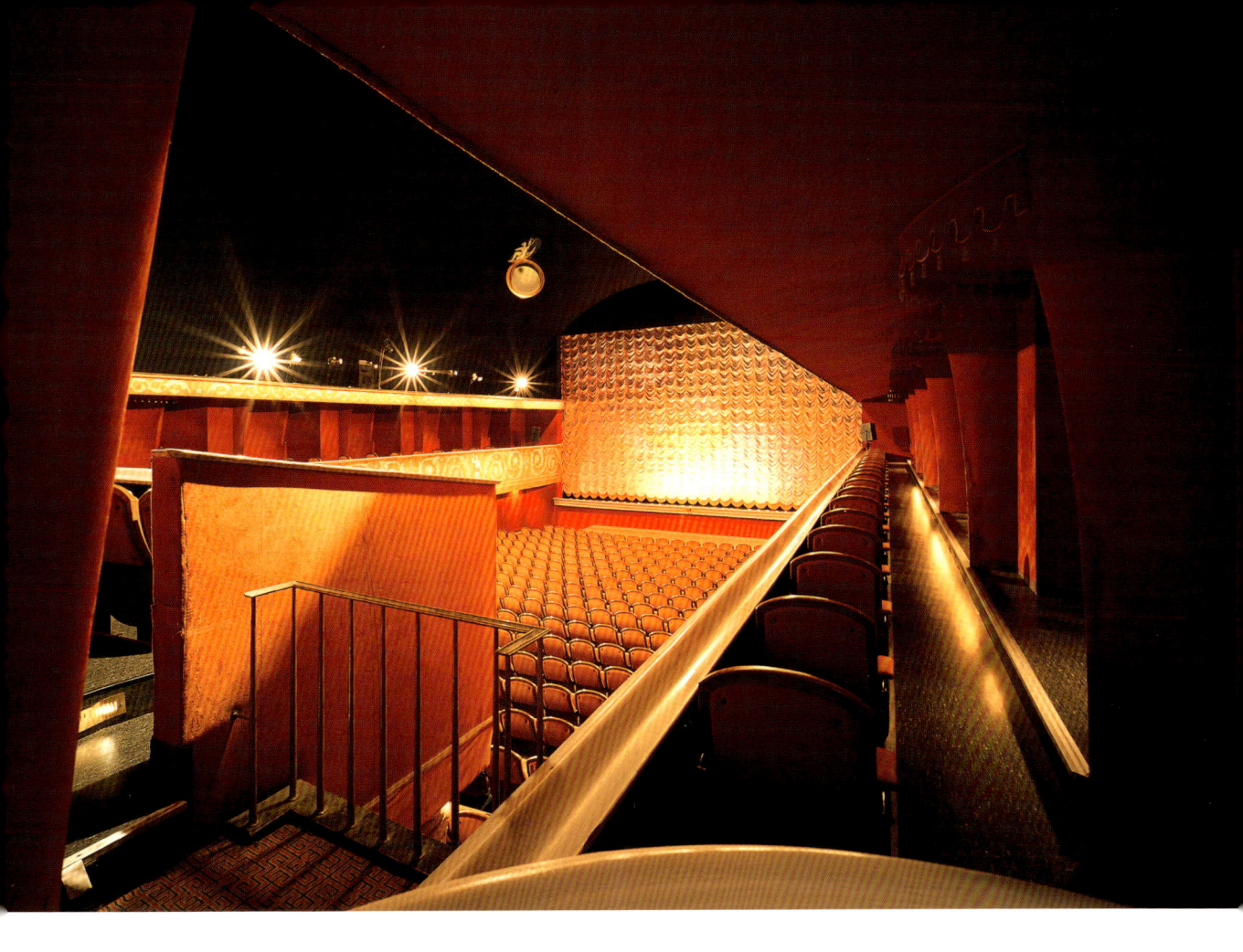

上階バルコニーのボックス席から劇場を見る。バルコニー席は椅子から壁・天井・天蓋に至るまで、赤で統一されている。

The stage as seen from a box seat on the upper-level balcony. In the balcony, everything from the seats to the walls, ceiling and ceiling canopy is a uniform red.

階段手摺端部のライオン。当初は手摺棒とともに赤く塗られていた。ほかに蛇頭の飾りもあった。

A lion design on the end of a staircase handrail. Originally, these along with the handrail posts were painted red. There were also snakehead decorations.

E.G. ASPLUND

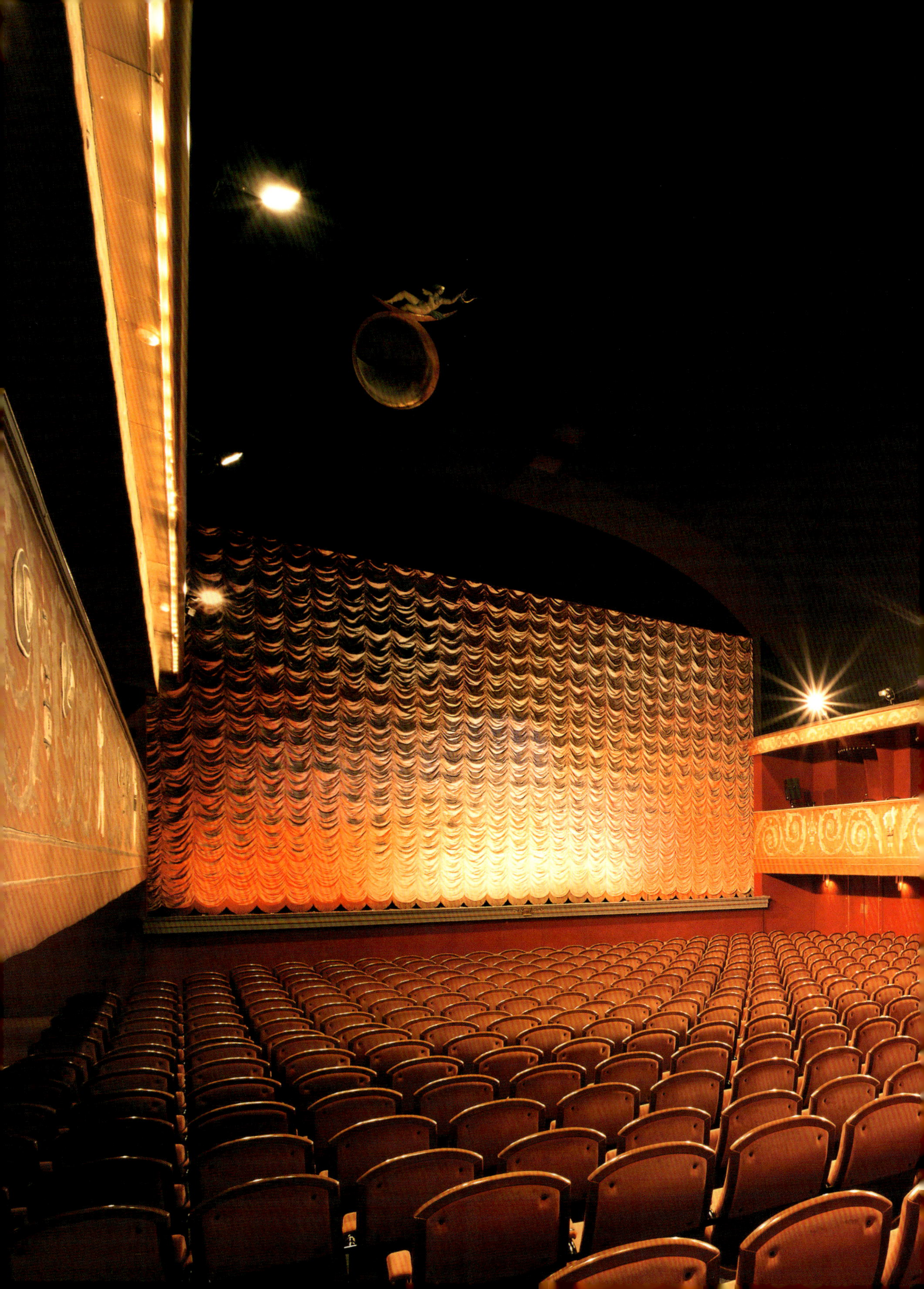

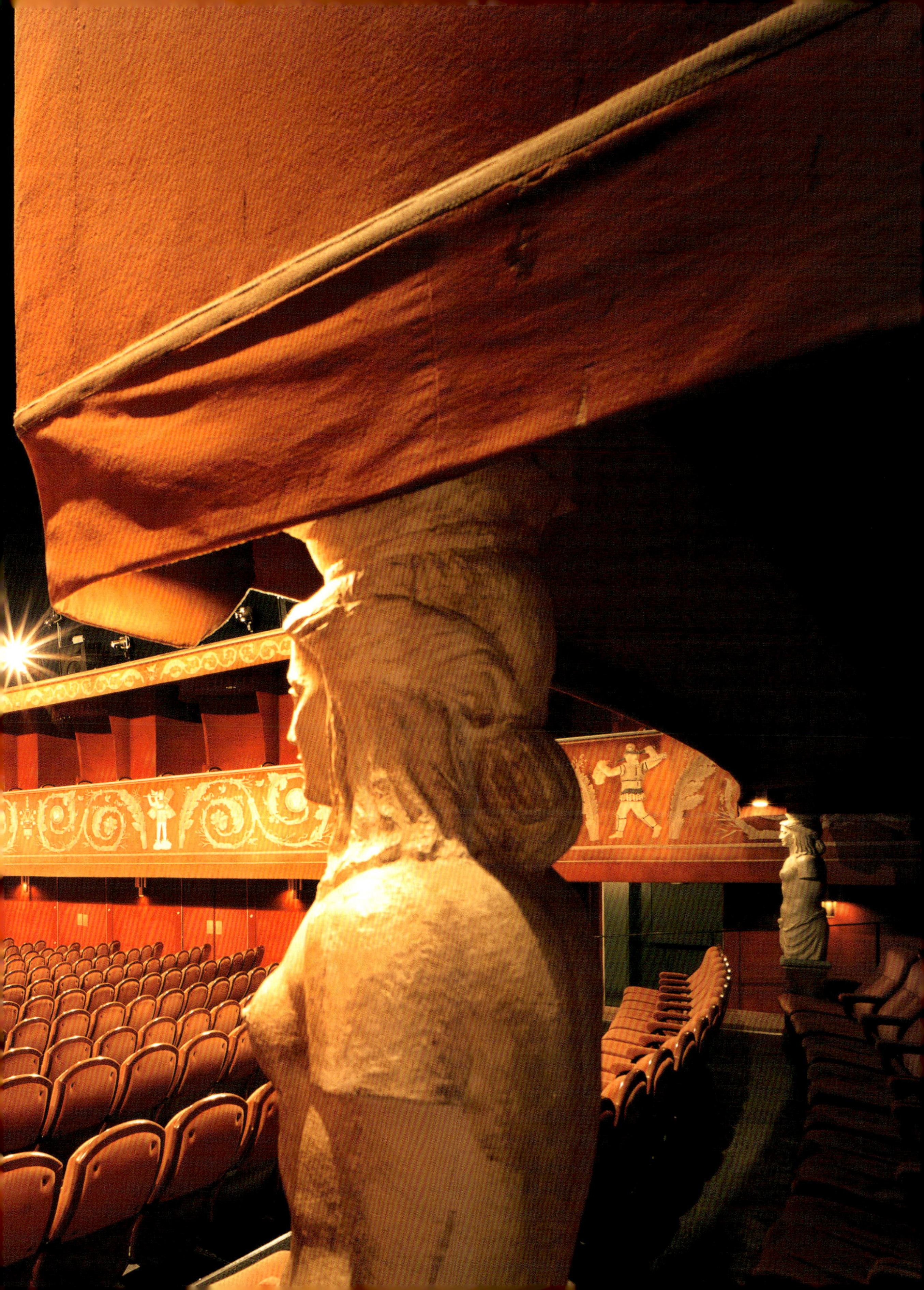

カール・ヨーハン学校 1915–24 イェーテボリ
Carl Johan School, Göteborg

スウェーデン第2の都市イェーテボリにある「カール・ヨーハン学校」増築の設計コンペが1915年に行われ、アスプルンドは2等だったが、なぜか設計を担当することになった。隣接する既存の2階建て校舎に対し、敷地の形状に合わせるようにして、直角よりわずかに軸を振って3階建ての体育館棟と5階建ての教室棟からなる新校舎を接続している。

巨大な切妻のヴォリュームに、正方形の窓を等間隔に張りつけた硬い表情の教室棟の外観は、わずかに1階の開口部周りで変化がつけられているとはいえ、学校建築として求められた要求に対する生真面目すぎる回答だったといえよう。全面に貼られた黄土色のレンガは、既存の建物との調和をはかったものである。アスプルンドは前面道路に面した妻側のファサードを、外観における最大の見せ場と考えていたようだ。基壇からペディメントにまで到達するほどの長いオーダーを構想したり、ピラスターで分割したりと何通りものスタディを行っているが、最終的にはいちばんシンプルな案を選んでいる。

インテリアは、新古典主義の時代背景が反映され、教室部分はやや格式ばった印象である。ところが、教室棟の屋根裏に相当する5層目の講堂や、体育館棟の屋根裏の図書室は、ヴォールト天井を採用して柔らかい印象になっている。特に図書室は、室内につくられた段差による空間の流動性と低めの天井に設けられたトップライトから入る光の作用とによって、アスプルンドらしい親密な空間が実現している。

A design competition for an expansion to Carl Johan School in Göteborg, Sweden's second largest city, was held in 1915. Asplund won second prize, but for some reason he was chosen to oversee the project. To an adjacent, preexisting two-floor school building, Asplund connected a new three-floor gymnasium and a five-story wing of classrooms at a slightly off-center angle.

With the classroom wing's rigid exterior of equidistantly placed, square windows and the volume of its gigantic gabled roof, and despite the variation provided by the first-floor opening, the work seems to be an overly serious response to a request for school architecture. The ocher brick that covers the entire surface was gauged to create a harmony with the older building. Asplund considered the gable side of the facade, which faces the road in front of the school, to be the highlight of the exterior. In conceiving an order long enough to reach from the podium to the pediment, Asplund studied many ways to partition the plaster, but eventually opted for the simplest method.

The interior reflects the then in-vogue neoclassical style and the classroom section seems rather formal. Yet, the fifth-level auditorium, which corresponds to the attic of the classroom wing, and the study, in the attic of the gymnasium, with their vaulted ceilings give the structure a soft touch. In the study, in particular, the fluidity of the space, rooted in the step in the room, and the light that shines in through the skylight in the low ceiling creates the intimate type of space characteristic of Asplund's work.

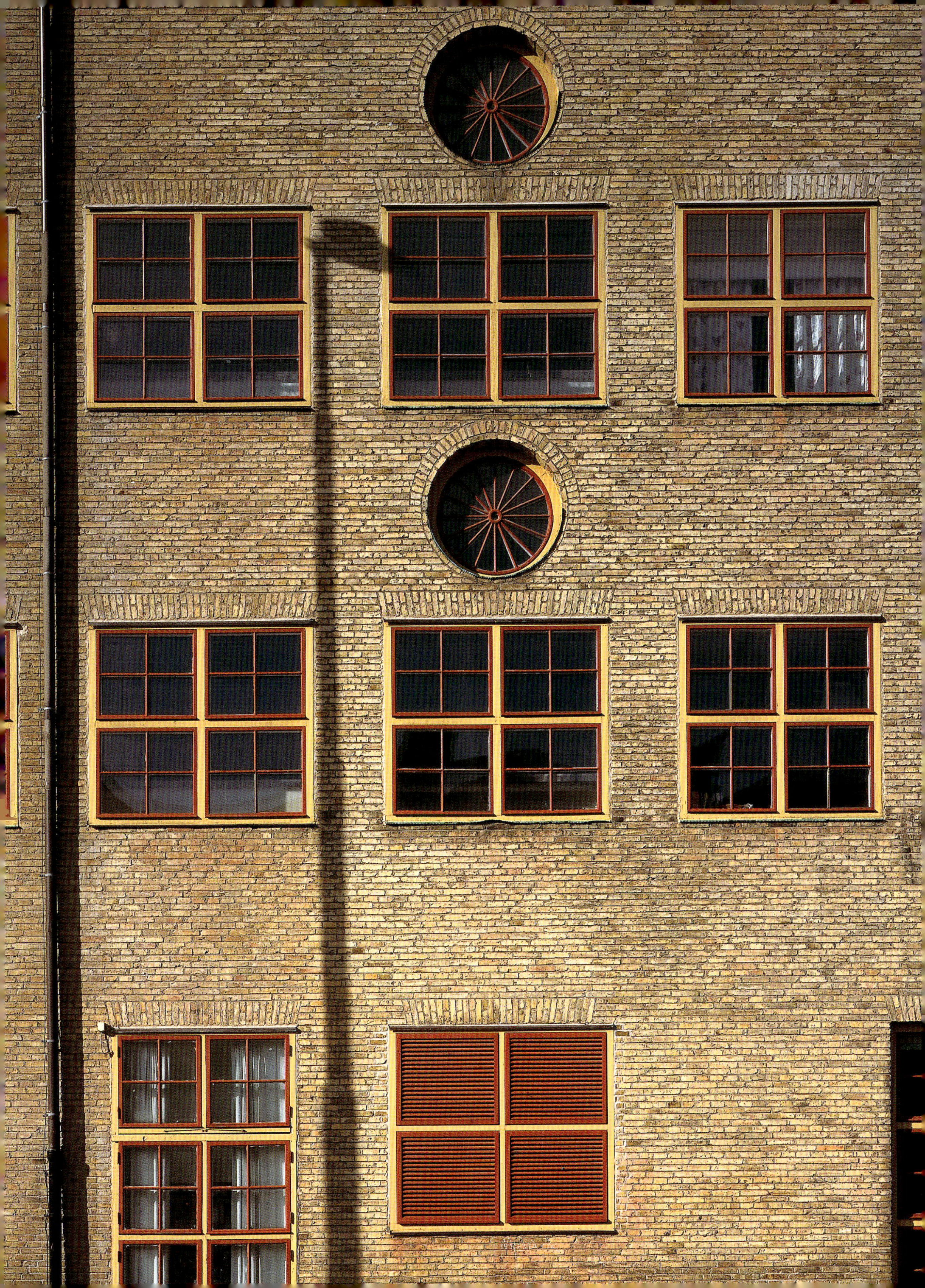

北西側コーナー部分は、「錯視」を利用した視覚的効果が計算されている。前面道路の緩やかな上り勾配と校舎の出隅を鈍角とすることによって、実際より建物を大きく見せ、記念碑性を高めている。

The northwest corner of the building incorporates a visual illusion. The gradual incline of the anterior road and the obtuse angle of the external corner of the structure make it seem larger than it is, while also increasing its monumental nature.

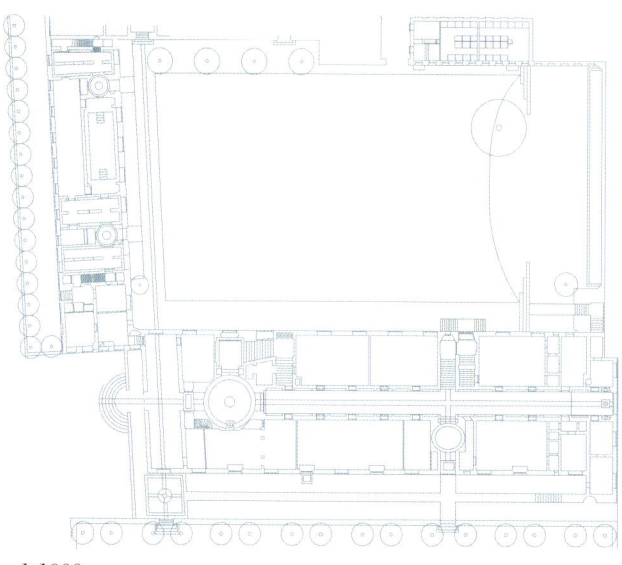

First-floor plan

1:1000

道路側より見た校舎全景。妻壁の破風には古典主義様式が採用されている。

A panorama of the school as seen from the road. Classical touches complement the gabled sections of the walls.

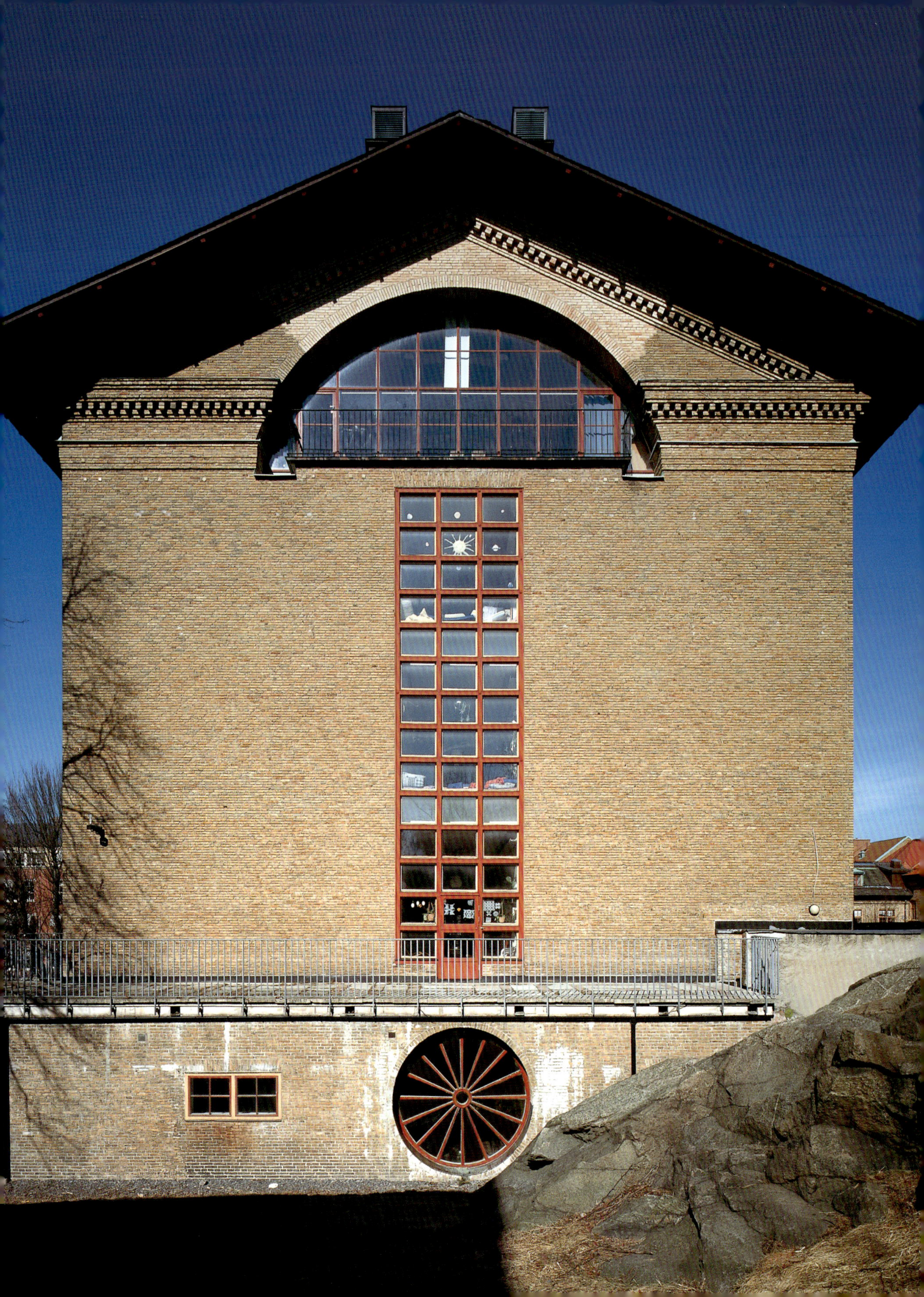

1階廊下南端部の丸窓とつぼ型水飲み器。丸窓から射す光が放射状の影を投影する。何気ない巧みな光の演出。

The vase-shaped drinking fountain and round window at the end of the first-floor corridor. As it streams through the window, the light creates a radial-patterned shadow in a moment of casual brilliance.

最上階美術教室のアーチ型開口部の形がそのまま校舎南側立面に表れている。

The arched opening to the art classroom on the top floor is clearly visible on the south elevation of the school.

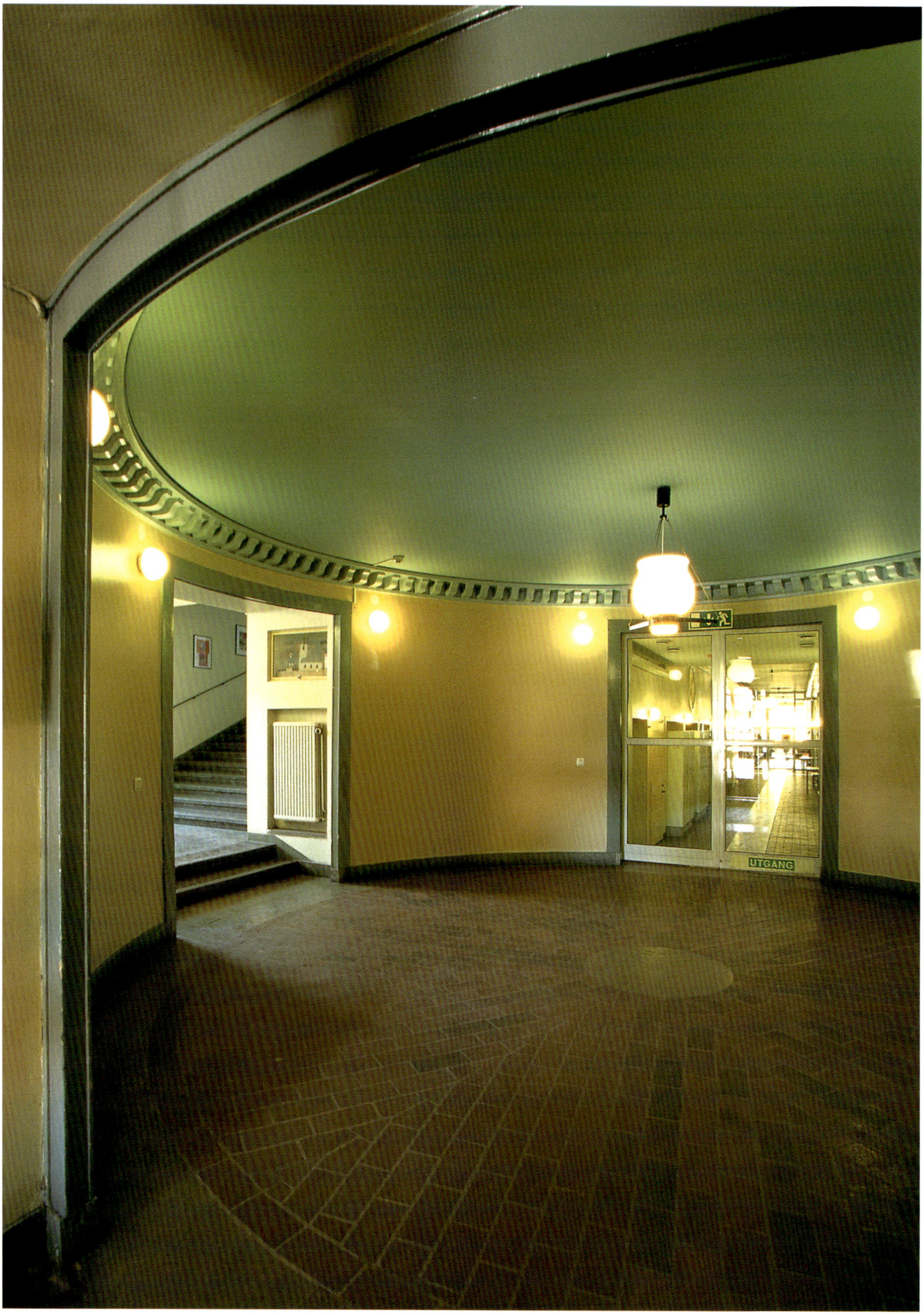
UTGANG

鶯色の天井、からし色の壁、れんが張りの床による円形エントランスホール。起点としての象徴性が与えられている。

The first-floor entrance hall with its brownish-green ceiling, mustard-yellow walls and brick-covered floor. As the source of flow lines, a touch of symbolism is added to the space.

玄関の円形ホールから2階に通じる階段。両側の壁が上に行くにしたがって狭くなり、実際より踊り場が遠くに見える。

The staircase leading to the second floor from the circular entrance hall. The two walls grow narrower as they lead upward from the frontage, making it seem as if the landing is farther away than it is.

階段室踊り場に設けられた丸窓とアーチ状の境界壁と側壁。

A round window and arched boundary and side walls surround the staircase landing.

169　E.G. ASPLUND

校舎に2カ所ある最上階階段室ホール。

The top-floor hall in the school, which has two staircases.

2階廊下北端部の床の高低差を利用し設置されたつぼ型水飲み器。

The vase-shaped drinking fountain is positioned to take advantage of the difference in floor levels at the north end of the second-floor corridor.

Lamp detail

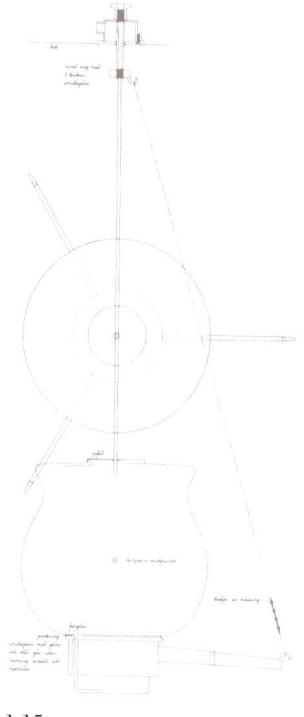

2階廊下より階段室を望む。廊下部分の階段垂れ壁を小判型に穿つことにより、階段室と廊下との一体感を生み出し、視覚的な連続性も獲得している。

A view of the staircase from the second floor. By making an oval opening in the hanging wall, a sense of unity and visual continuity is created between the staircase and the corridor.

1:15

2階廊下。両側に扉や収納壁、ベンチが
リズミカルに並ぶ。

The doors, storage walls and benches
are rhythmically arranged along both
sides of the second-floor corridor.

171 E.G. ASPLUND

トップライトのある最上階講堂。収容人数100人程度。トップライトからの光が天井の圧迫感を和らげる。

The top-floor hall is equipped with a skylight. The hall holds about 100 people. The light that flows in the space works to ease the sense of pressure created by the ceiling.

前面ガラス張りの最上階の美術教室。大きなガラス面がこの教室に開放感を与えている。

The anterior glasswall in the top-floor art classroom. The large glass wall adds a sense of release to the space.

講堂舞台袖壁の階段。天井の曲面と階段。舞台枠によって切り取られた袖壁にアイアンワークの手摺がやわらかい曲線を描く。

The staircase next to the wing wall of the stage in the auditorium. The ironwork handrail adds a soft, curved line to the wall, which is defined by the rounded surface of the ceiling, the staircase and the frame of the stage.

体育館棟2階にある職員用サロン。真っ赤な壁に灰水色の天井、シンプルな円柱が新鮮な印象を与え、天井は、中央の円形部分をつや消し塗料で塗り分けている。

The salon for staff members on the second floor of the gymnasium. Along with the greyish blue ceiling and the bright red walls, the simple round columns seem refreshing. The blue-gray ceiling is divided in two parts, with the round, center section painted in matte.

体育館棟3階図書室。階段下の司書席から閲覧室が見わたせる。

The third-floor library in the gymnasium. The reading room can be surveyed from the librarian's desk at the bottom of the stairs.

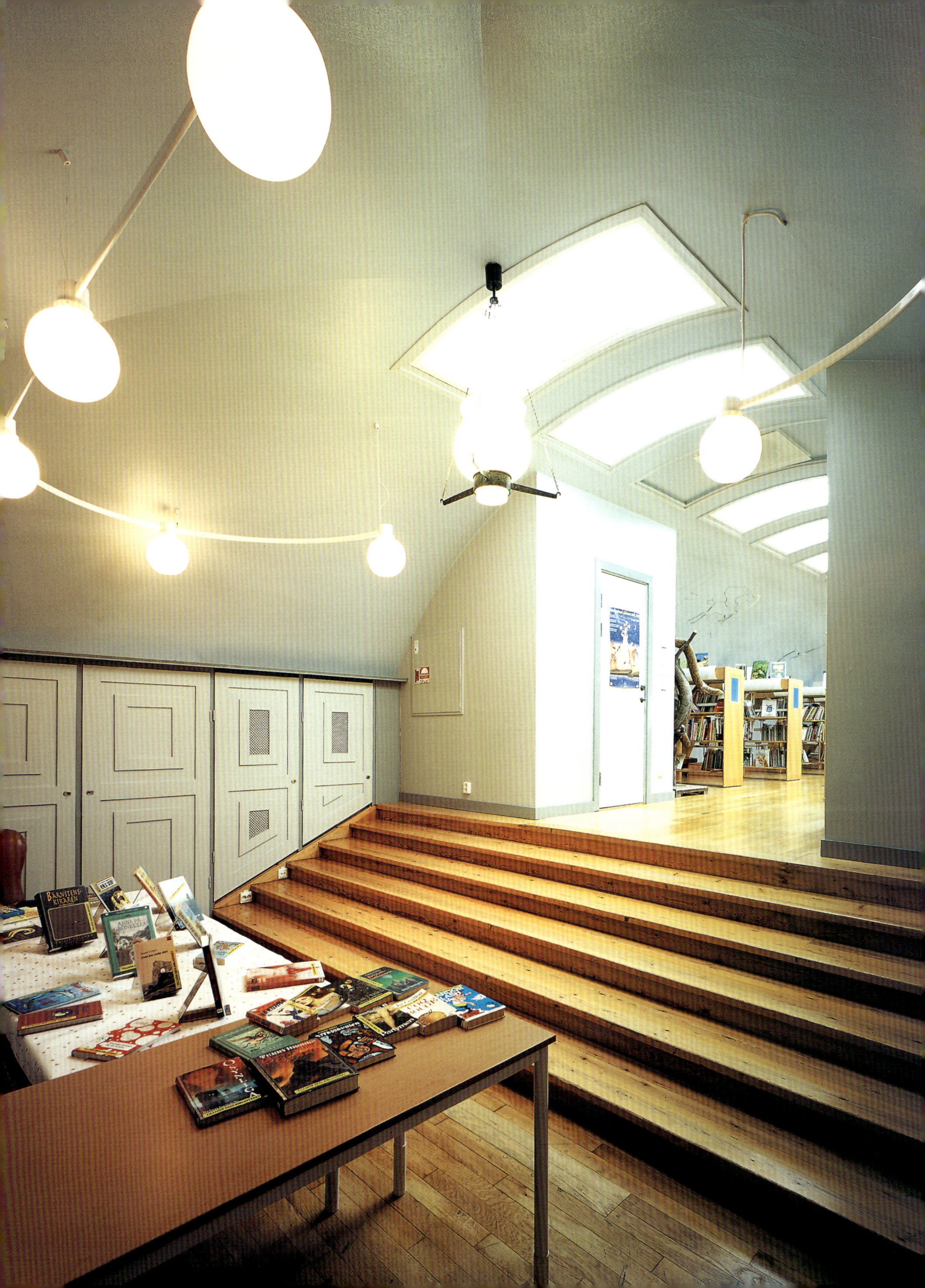

ストックホルム市立図書館 1920-28 ストックホルム
Stockholm City Library, Stockholm

アスプルンドは当初、この建物の設計コンペの準備委員を委託され、1920年に公共図書館の先進国アメリカへ視察に行っている。帰国後になぜか設計者として指命された彼は、開架式閲覧室を円柱形の大きな一室とする計画案をまとめた。その周囲を諸室が矩形に取り囲む明快な幾何学的構成は、ブレやルドゥー、パッラーディオなどの先例を意識したのだろうが、結局はこの形態が利用者にとって使いやすいと判断したのであろう。

初期案ではドーム型屋根のトップライトから、中央の大閲覧室に光が降り注ぐ計画だった。最終的にはフラットな屋根が採用され、ハイサイドライトに変更されている。初期案では、玄関にコリント式のオーダーがつけられていたが、最終案ではそうした装飾的要素がほとんど削られた。幾何学図形による単純な構成に造形のポイントが絞られ、結果的に近代的な表現に接近したのだが、立面の寸法は新古典主義の時代背景を反映して、黄金比に基づいている。外壁のコーニスと玄関ホールに施されたレリーフ、玄関の額縁の形状などはエジプト風である。

大通りから階段をあがり館内に入ると、さらに階段が延び書庫の一部が正面に見える。その階段をあがると、徐々に別世界に入るような高揚感に包まれていく。ハイサイドライトからの柔らかい光が満ちる室内に、頭から入っていく非日常的な空間体験の効果である。本の背表紙がぐるりと見渡せる館内は、本の存在感と探しやすさという基本的な機能が、そのままインテリアの表現へと昇華した、見事なデザイン的解決を示している。

In 1920, Asplund, who had been commissioned to serve on the committee overseeing the design competition for this building, made a visit to the U.S., the most advanced country in terms of public libraries. Upon his return, he was for some reason appointed designer of the project and submitted his proposal for a large, cylindrical space. The distinctly geometrical structure of the building has an intentional historical precedent in the work of Boullee, LeDoux and Palladio, but ultimately Asplund adopted the form for the ease it offered library patrons.

His original proposal called for light to stream down into the central reading room through a skylight in a dome-shaped roof. In the end, however, a flat roof was used and the skylight was replaced with high side lights. In an early plan, Corinthian order was used for the entrance, but in the final plan, ornamental elements of this type were almost completely removed. The design hinges on a simple structure based on geometrical shapes, resulting in what approaches a modernist expression, but the dimensions of the elevation surface reflect the neoclassicism that was in favor during the period and are based on the golden ratio. The cornice on the exterior walls and the relief that decorates the entrance hall, and the shape of the architrave in the entrance are all Egyptian in style.

After ascending the stairs and entering the building, another staircase leads to a portion of the stacks. As one climbs this staircase, one is gradually overtaken by a sense of euphoria. The soft light that flows into the space through the high side lights creates an extraordinary spatial experience. As one takes a sweeping look over the spines of the books, their presence and being able to search through them easily is a sign of the splendid design.

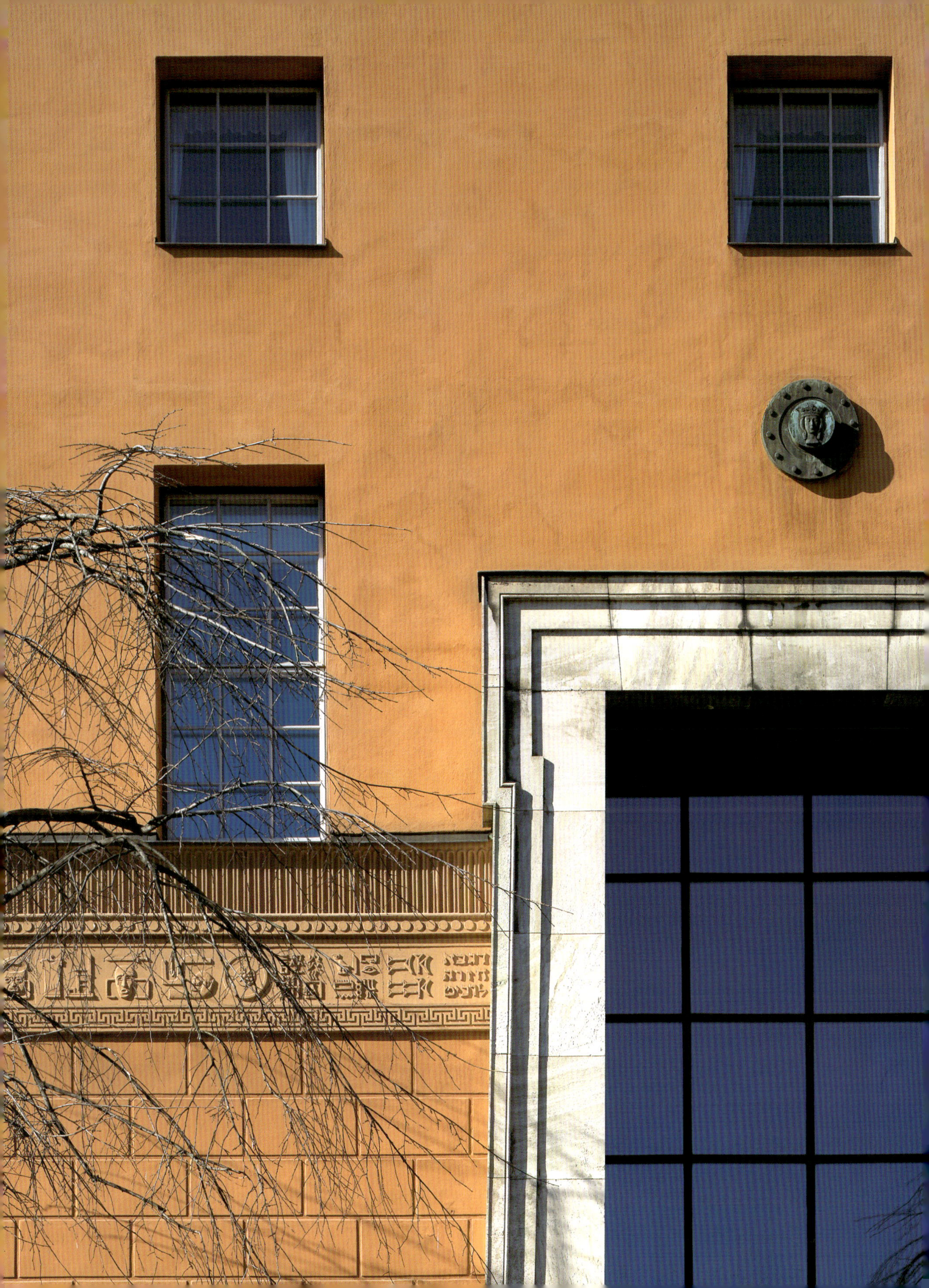

Facade (1920-28)

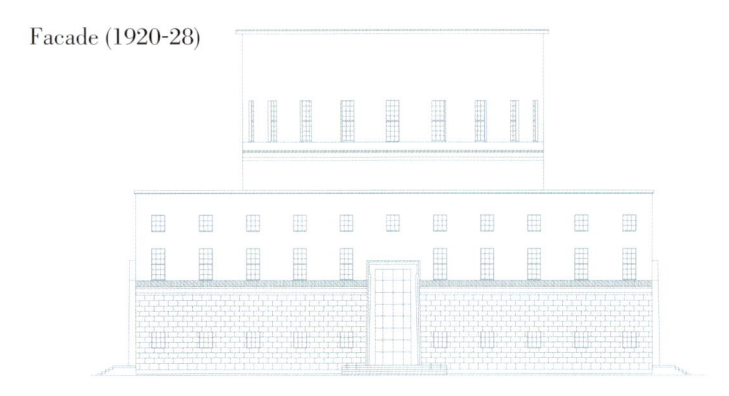

First-floor plan (1920-28)

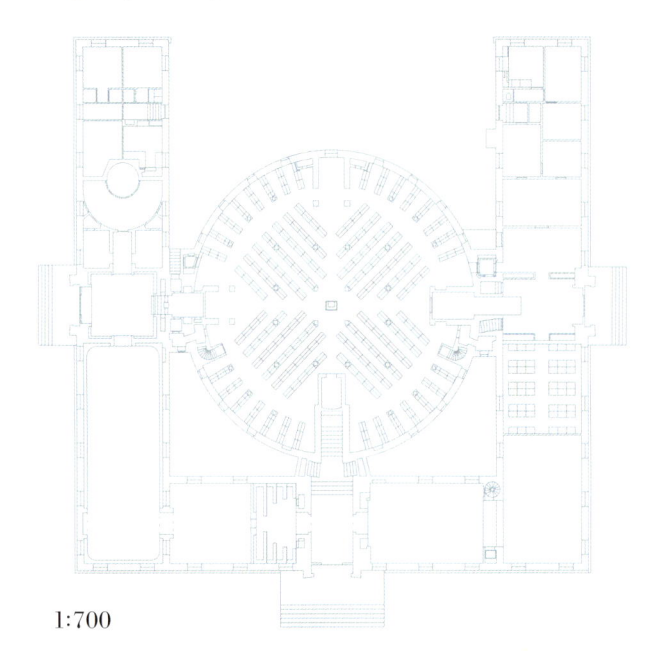

1:700

アスプルンドは図書館周辺のランドスケープ計画も行っている。公園内池からの図書館遠望。

The landscape around the library was also designed by Asplund. This is a broad view across the pond in the surrounding park.

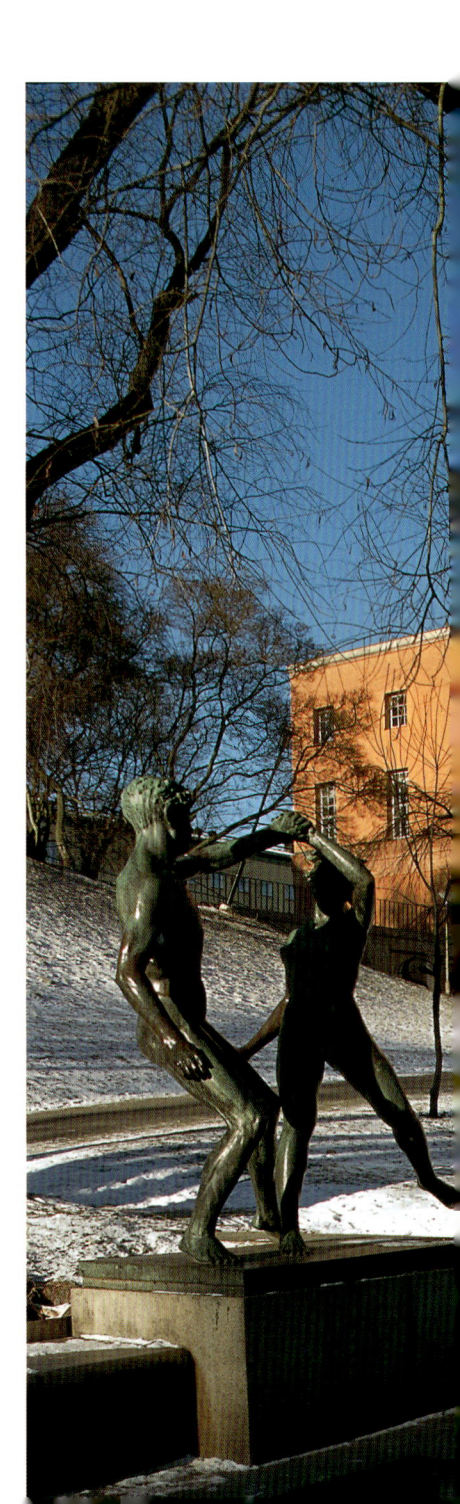

東側公園からの雪景色。円筒と矩形による構成。

The view from a park on the east side. The structure of the building consists of a cylinder and a rectangle.

STOCKHOLM PUBLIC LIBRARY
ARCHITECT GUNNAR ASPLUND 1928

正面を北面道路側アプローチから見る。
わずかに上部が絞られた門型の入り口
へと視線は導かれる。

The front entrance as seen from the
approach along the street on the north
side. The slightly higher top section
draws the eye to the gate-shaped
entrance.

SVANSTRÖM
STOCKHOLMS STADSBIBLIOTEK
ARKITEKT GUNNAR ASPLUND 1928

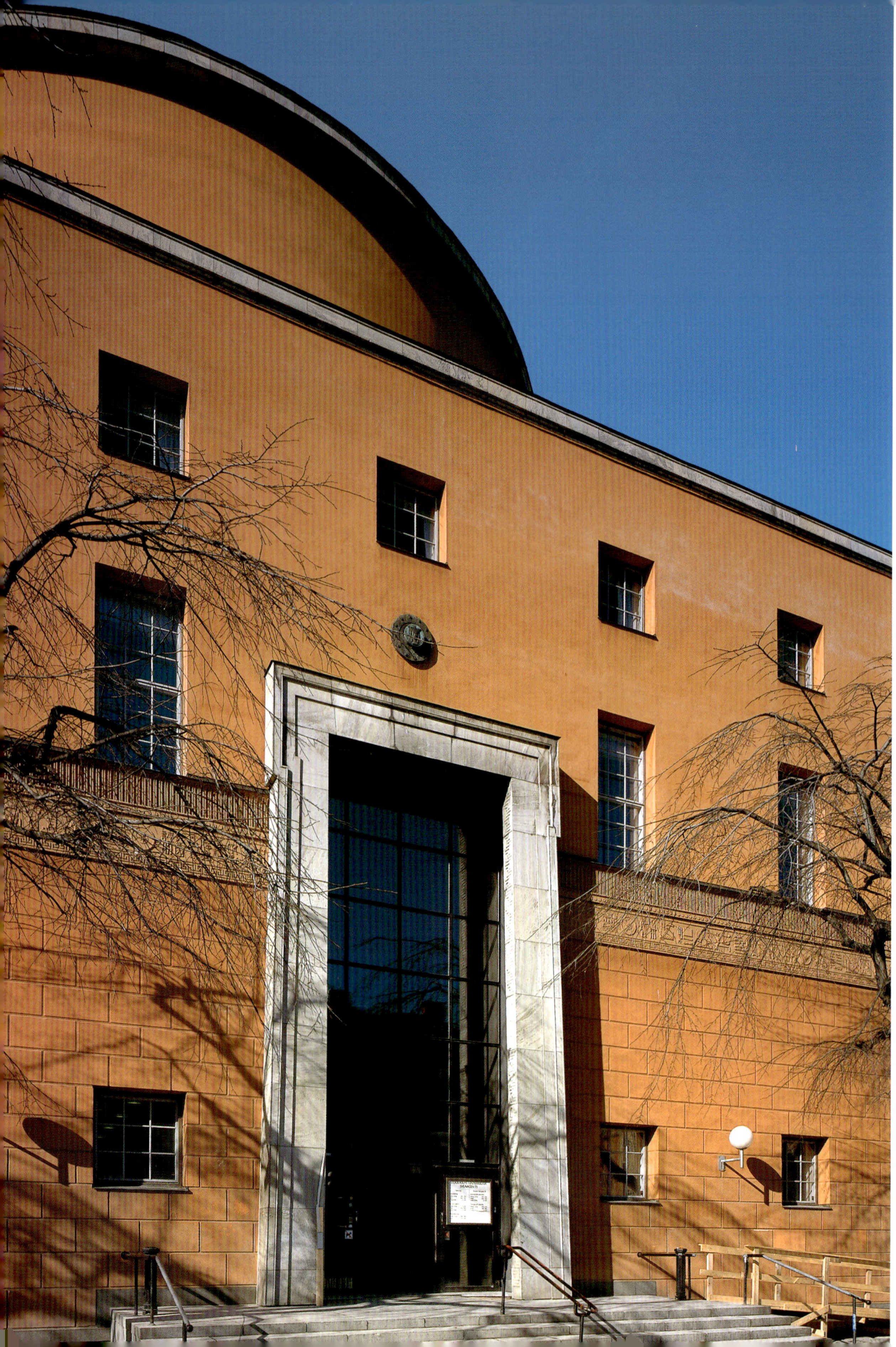

古典主義様式による構成が図書館に権威的な印象を与えている。四周を取り巻くコーニスのレリーフはエジプト様式。それは石造りの門とともに、学問の象徴としてのモチーフとなっている。

The classical style of the building gives the library an authoritative air. The cornice relief, which girdles the building, has an Egyptian style. Along with the stone entranceway, the motif is meant to symbolize learning.

眼が暗さに慣れるにつれ、黒漆喰に塗り込められた壁からエジプト風レリーフが浮かび上がる。ここでは繊細な光の導入という意味で、黒い壁が劇的な効果を生んでいる。

As one's eyes adjust to the darkness, an Egyptian-style relief coated with black plaster emerges from the walls. The subtlety of the light in the space gives the black walls a dramatic appearance.

エントランスホール奥のロトンダへと通じる正面階段。巨大なコードペンダントが、円筒の大空間（開架閲覧室）を明るく照らし出す。

The front staircase leading to the rotunda at the rear of the entrance hall. A huge cord pendant brightly illuminates the large space (open-stack reading room) in this cylindrical area.

エジプト様式のレリーフの光と影が空間をドラマチックに演出している。

Light and shadow play across the Egyptian relief to create a dramatic effect.

185 E.G. ASPLUND

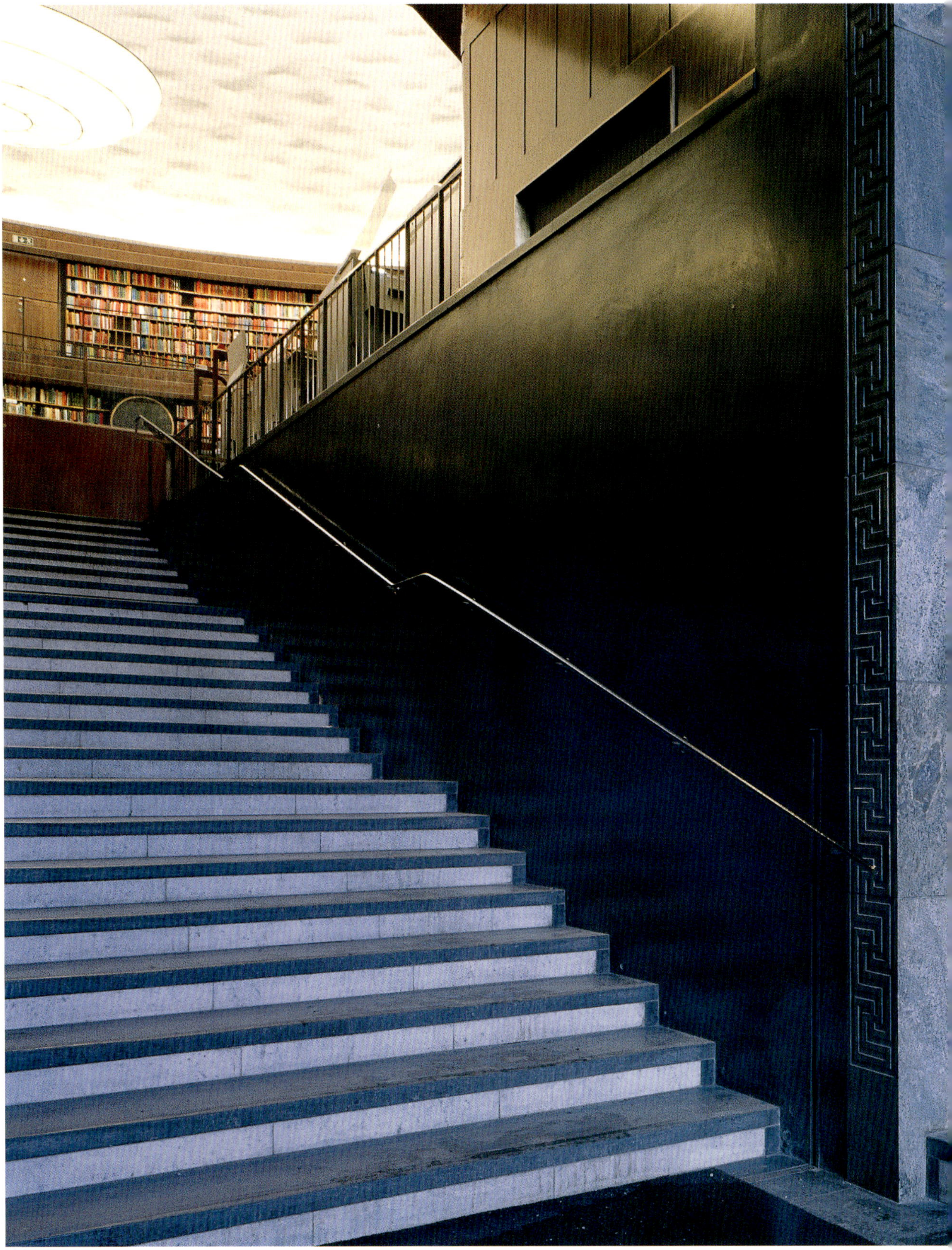

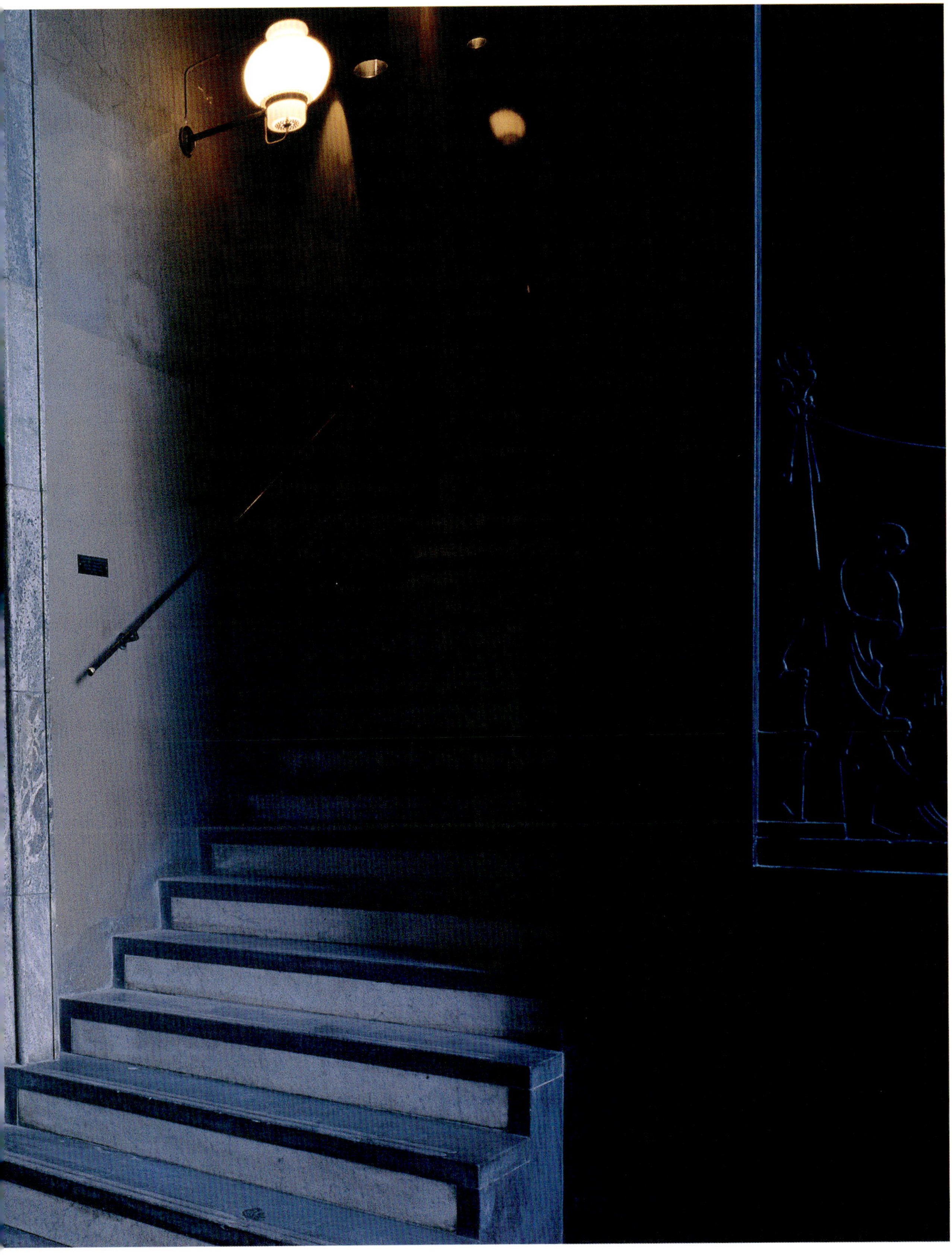

Uppslagsverk

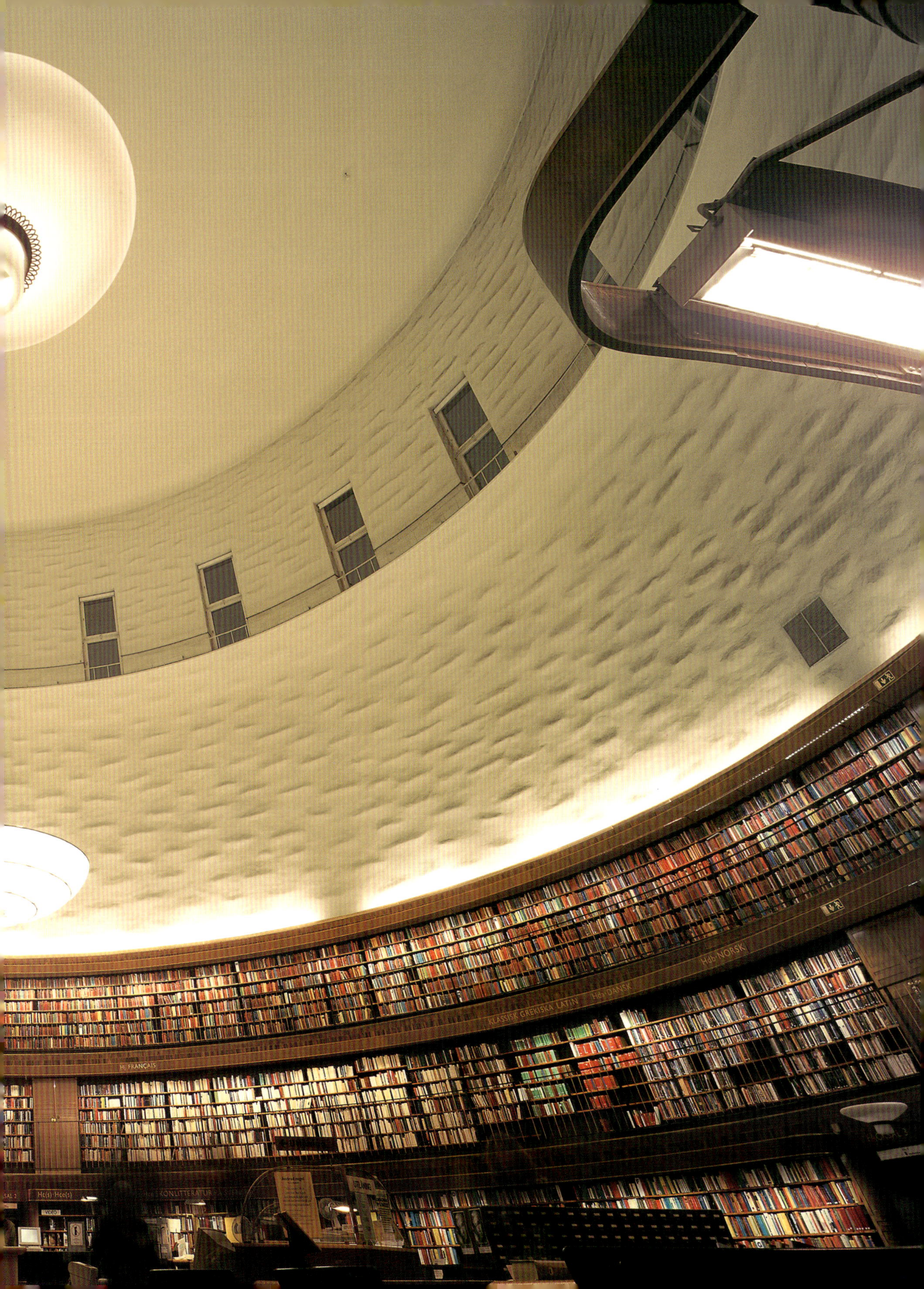
H. FRANÇAIS
KLASSISK GREKISKA LATIN
Hdb NORSK

2層目から見た開架閲覧室全景。巨大なロトンダの圧倒的な存在感。内壁に見える
無数の横長凸面が適度に光を乱反射させ、大空間を引き締めている。

A full view of the open-stack reading room from the second level. The huge rotunda
has an overwhelming presence. The long, horizontal inner wall with its countless convex
surfaces reflects a moderate amount of light, helping to define the large space.

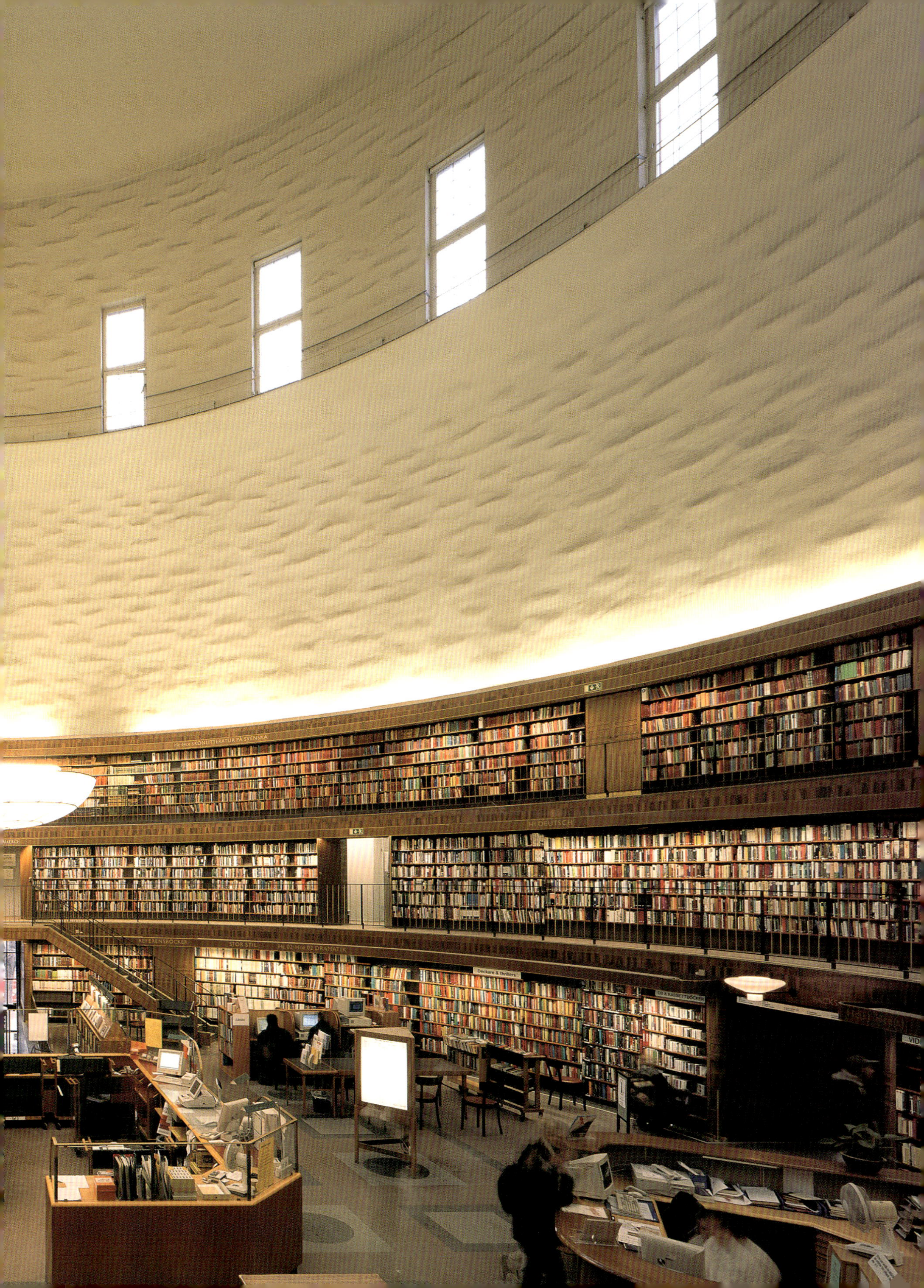

円周書架2層目にはめ込まれた大時計。

A large clock is inlaid in the circular book shelves.

ロトンダ中央よりエントランスホールを見る。連続する円周書架の下を潜り抜ける大階段は、外への明快な動線となっている。階段を下りる人がシルエットとなって美しく浮かび上がる。

The entrance hall as seen from the center of the rotunda. The large staircase passes below the succession of circular book shelves, forming a clear flow line toward the outside. Beautiful silhouettes are created as people descend the staircase.

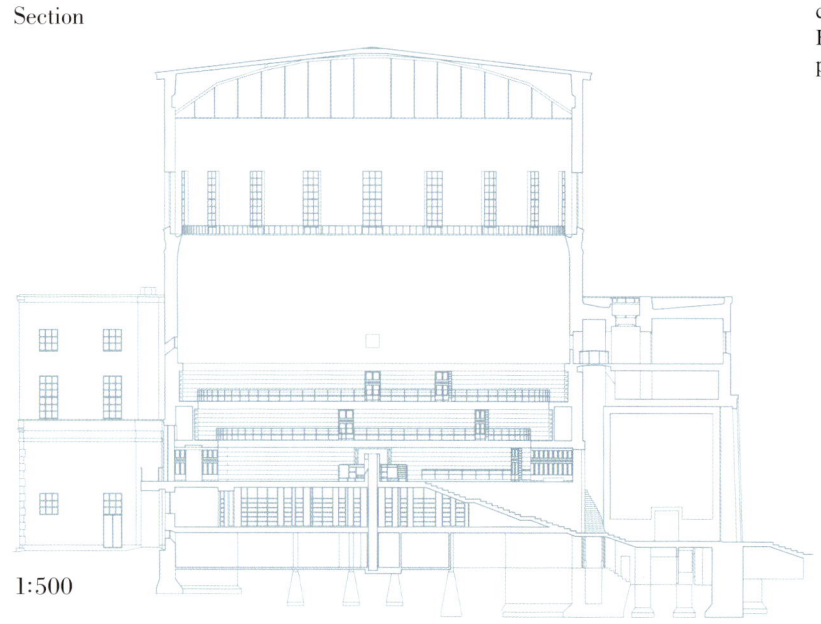

Section

1:500

ENGLISH

SVENSKA

円周書架端部のディテール。ウォールナットに象嵌された真鍮の装飾が美しい。

Detail of the end of the circular book shelves. The brass ornamentation inlaid in the walnut is gorgeous.

ロトンダの外周に配された閲覧室。高窓からの採光による落ち着いた雰囲気。

The reading room located outside the rotunda. A tranquil atmosphere is created by the natural light that spills into the space from the high windows.

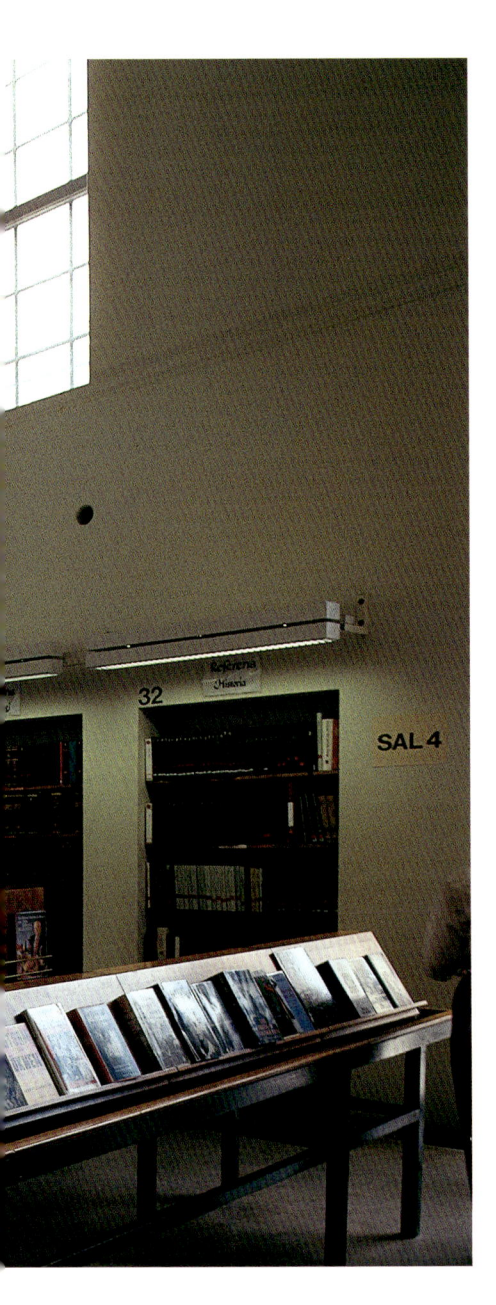

2層吹抜けの閲覧室。

The reading room on the second-level breezeway.

閲覧室と上階書架を結ぶ優雅な螺旋階段。

The spiral staircase that connects the reading room with the stacks on the second floor.

星座が描かれた子供図書館の読書室天井。

The reading room in the children's library with constellations painted on the ceiling.

子供図書館ラウンジ。大きな開口部からの光が差し込む開放的な空間。

The lounge in the children's library. Light pours through the large opening in the wide-open space.

子供図書室奥のおとぎ話の部屋。子供たちは半円形の部屋の形に合わせて作られたベンチに座り、語り部によるおとぎ話に耳を傾ける。

The fairy-tale room in the rear of the children's library. As they sit on benches that fit the shape of the semicircular room, the children are taken to fantastic worlds by a storyteller.

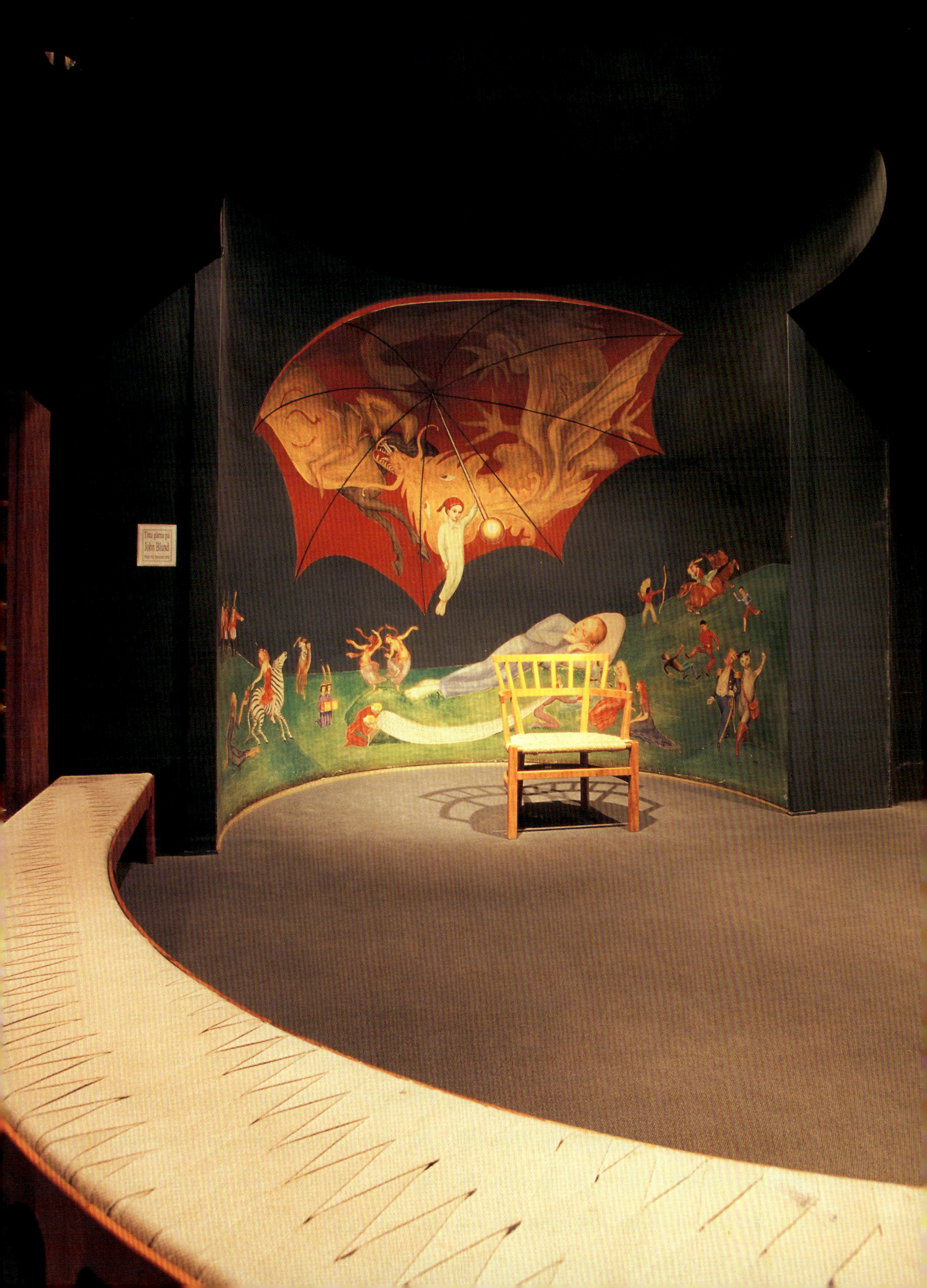
John Blund

イェーテボリ裁判所増築　1913, 1919, 1934-37　イェーテボリ
Göteborg Law Courts, Göteborg

　イェーテボリのグスタフ・アドルフ広場に面した裁判所の増築である。1913年のコンペで1等を獲得したアスプルンドは、以後30年以上にわたり、発注者側の要求や広場の整備計画の変更に合わせて提案をくり返すことになった。既存建物は1672年に巨匠N.テッシンによって建てられ、その後数回の増築を経て、中庭を囲む3階建てになっていた。

　コンペ応募案は、ナショナル・ロマンティシズムの時代背景を反映している。1915年と16年の計画案では、クラシシズムの色合いを強め、24年と25年の案では、既存建物の表現に統一した別棟を接続した。34年の案もこの延長上にある。ところが1935年から36年にかけて、根本的な発想の転換が起きた。増築部分は目の醒めるような近代建築へと姿を変えたのである。中庭側の大きなガラス面、広場のような吹抜けのホール、木の質感を生かした壁面、トップライト、透明なエレベーター・シャフト。裁判所を訪れる人の重苦しい気分を吹き飛ばす、さわやかな空間である。

　あえて表現を統一しなかった外観には、竣工当時から厳しい批判があったという。実際はどうか。高さ方向の要素や色彩を既存部分に合わせ、一体感を表現する。窓の位置は各スパンのなかで、そっと既存建物の側に寄り添っている。既存建物に対する敬意と愛情がさりげなく示されながら、新しい時代の表現を恥じることなく、声高に主張することもなく、リアリティに基づいて素直に表現する姿勢が見られる。アスプルンドにしかできなかったであろう、知性のあり方を見る思いがする。

This project was an expansion of a courthouse building that faces Gustav Adolph Square in Göteborg. For more than thirty years, Asplund, who won first prize in the design competition in 1913, repeatedly made proposals to fit the builder's requests and changes in the square's development plans. The preexisting structure, created by the master architect Nicodemus Tessin in 1672, underwent a series of expansions over the years to become a three-floor building surrounding a courtyard.

　The proposals Asplund first submitted to the competition are reflective of the National Romantic ethic that was popular at the time. In the 1915 and 1916 plans, there is a strong sense of classicism, and the proposals of 1924 and 1925 called for a separate wing that was similar in style to the original building. The 1934 proposal was a continuation of this. Then in the 1935-36 plan, a fundamental conceptual shift occurred. The addition had suddenly taken the eye-opening form of modern architecture. This included elements such as a large glass surface in the courtyard, a plaza-like, open-ceiling hall, walls with a wood texture, a skylight and a transparent elevator shaft. The refreshing space worked to dispel court visitors' glum feelings. The exterior, which Asplund did not design to match the interior, was the subject of severe criticism from the time construction was completed.

　How does it stand up today? In terms of the height and color of the preexisting building, Asplund's work is meant to create a sense of unity. In each span, the windows are positioned to nestle up to the old building. While there is a nonchalant type of reverence and affection for the older structure, Asplund is not ashamed to announce a new era, and without overly asserting itself, the design is straightforward and realistic. It is a work that displays Asplund's special intelligence.

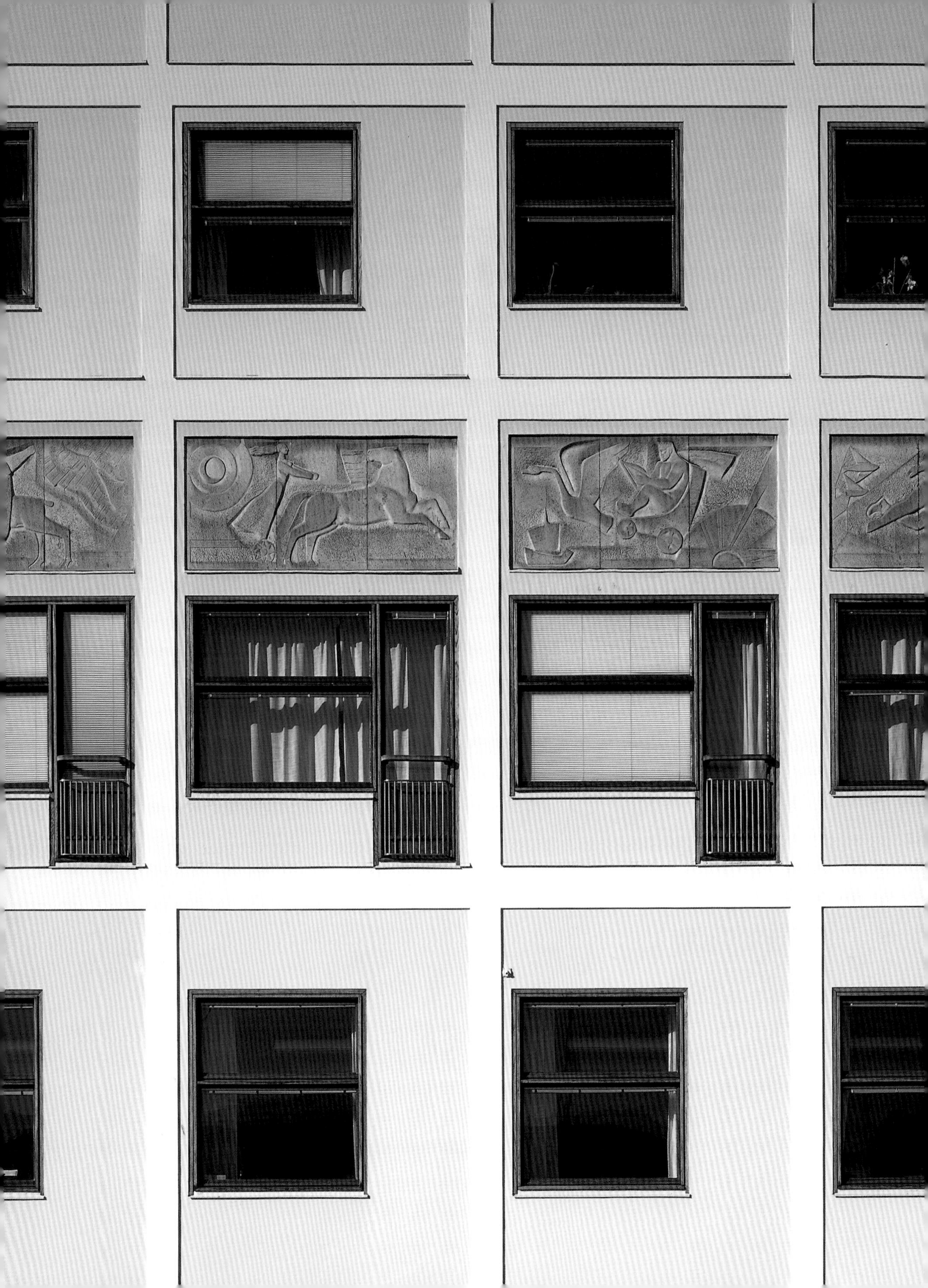

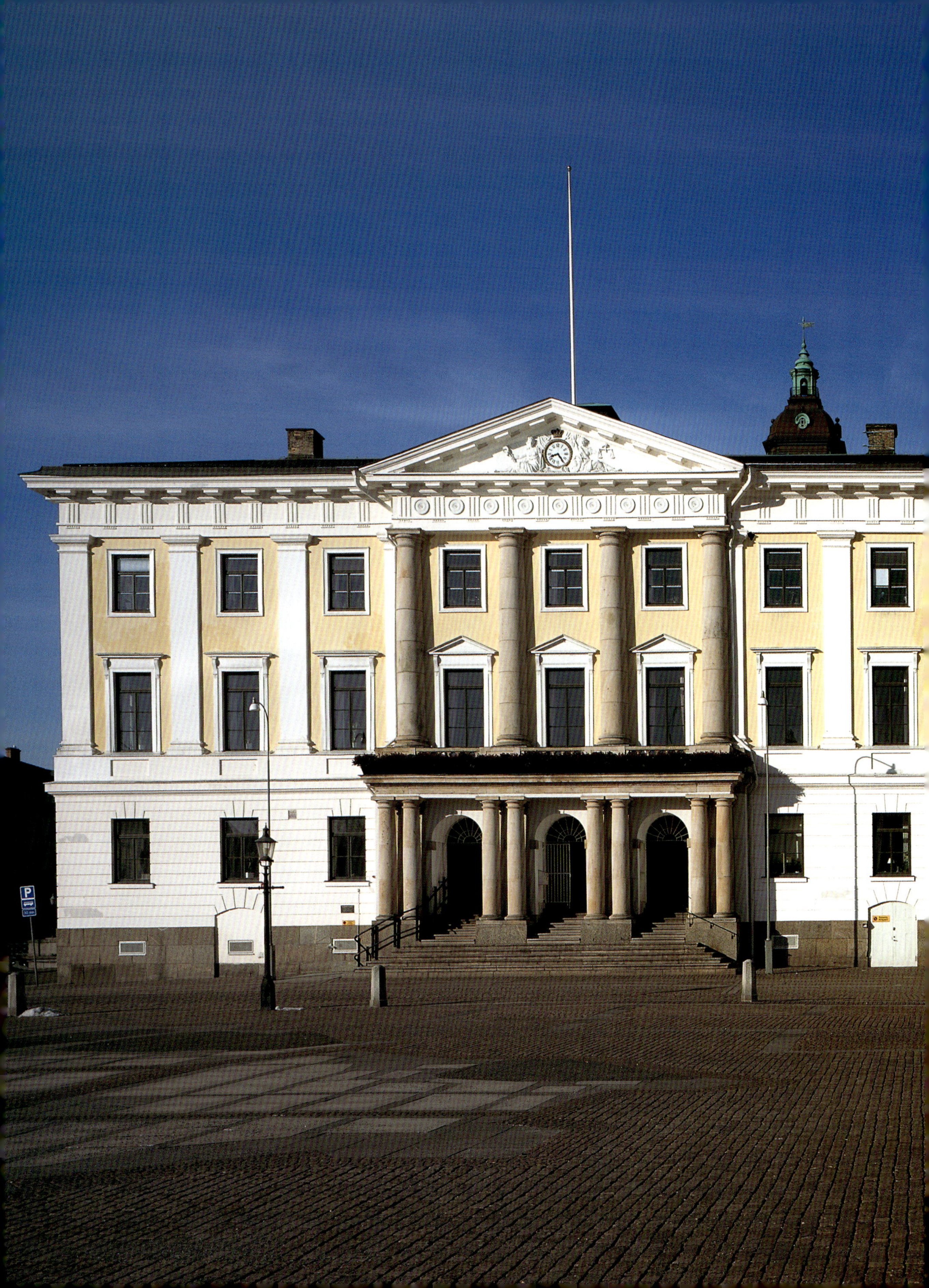

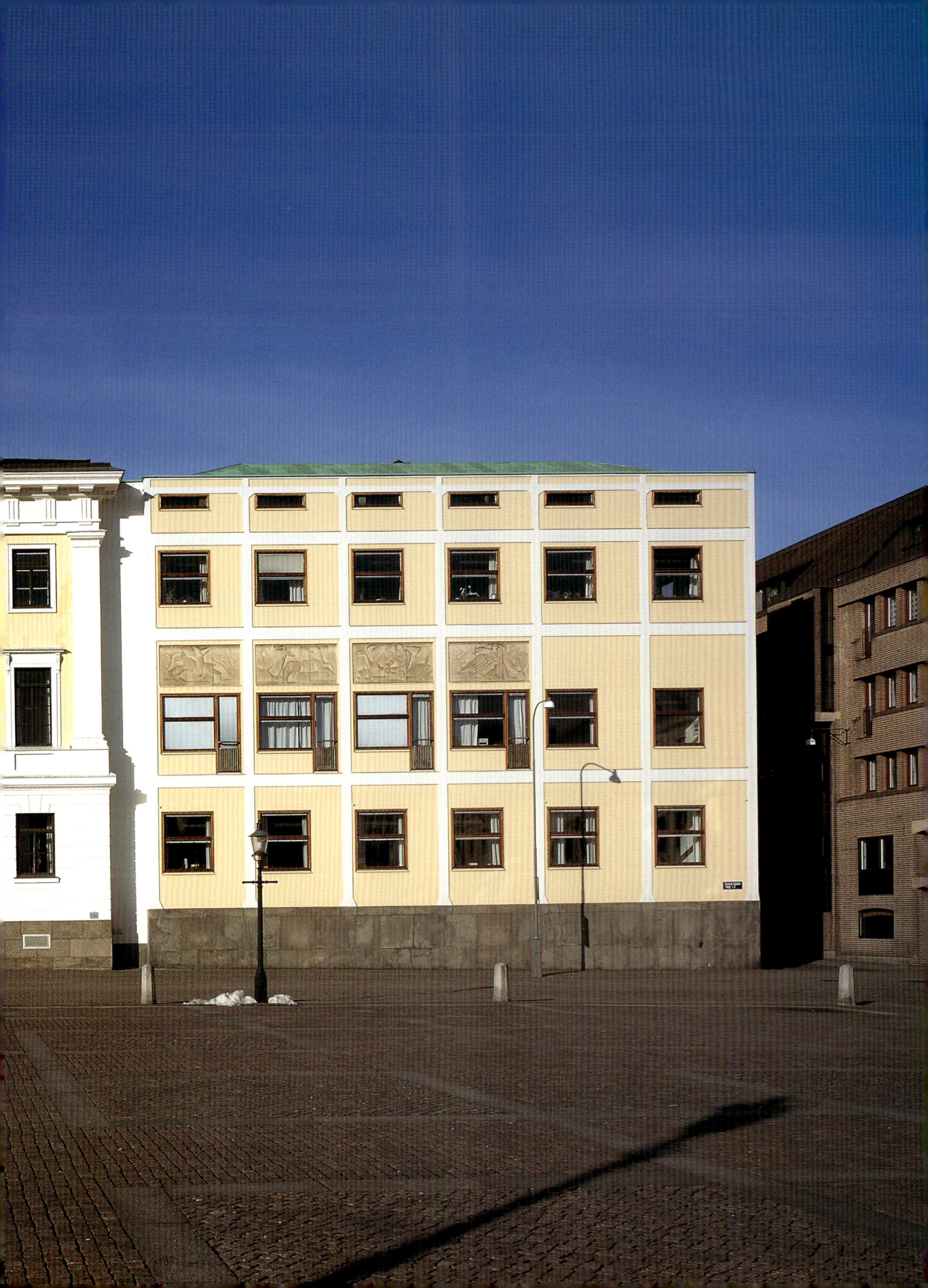

グスタフ・アドルフ広場から見た裁判所。
グスタフ・アドルフの彫像を中心に、公共
施設が取り巻く。

The court building as seen from across
Gustav Adolf Square. The statue of
King Gustav II is surrounded by public
facilities.

1925

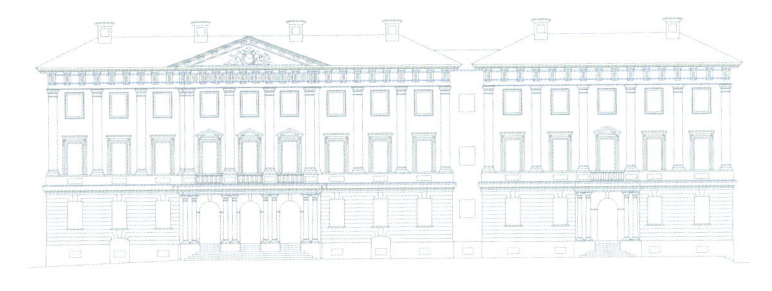

1934

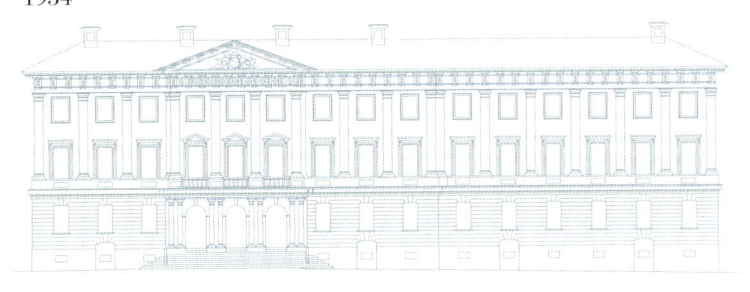

1936 (final plan)

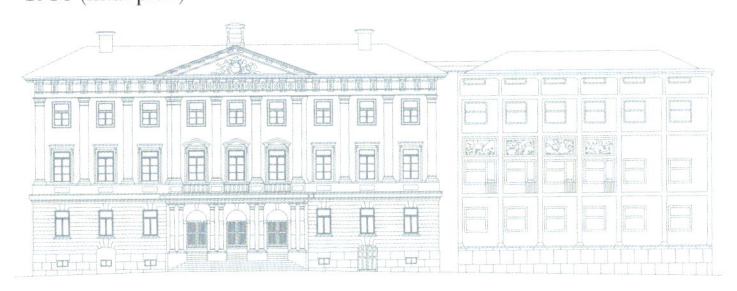

1:600

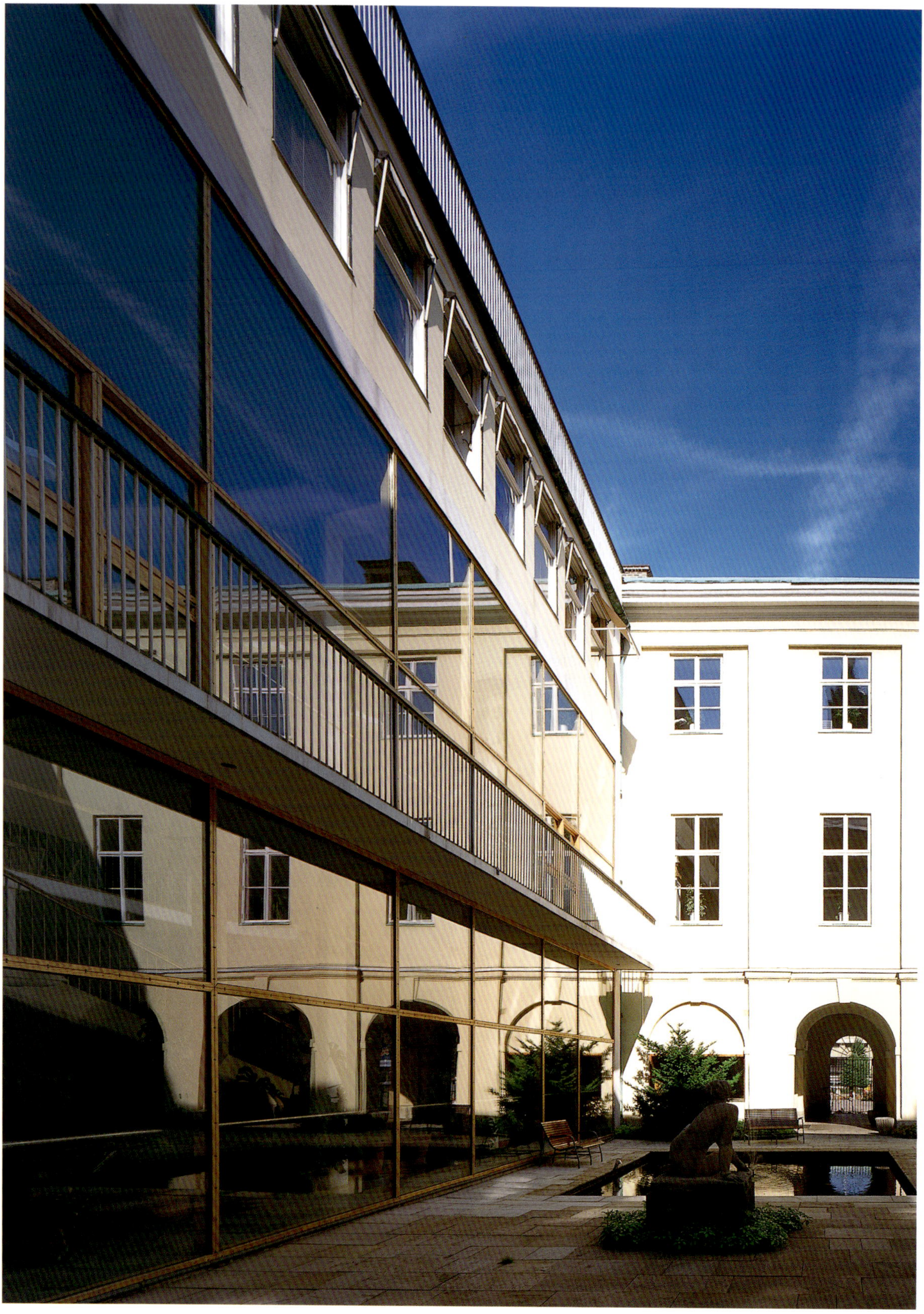

中庭に面した南側開口部。中庭の池の水面がリフレクターとして機能し、中庭に差し込んだ光を館内に導く。

The opening on the south side of the building facing the courtyard. Reflecting off the surface of the pond, sunlight floods the interior of the building.

2層分の大きな開口部により、内部は温室のようにさんさんと太陽が降り注ぐ。右側アーチの奥が増築部分の入り口。

The sun shines brightly through the large, two-layered opening, making the interior like a hothouse. To the rear of the arch on the right is the entrance to an extension.

Section

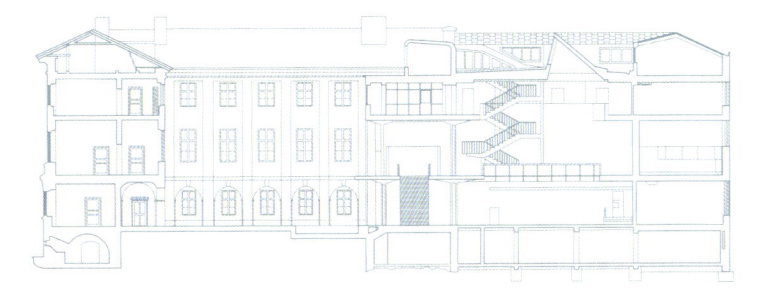

Second-floor plan

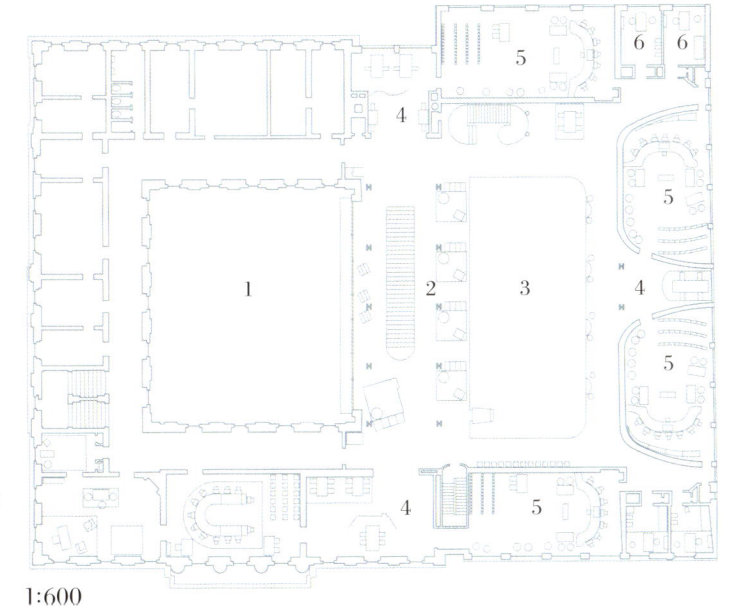

1. Courtyard
2. Waiting room
3. Hall
4. Anteroom to courtroom
5. Courtroom
6. Conference room

1:600

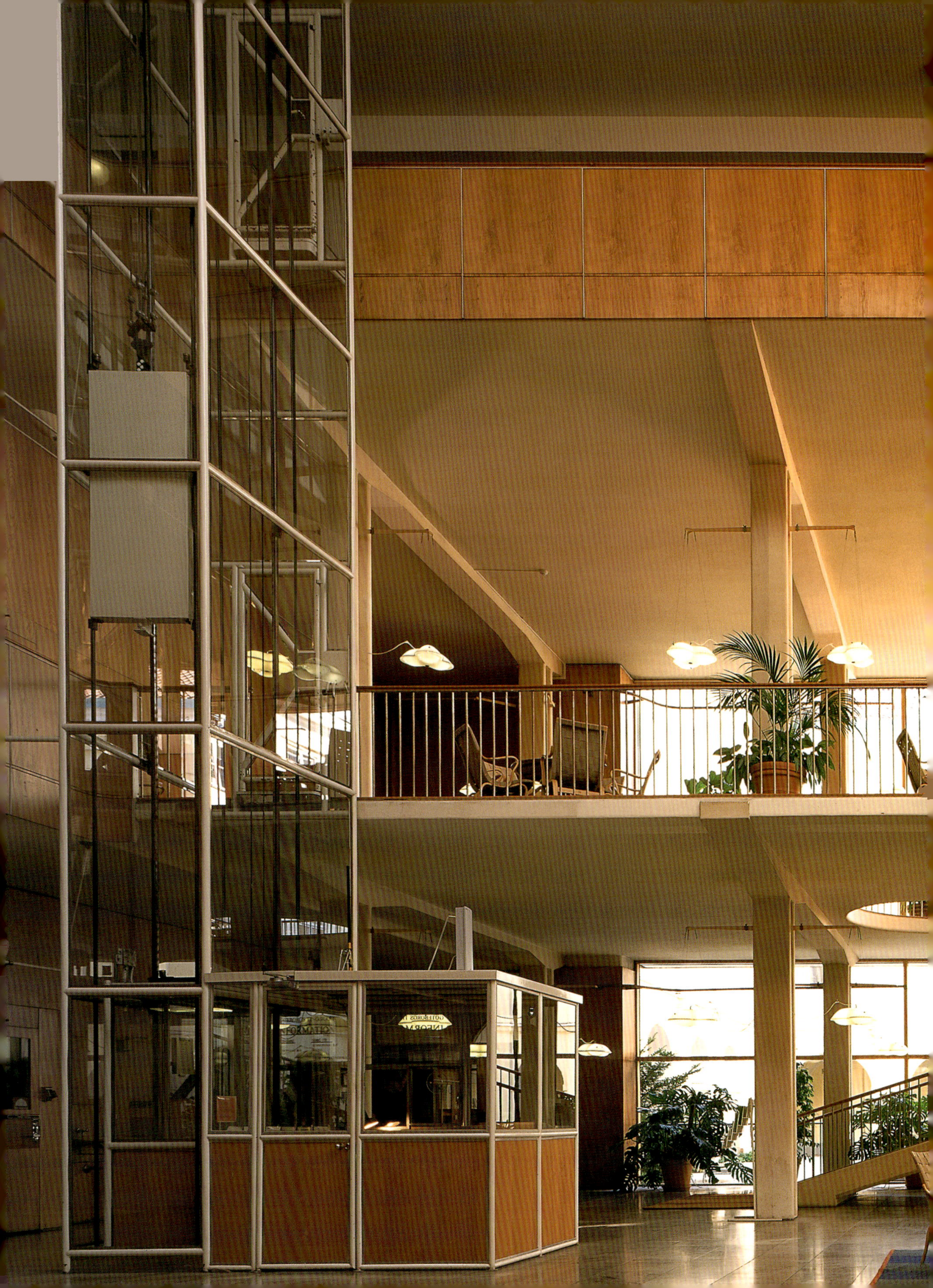

ADEL
PRÄST
Domkapitel
BORGARE
Rådhusrätt
BONDE
Häradsrätt
"ENVARS RÄTT ATT DÖMAS AV SINA LIKAR"

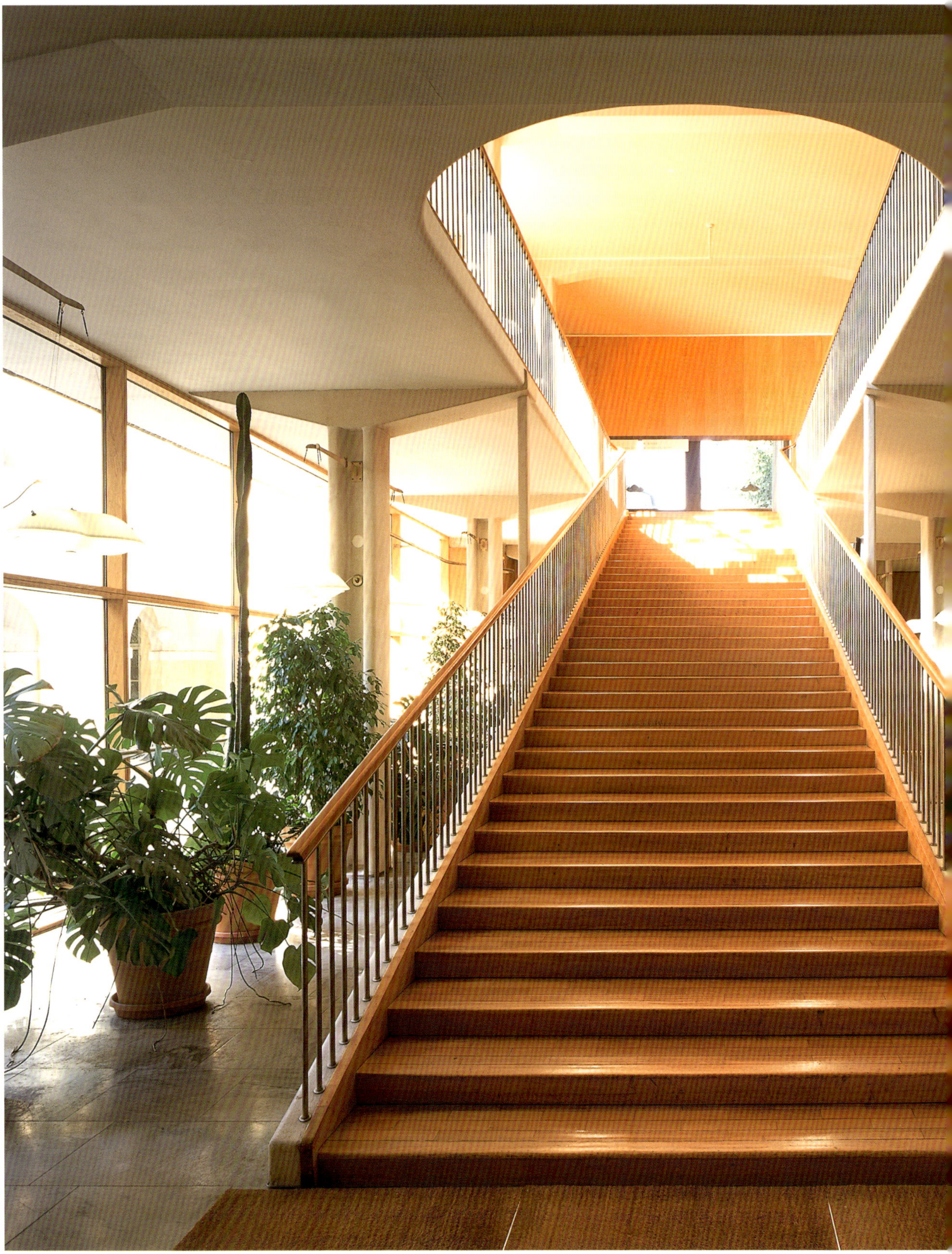

2階待合室への緩やかな直階段。アスプルンドは裁判所を訪れる人の心理状態を配慮し、階段の勾配を何度も検討したとされる。

The gently inclined, straight staircase that leads to the second-floor waiting room. Keeping in mind the mental state of courtroom visitors, Asplund apparently spent a great deal of time calculating the angle of the staircase.

2階通路からのメインホール全景。

A full view of the main hall from the
hallway on the second floor.

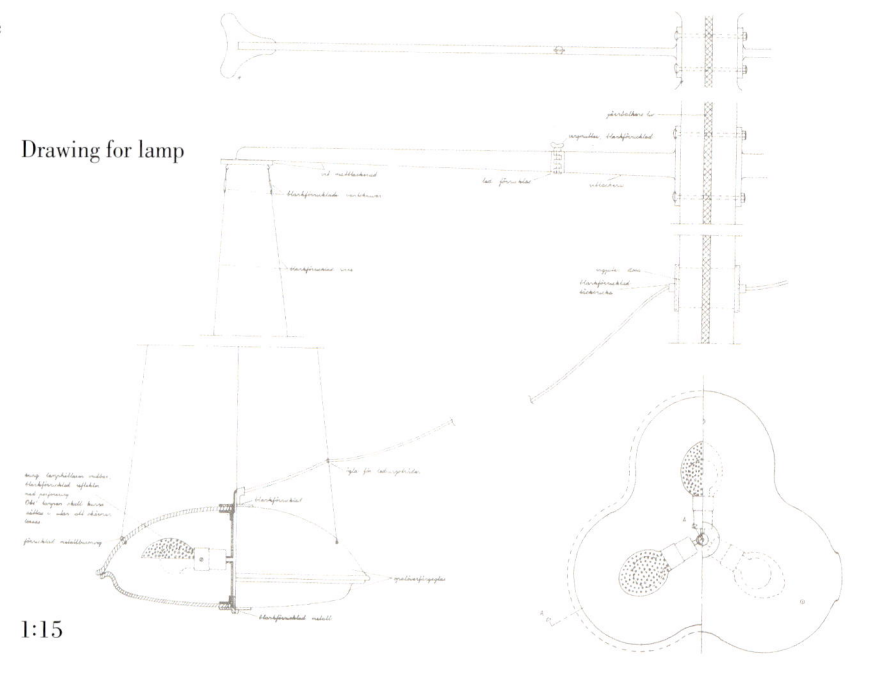

Drawing for lamp

1:15

総ガラス張りのエレベーター。丸パイプによる巧みな構成。
The all-glass elevator is ingenuously structured using round pipes.

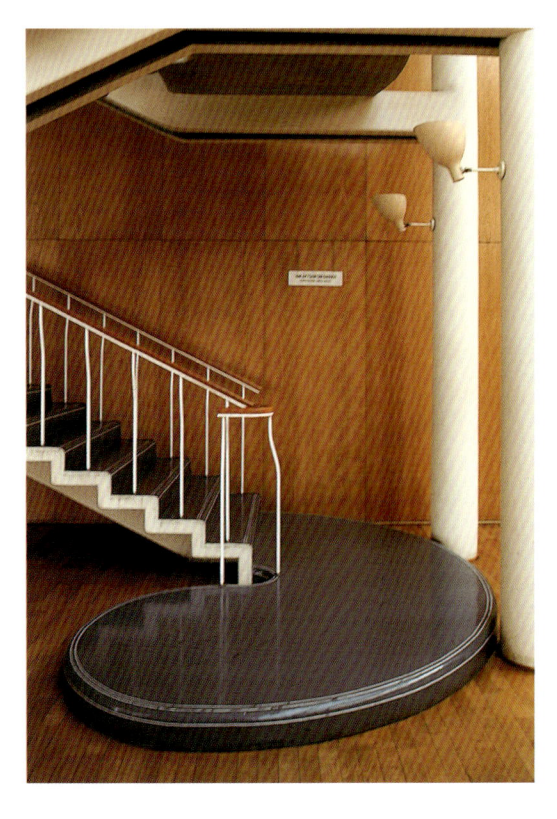

端正なプロポーションによる彫塑的な階段。すべてが曲面で仕上げられている。端部には木製文字盤の大時計。

The exquisite proportions of the sculpted staircase. The entire staircase consists of rounded surfaces. To the side of it is a large, wooden-faced clock.

215 E.G. Asplund

柱から両側に天秤棒のように突き出した
ロッドの先に有機的な形の照明器具が
下がる。

On the end of a rod that protrudes
like a shouldering pole from the
column hangs an organically-shaped
light fixture.

通路に設けられたガラス製水飲み器。

A glass drinking fountain in one of
the hallways.

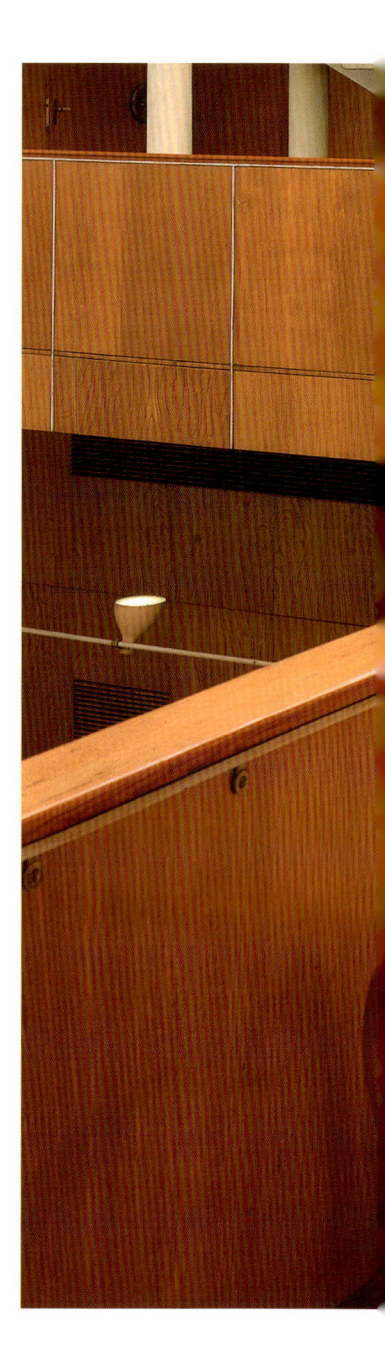

2階通路手摺を利用した待合スポット。一部切り抜かれた幕板の部分から階下の様子がうかがえる。

A waiting area that incorporates the handrail in the second-floor hallway. From the cutaway section in the paneling, the lower level is visible.

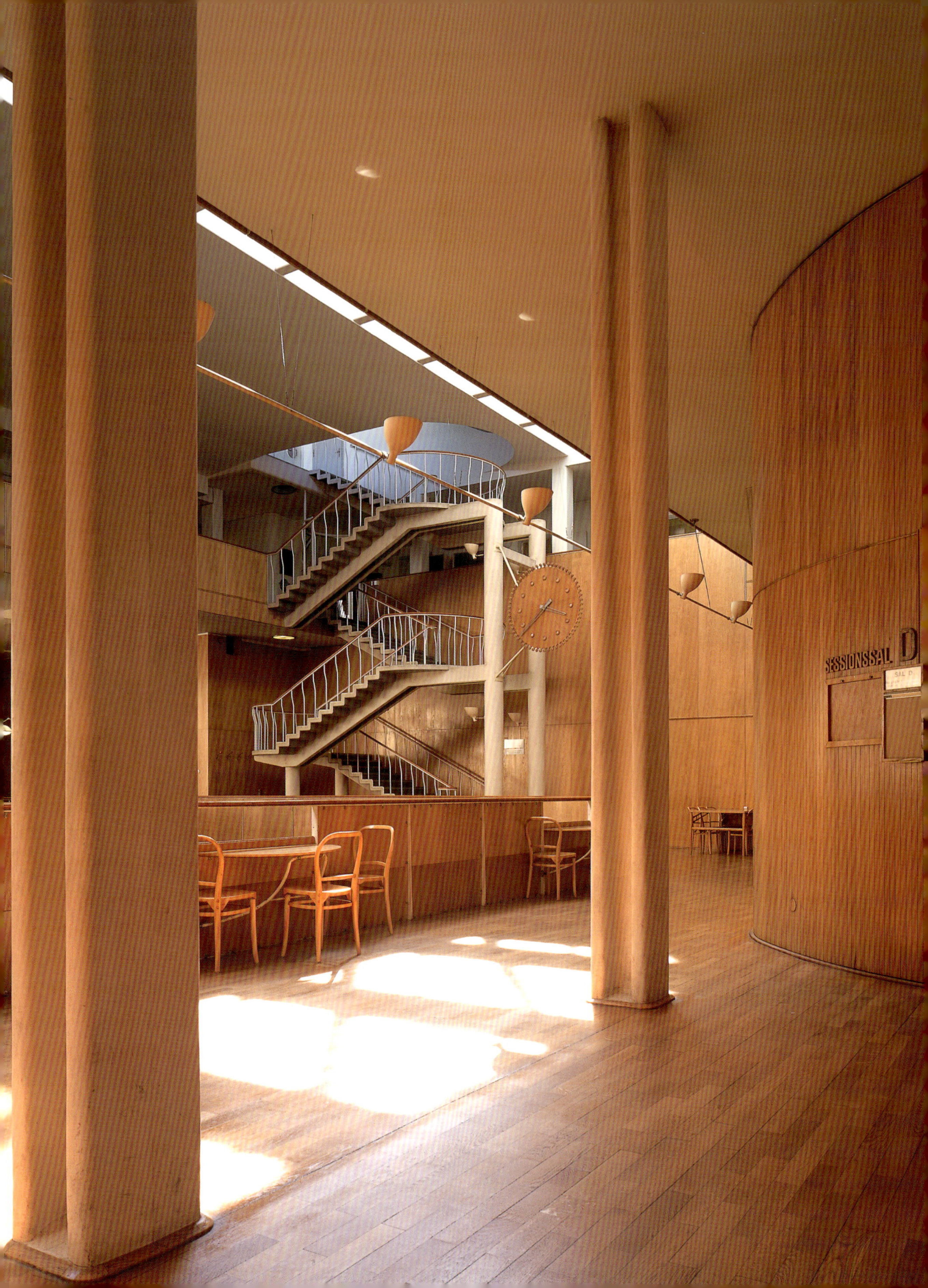
SESSIONSSAL D

曲面壁をもつ第3法廷内部。壁も家具もすべて滑らかなデザインで統一されている。

The interior of the No. 3 Courtroom, with its rounded walls. The walls and the furniture are unified with the same smooth design scheme.

第3法廷出入り口から通路を見る。手前の法廷入り口から奥の彫塑的な階段まで、曲面を多用した仕上げが空間に統一感を与えている。

A view of the hallway outside the entrance to the No. 3 Courtroom. From outside the entrance to the sculpted staircase in the rear, the versatile use of rounded surfaces adds a sense of unity to the space.

1階ホールよりアトリウムを眺める。ホールの上部には、吹抜けを横切るトップライトが配置され、北側にも採光をもたらしている。2階スラブ裏を照らすためのアッパーライトが巡る。

A view of the atrium from the first-floor hall. In the upper part of the hall, there is a top skylight that cuts across the breezeway, while on the north side, natural light streams into the space. The upper light shifts to illuminate the back of the second-floor slab.

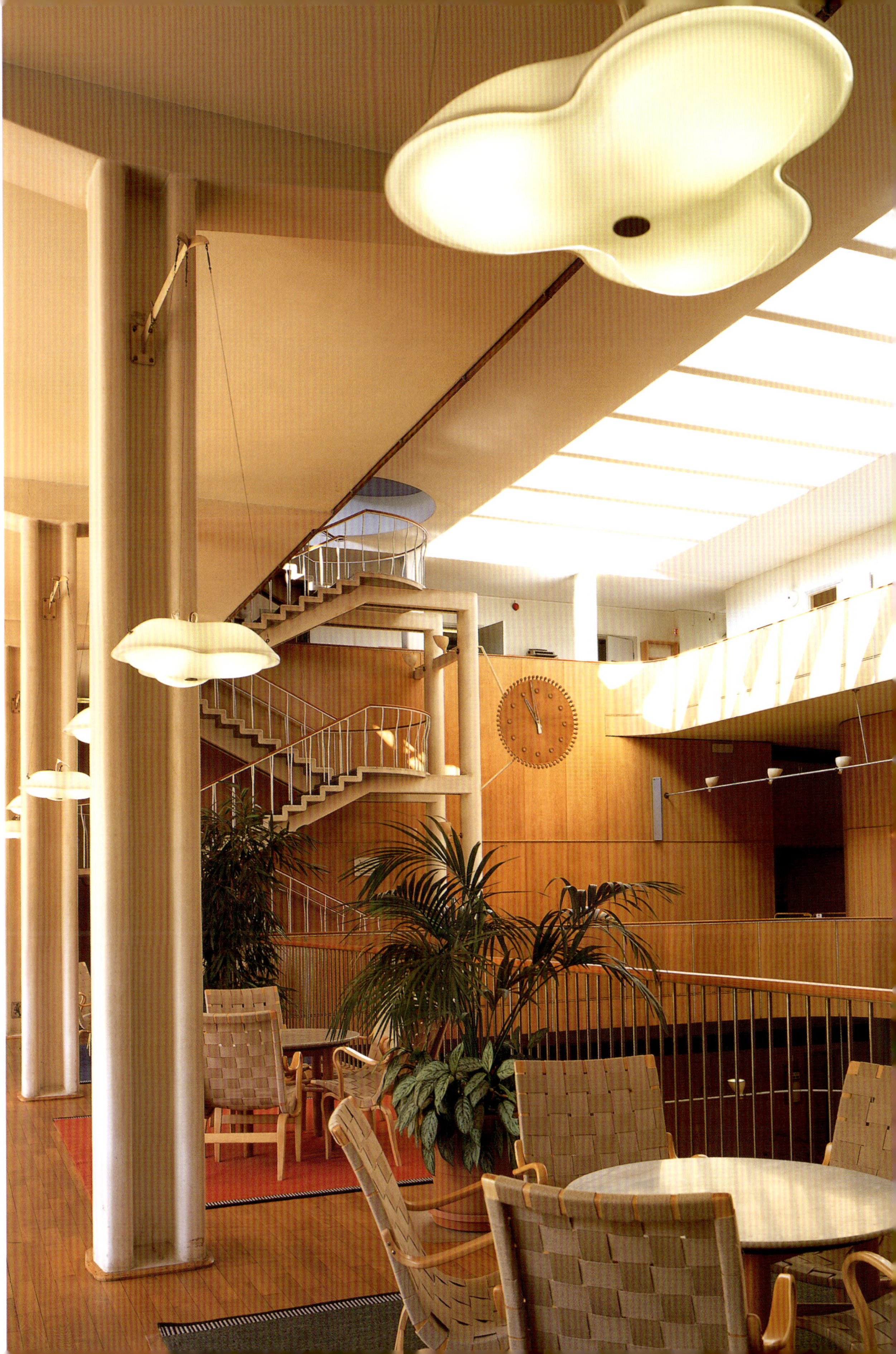

国立バクテリア研究所本館　1933–37　ソルナ
State Bacteriological Laboratory, Solna

ストックホルム郊外のソルナの広大な敷地に、10棟以上の施設が建ち並ぶ。1933年に行われた指名設計コンペで1等を獲得したアスプルンド案をもとに、配置計画に変更が加えられ、諸施設が実現に至った。適度な間隔がとられた分棟配置は、実験用バクテリアの不用意な伝染を防ぐため、コンペの段階ですでに条件になっていたことである。

守衛所のある正門から入ると、3階建ての本館が見える。館内に入ると3層吹抜けの大きなホールとなっており、正面に巨大な冷蔵庫がそびえ立つ。白を基調とした室内と、最上部のハイサイドライトから入る青白い光の作用で、アスプルンド作品にしてはやや冷たい印象を受ける。研究所の機能が要求する清潔さと、執務空間としての実用性に対し、シンプルな内装で素直に応えた結果であろう。ホールに入ると向かって右側に見える優美な弧を描くらせん階段、滴り落ちる水滴のようにも見える照明器具の温かい白熱球の明かり、プランの軸線の振れによる視角の変化、柔らかいクリーム色に塗られた吹抜け上部の天井など、アスプルンドらしい工夫によって、研究所にありがちな冷厳で退屈なイメージが払拭されている。

外観をれんが仕上げとしたから、彼が近代建築より後退したと見ることは早計であろう。緑豊かな郊外の敷地にふさわしい表現を模索しただろうし、室内の白を基調とした仕上げに対するコントラストを意図したのかもしれない。「白い箱」をつくらなければならない、という強迫観念とはアスプルンドは無縁であった。シンメトリーを崩した造形、レンガの外壁と面をそろえて納めた白い窓枠など、アスプルンド流の近代が随所に表現されている。

Over ten buildings stand on this expansive lot in Solna, in the suburbs of Stockholm. Based on Asplund's proposal, awarded first prize in a limited design competition held in 1933, a decision was made to change the site plan and build a group of structures. The need to maintain a distance between the buildings in order to protect against the inadvertent transmission of experimental bacteria was one of the original conditions specified for the competition.

After entering the front gate, the three-floor, main building comes into view. Inside the building, there is a large hall with a three-story breezeway and a huge refrigerator. Due to the effects of the white interior and the pale sunlight that seeps through the high side lights at the top of the space, the overall effect is rather cold for an Asplund work. Along with the cleanliness that is required for a laboratory and the utility of the administrative offices, the simple interior suggest compliance. As one enters the hall, on the right side, one discovers the exquisite arc of a spiral staircase. Elements such as the bright light given off by the hot, white globe-shaped fixtures, the change in perspective created by the off-kilter axis line, and the soft cream-colored ceiling in the upper part of the breezeway, are all characteristic Asplund devices. Together they work to dispel the idea that laboratories are grim and dreary.

From the exterior alone, it would be wrong to conclude that Asplund had regressed beyond modern architecture. He was searching instead for an expression that would fit this lush, suburban lot, and chose white to set the tone of the interior and create a contrast. The notion that an architect must create a "white box" was totally alien to Asplund. With a design that undermines symmetry, and aspects like the white window frames to match the brick of the exterior wall and facade, Asplund's modernism is in evidence everywhere.

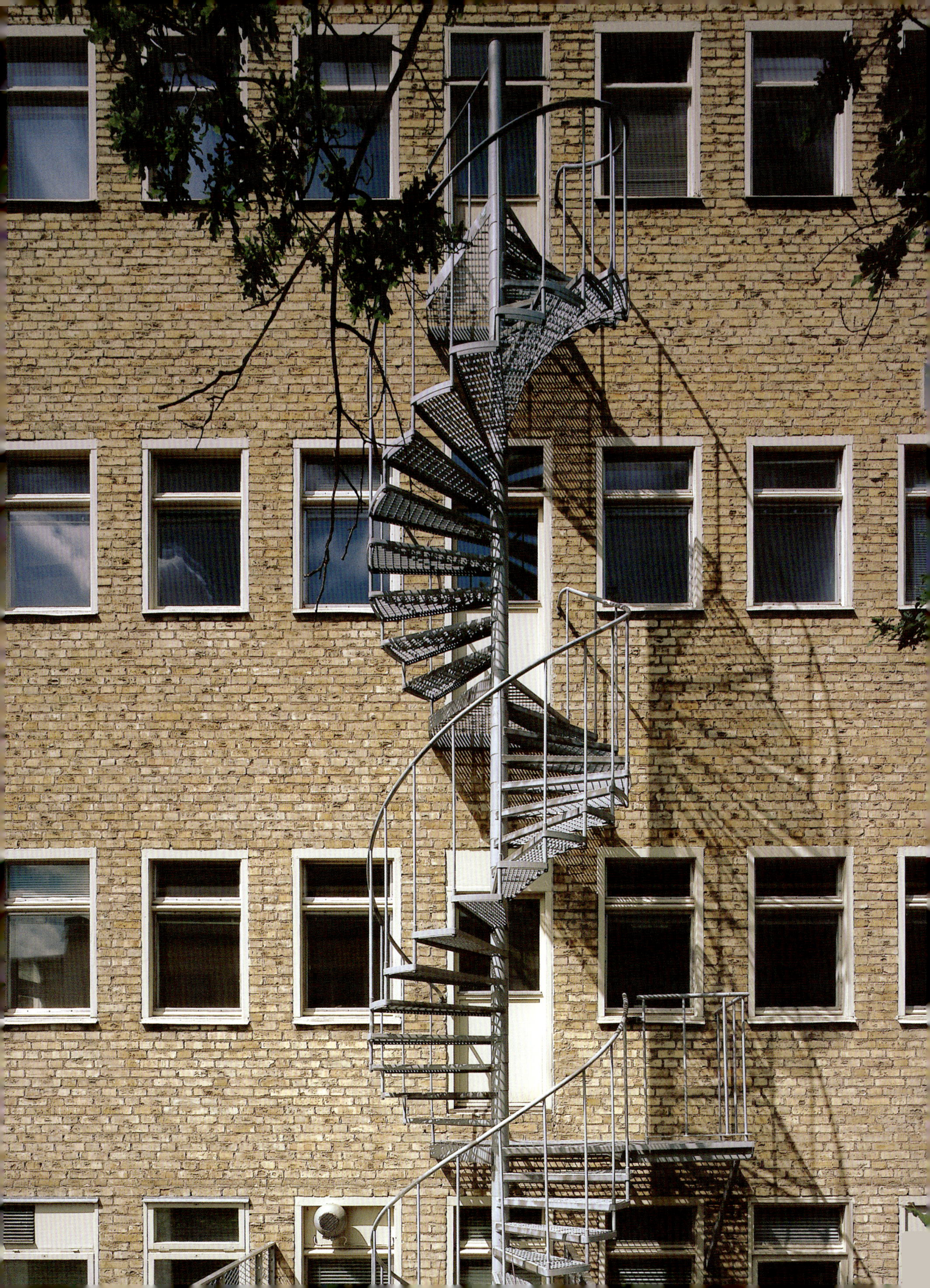

西側アプローチからの全景。左につながる管理事務棟は少し斜めに振って接続され、軸線は南側外壁線と直行してアトリウムの形状を規定する。右は図書室。

A panoramic view of the west approach. The administrative wing is connected to the main building on the left at a slight slant. The axis line regulates the form of the atrium by connecting directly to the exterior wall line on the south side. The library is on the right.

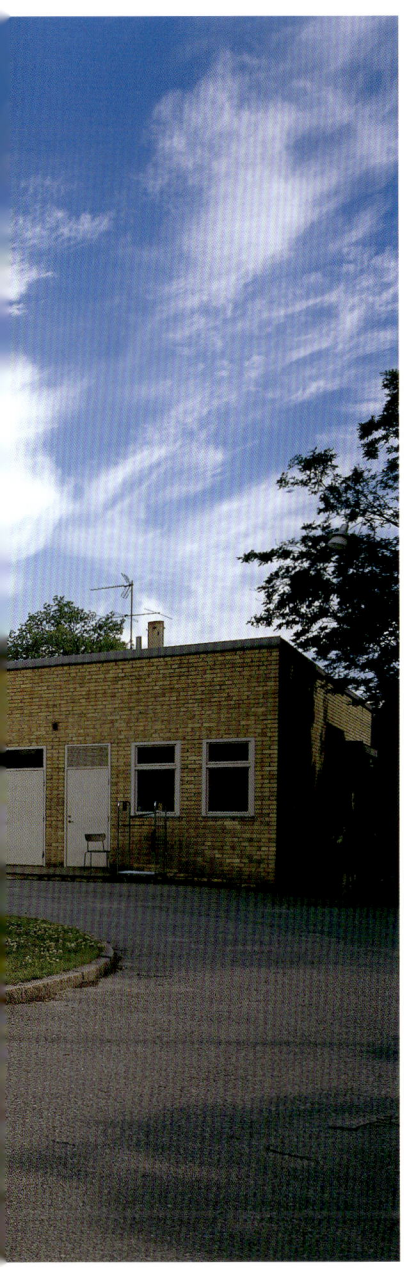

南側外観。左手前低層部は後の増築。

An external view of the south side of the building. The lower tier on the left is a later extension made to the building.

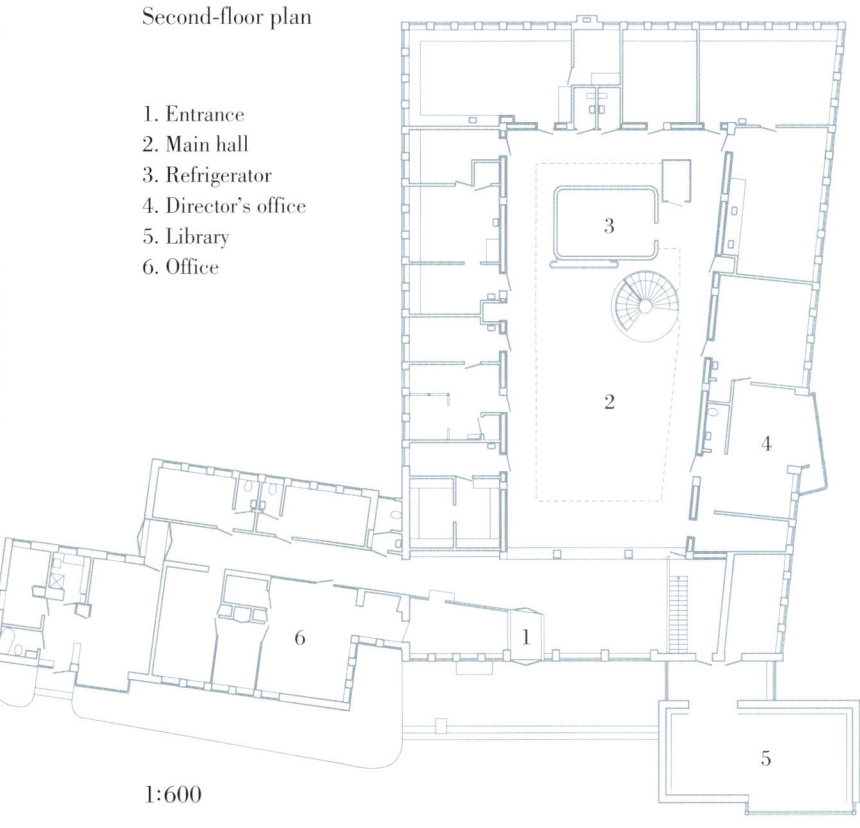

Second-floor plan

1. Entrance
2. Main hall
3. Refrigerator
4. Director's office
5. Library
6. Office

1:600

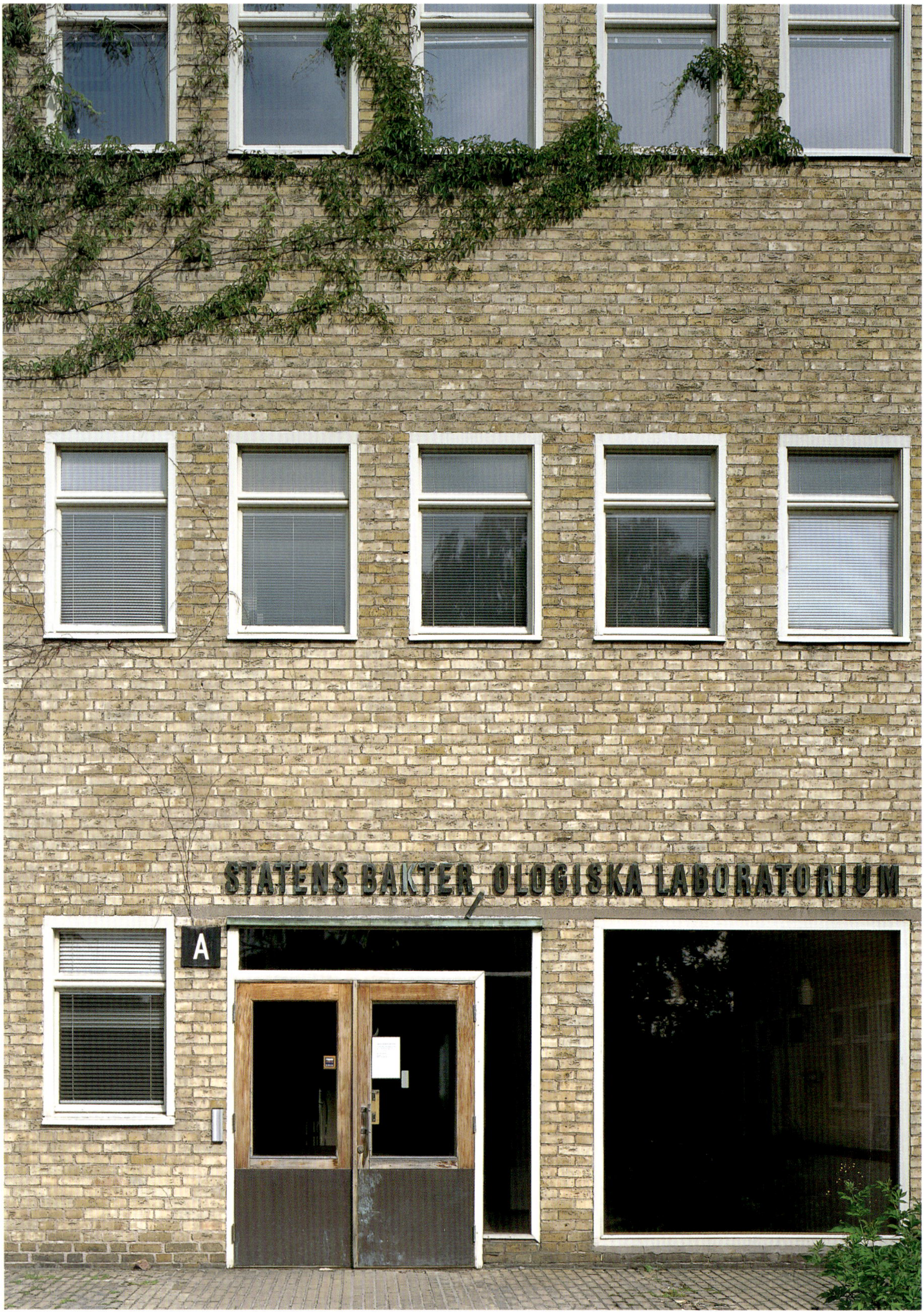
STATENS BAKTERIOLOGISKA LABORATORIUM
A

端正なプロポーションの開口部とエントランス周り。木製の窓枠はれんがの外壁と面が揃うように納められている。

The proportions of the building's entrance and external openings are very precisely designed, and the wooden window frames are flush with the surface of the exterior brick wall.

所長室から見たバルコニー付き出窓。

The view from the director's office, with a balcony attached to the bay window.

絶妙な割付で並ぶポツ窓のリズムを破るかのように、斜めに突出した2階所長室の出窓。

The bay window of the second-floor director's office protrudes at an angle, breaking the rhythm of the perfectly spaced rows of windows.

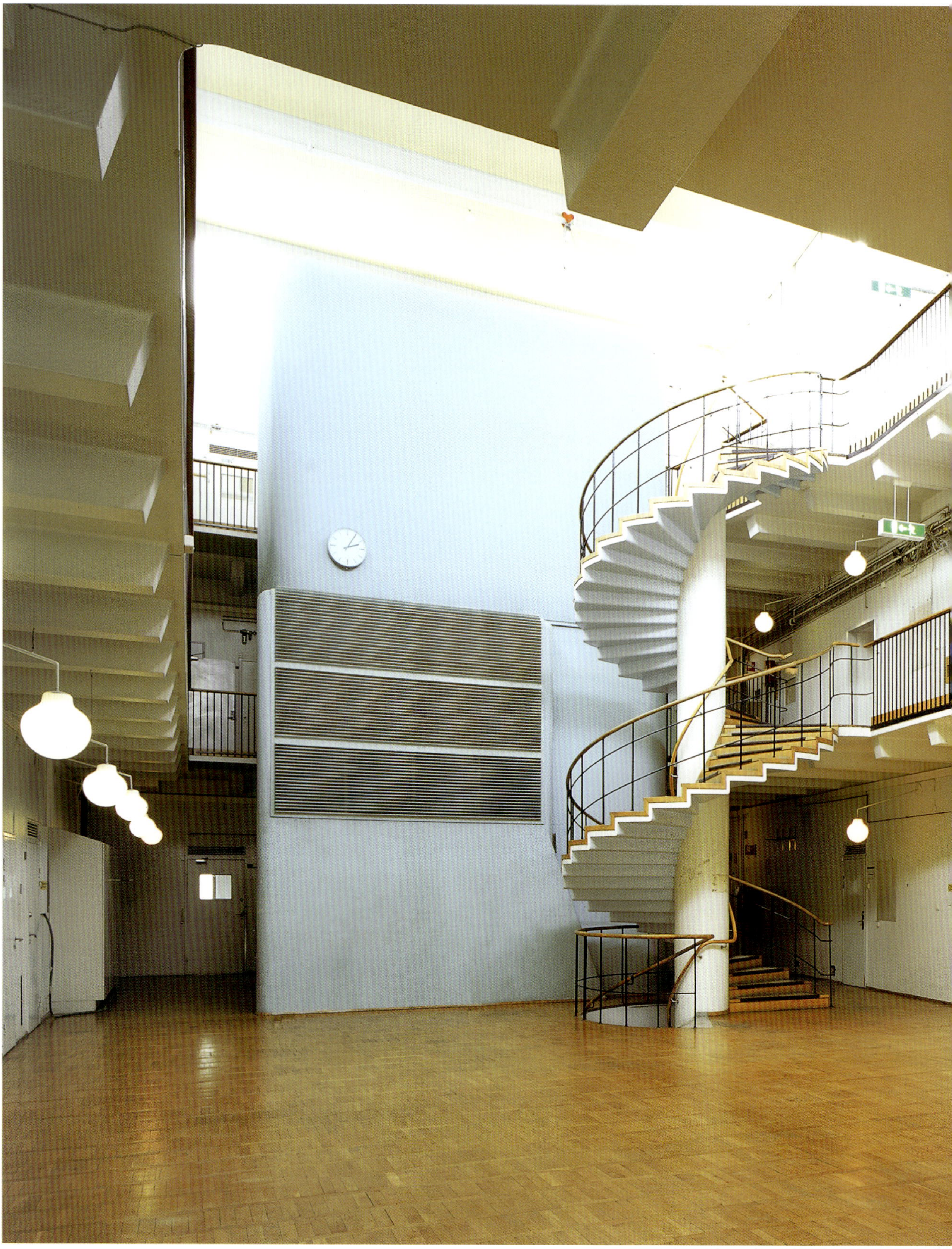

2階大ホール入り口側からのアトリウム全景。左右の壁がわずかに振れたアトリウム空間の不思議な遠近感。水色の巨大冷蔵室と繊細な螺旋階段の対比によって空間を引き締めている。

A full view of the atrium from the entrance on the second-floor of the large hall. The slight fluctuations in the left and right walls add an odd perspective to the space. The huge, light-blue refrigerator and the delicate spiral staircase play off each perfectly.

螺旋階段を上るとハイサイドライトが巡る4階に出る。奥の小さな螺旋階段は屋上への昇降用。

The spiral staircase leads to the forth floor, a space that is surrounded by high sidelights. The small spiral staircase in the rear leads to the roof.

壁から斜めにもち出されたロッドの先端に下がるガラスのボウルは、まるで注射針の先から落ちようとする薬液のしずくのようだ。

The glass bowls, which hang from the end of rods extending at an angle from the wall, resemble a drop of medicine about to fall from the end of a syringe.

屋上に通じる小螺旋階段。小規模ながら機能的で美しい。

The small spiral staircase leading to the roof. Though small in scale, the structure is functional and attractive.

垂直動線である螺旋階段は緩やかな勾配となっており、段裏は曲面処理されている。さわやかな水色は、天井の黄色とも相まって医療施設らしい清潔な印象を与えている。

The spiral staircase, the atrium's vertical flow line, inclines gently and the reverse side of the stair treads are curved. In combination with the yellow of the ceiling, the refreshing light-blue color creates an image of cleanliness that befits a medical facility.

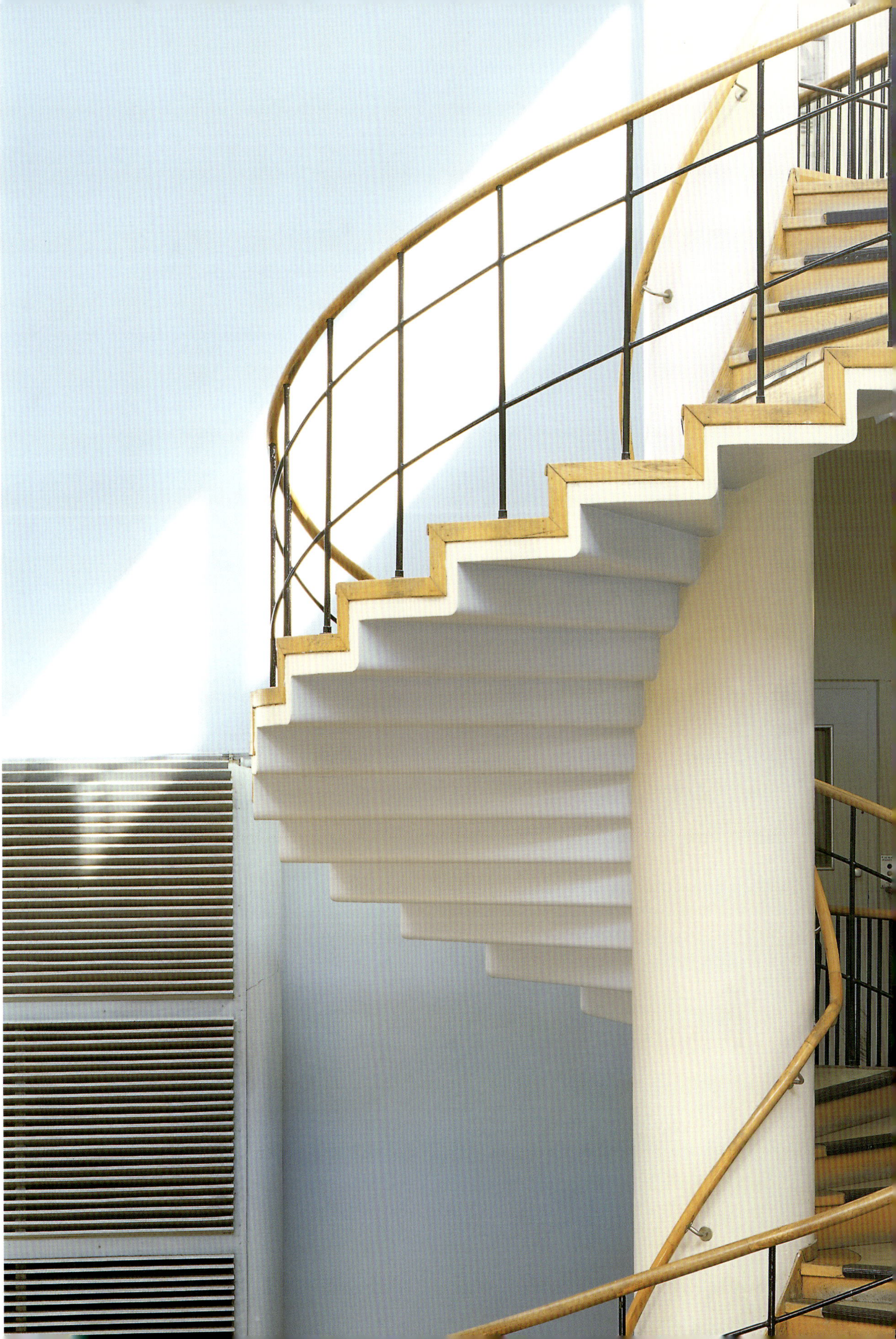

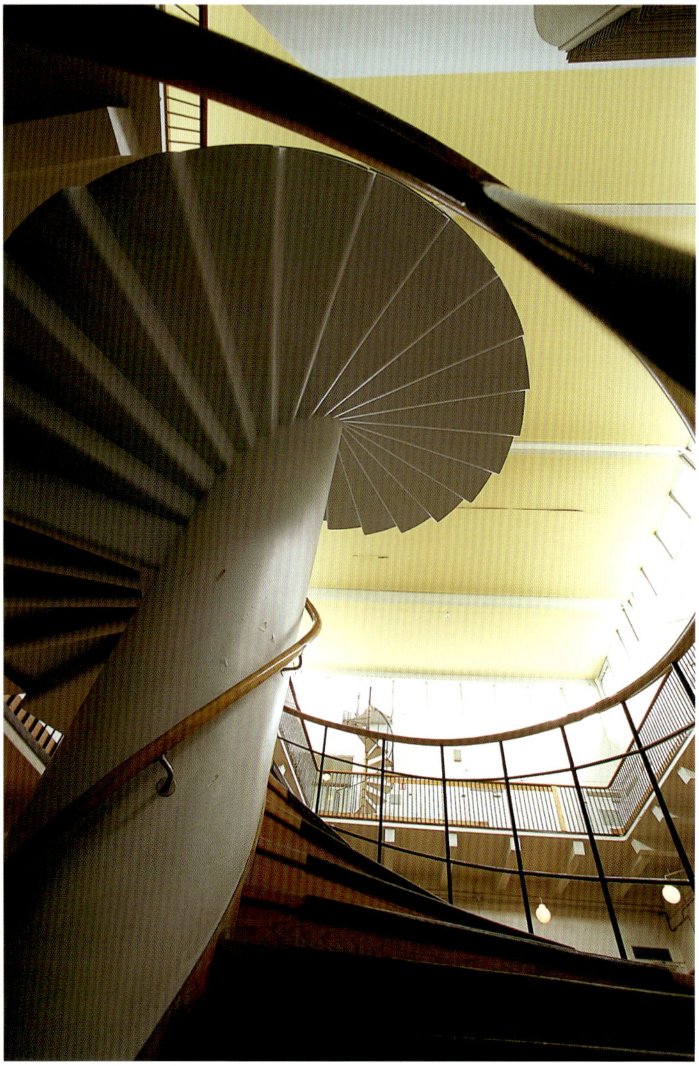

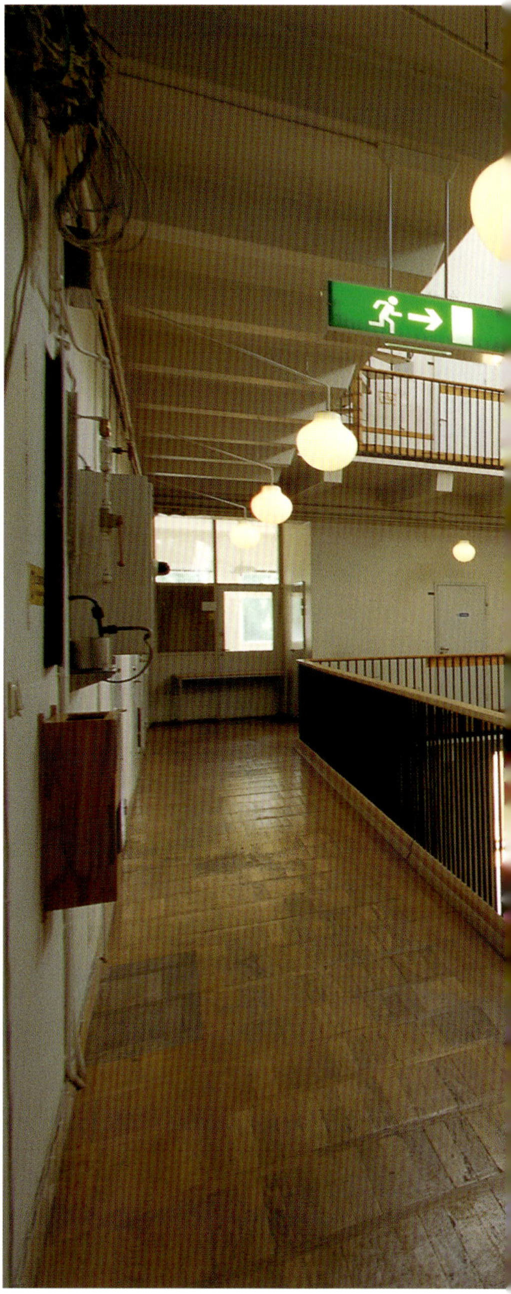

3階アトリウム回廊と螺旋階段。回廊のスラブ裏が螺旋階段の段裏へとスムーズにつながり流れていく。

The third-floor hallway and spiral staircase. The back of the slab flows smoothly into the bottom of the staircase.

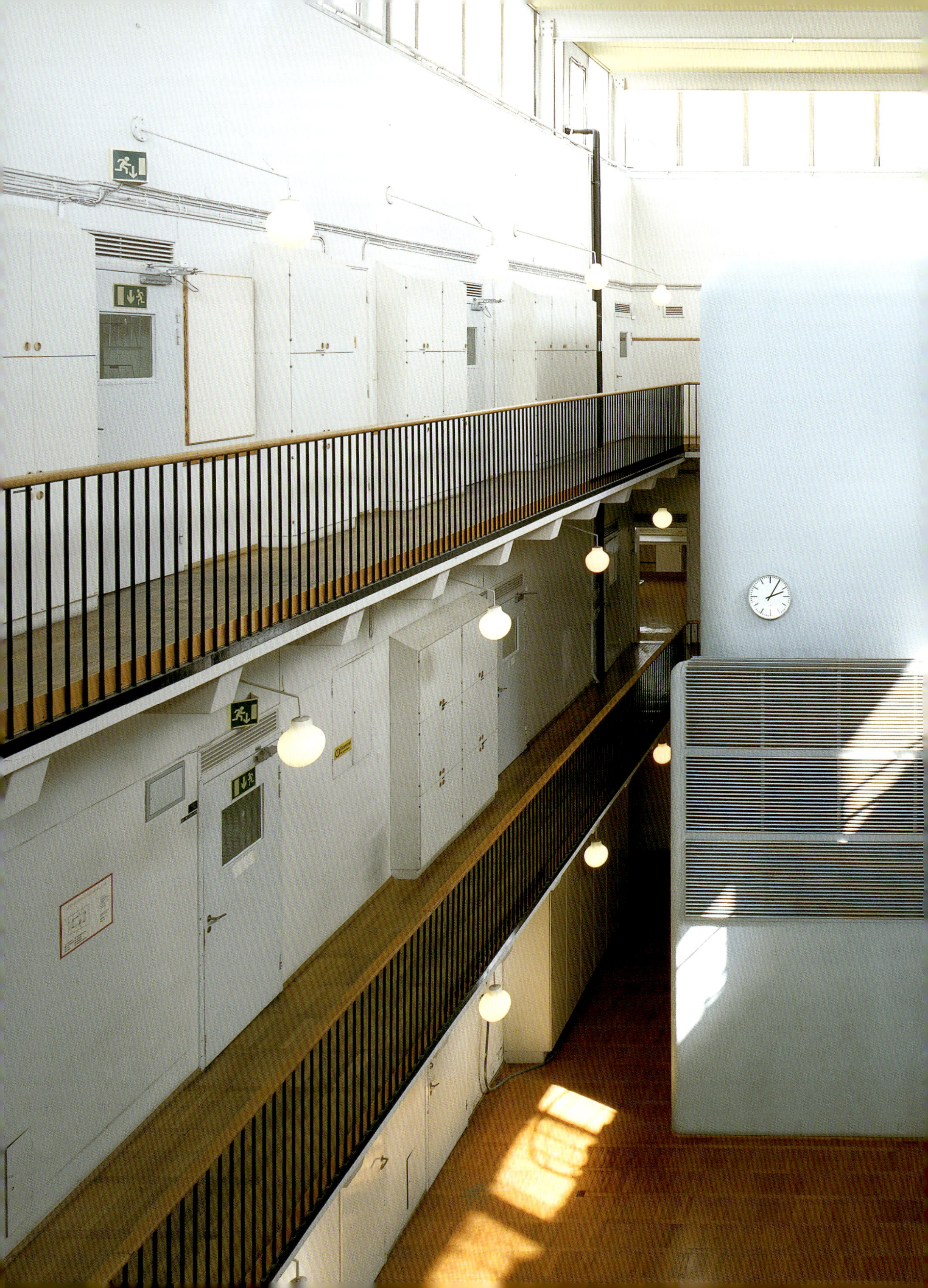

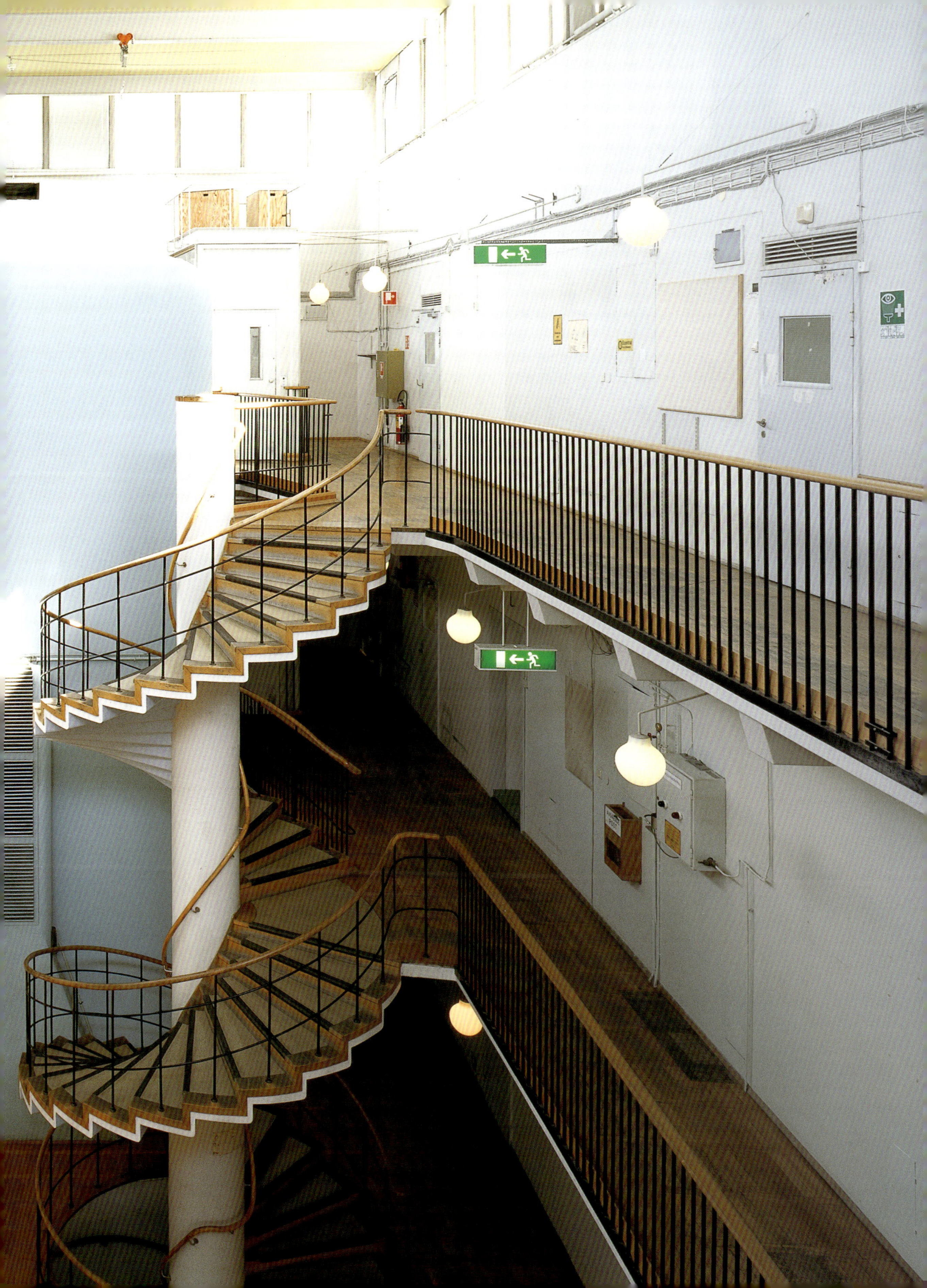

夏の家　1936-37　ステンネース
E. G. Asplund's Summer House, Stennäs

　ストックホルム郊外の沿岸地帯に建つ、アスプルンド自身の別荘である。敷地は背後の岩盤から、海岸に向かって下る傾斜地である。庭先まで近づくと一気に視界が開け、雑木林の影に隠れていた海が見える。休日を過ごす別世界に人を引き込む、劇的なアプローチの演出である。

　初期の計画案では農家を題材とし、3つの棟を接続する伝統的な形式だった。最終的にはふたつの棟を接続する形に納め、3カ所に設けた内部の階段で接続している。敷地の高低差を生かした空間構成は絶妙で、平屋建てではあるが視線や人の動きが高さ方向に展開する。それが外部に通じる5カ所のドアと結びつき、休日の楽しい活動が生まれるのだ。傾斜した敷地の最も高い位置にある厨房から最も低い居間まで、視線が一直線に廊下を通り抜ける。居間棟が軸を振って接続されるのは、入り江の陸の切れ目に臨める水平線に、視線を合わせるためである。

　主棟と居間棟のずれによって、さりげなく玄関が設けられ、このずれにより食堂からも海が見わたせる。天井高は低く抑えられ、小幅板の壁と天井があえて荒く仕上げられる。農家のかまどをデフォルメした居間の暖炉やラフな身振りの煙突など、随所で農家のたたずまいが演出される。とはいえ、内部も外部もともに白く塗装され、表現されているのは、あくまでもアスプルンド流の近代なのだ。

　伝統的な赤い民家を思わせる別棟、トイレ小屋、ボート小屋、道具小屋、ガレージなどの付属建物もすべてアスプルンドの設計である。

Built along the shore in the suburbs of Stockholm, this was Asplund's own summer house. The lot, a sloping piece of land, leads from a rock bed down to the sea. As one approaches the end of the garden, all at once one's field of vision opens and the ocean, hidden in the shadow of a growth of trees, comes into view. This dramatic touch has the power to transport vacationers to another world.

　In the initial plan, the house had a traditional form with three connecting wings based on a farmhouse design. Ultimately, the house came to consist of two connecting buildings linked by three interior stairways. The spatial structure, which makes use of the elevation difference on the lot, is splendid and though the house is single-storied, one's gaze and people's movements expand heightwise. The buildings are connected to the outside by five doors, allowing visitors to easily enjoy holiday activities. From the highest point on the lot, the kitchen, to the lowest, the living room, one's gaze passes straight through the corridor. The living-room wing is connected off the axis line to allow a view of the horizon - the break between the land and the bay.

　The off-center connection between the main building and the living-room wing allowed for the creation of a casual entranceway and afford a view of the ocean from the dining room. The ceiling, which has been kept rather low, and the narrow paneled walls have a rough finish. Elements such as the living room fireplace (an altered farmhouse furnace) and the rough chimney give the entire work an agrarian air. Yet, what is being expressed in the white-painted interior and exterior of the house is nothing less than Asplund's own brand of modernism.

　The traditional-style red annex and the other structures on the lot were all designed by Asplund.

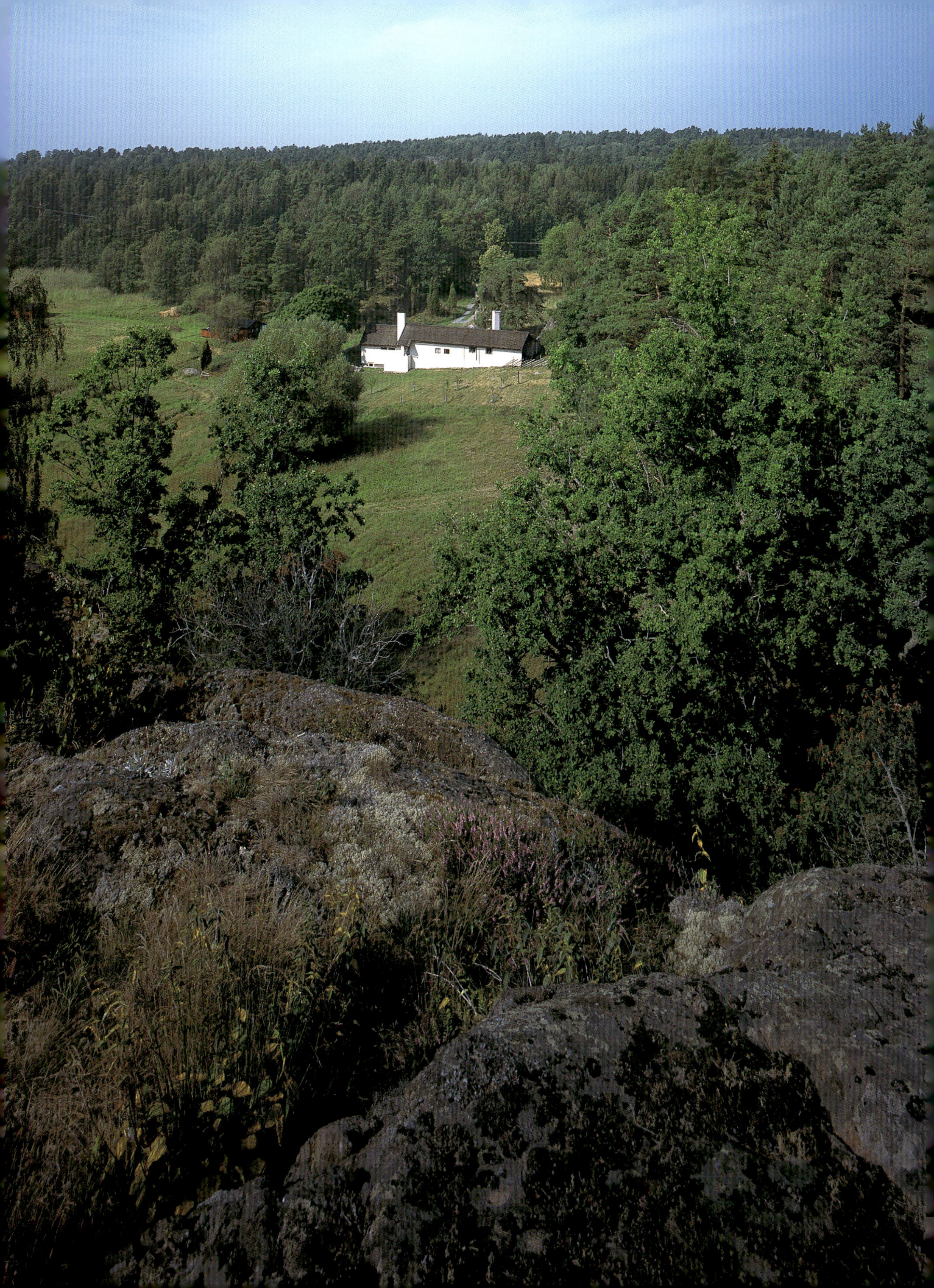

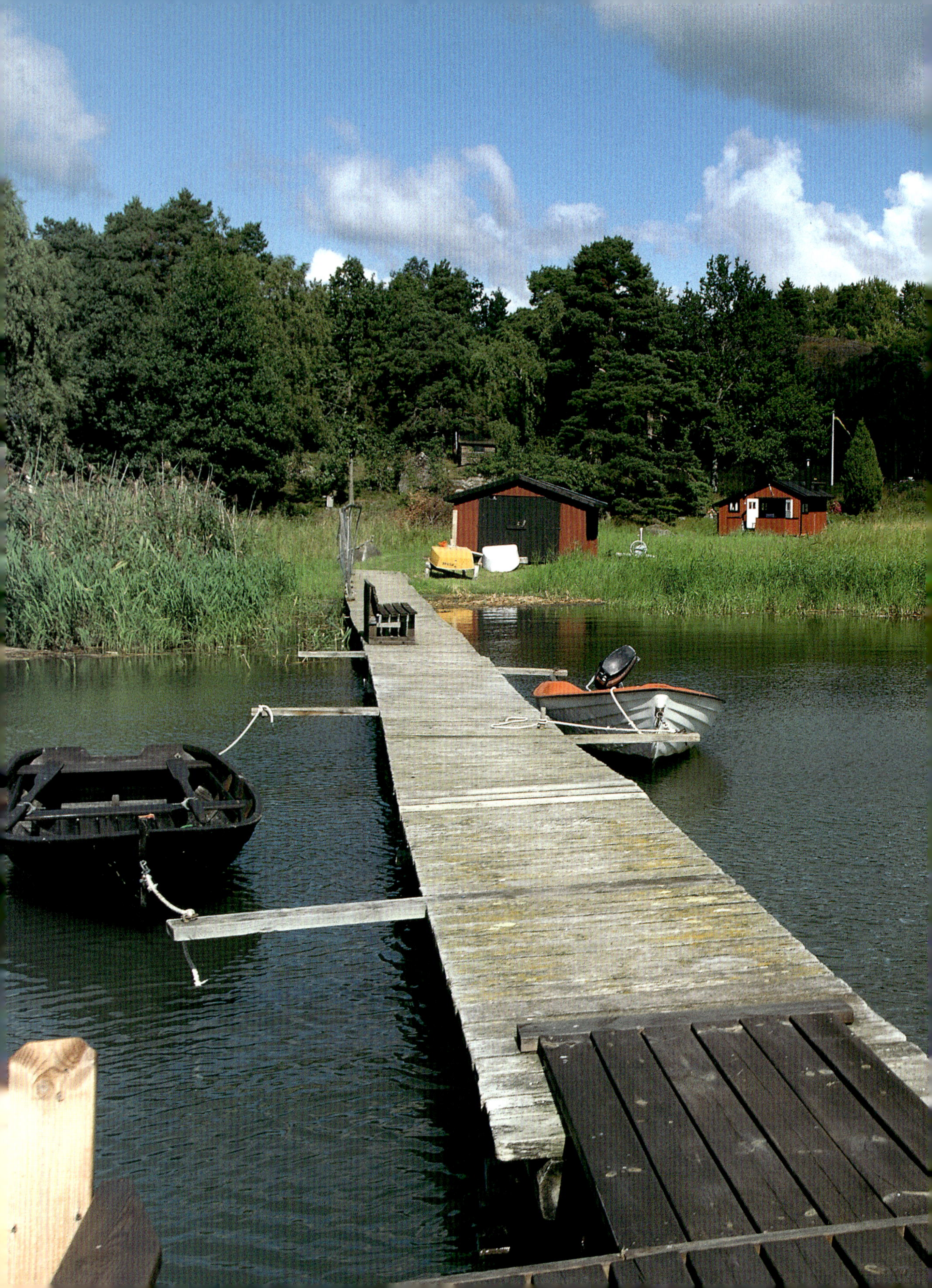

桟橋より見る。手前からボート小屋、別棟、夏の家、道具小屋。

The house seen from a landing pier. Beyond the pier, a boathouse, another wing of the house, a summer house and a toolshed are visible.

背後に迫る岩山からの眺望。
The scenery from a hill that looms above the summer house.

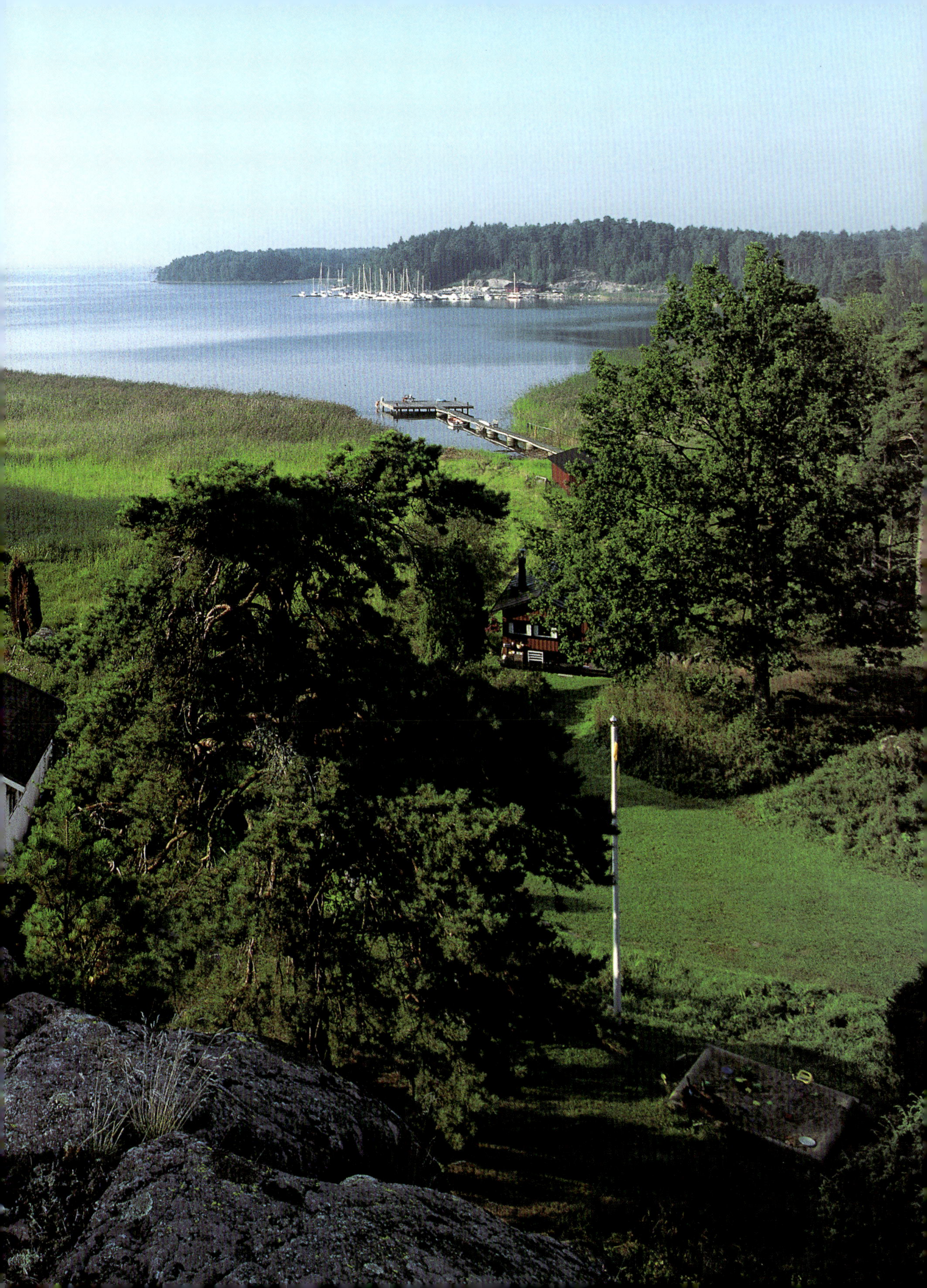

夏の家へのアプローチ。
The approach to the summer house.

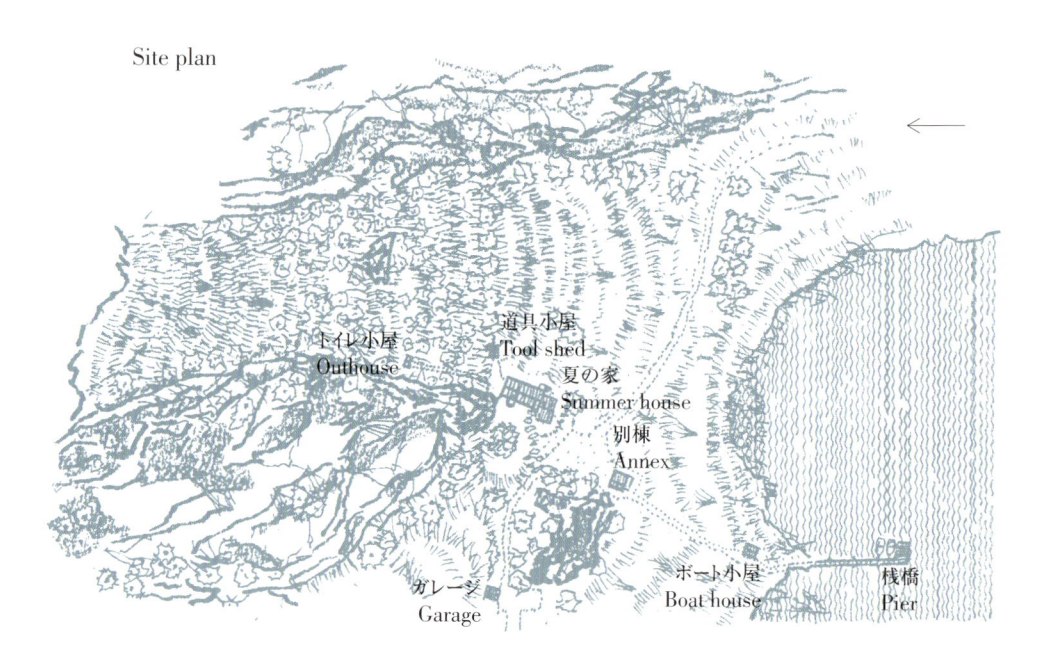

Site plan

トイレ小屋
Outhouse

道具小屋
Tool shed

夏の家
Summer house

別棟
Annex

ガレージ
Garage

ボート小屋
Boat house

桟橋
Pier

敷地西側の林からの遠望。大きな松のある前庭は戸外のダイニングスペースとなる。

A broad view from a woods on the west side of the lot. The front yard, with its large pines, can be used as an open-air dining space.

真夏の西側夕景。手前地面の石畳は、当時工事が進められていた森の火葬場の石工たちが、記念に運んだもの。その配置は、日本庭園の飛び石の影響を感じさせる。テラスの四角い窓の位置から、床レベルがリビングに向かって少しずつ下がっていることがわかる。

The west side of the house at dusk in midsummer. The paving stones in the foreground were brought to the house as a memento by the stonemasons who were working at the time on Woodland Crematorium. The way they are positioned recalls the steppingstones in a Japanese garden. From the position of the square windows in the terrace area, it is clear that the floor level of the house gradually descends as one approaches the living room.

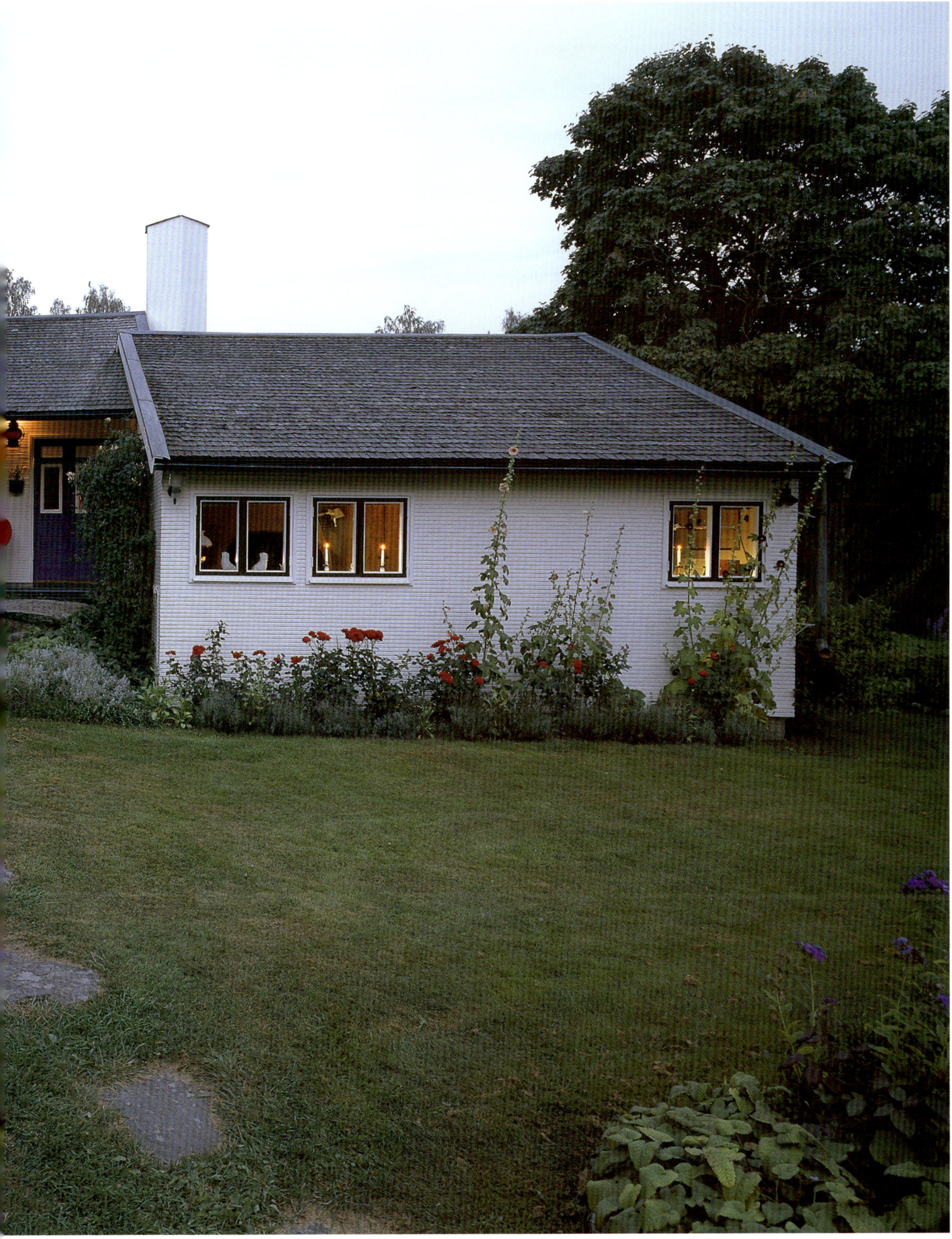

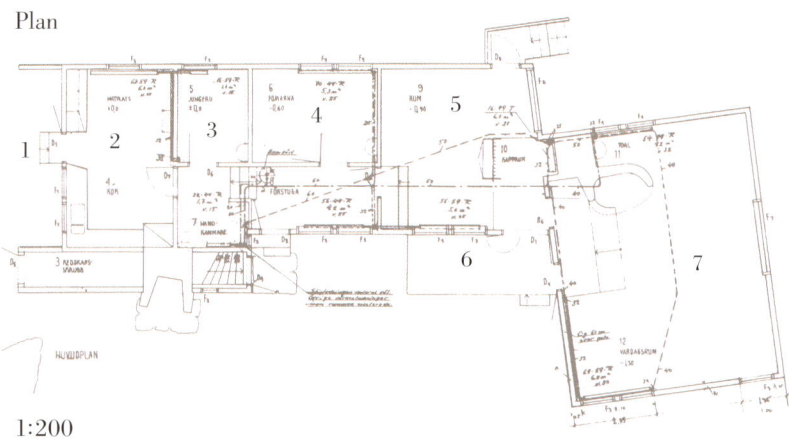

Plan

1:200

1. Outdoor space
2. Dining room with kitchen
3. Bedroom
4. Bedroom
5. Dining room
6. Terrace
7. Living room

Section

1:200

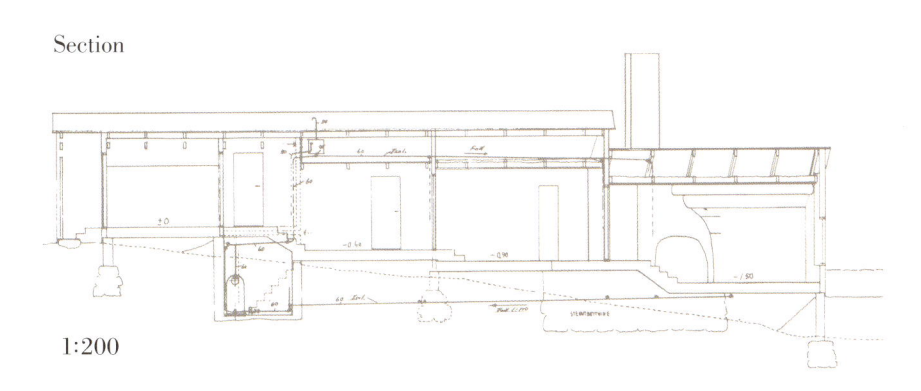

テラス西の前庭からの眺望。

A view of the front yard on the west side of the terrace.

リビングより岩山方向を望む。外装は細い見付幅の羽目板張り。テラスの床は、同じ板を透かし張りで用いている。

The view toward the mountains from the living room area. Wooden paneling with a narrow aspect width has been used for the exterior. The floor of the terrace uses the same type of panels in a slit-boarding style.

南東側より外観全景。夏の家が斜面に沿って建てられていることがわかる。

A full view of the exterior of the house from the southeast. From this vantage point, it becomes clear that the summer house was built along the same incline.

ダイニングとリビングとの取り合い部分。外部階段からも直接出入りができる。外部階段の段板を手摺壁に貫通させ、その断面を出す。アスプルンドのデザイン・アイデアのひとつ。

The point where the dining room meets the living room. The exterior stairs can be used to directly enter the house. The stair tread on the staircase penetrates the handrail wall to create a cross-section. This was one of Asplund's unique design concepts.

キッチン奥にある外部スペース。入り江方向を眺める。

The exterior area behind the kitchen as seen from the side of the hill, facing an inlet.

251 E.G. Asplund

夕日に照らされた西側テラス。右手のドアからダイニングに入る。椅子はアスプルンドのお気に入りだったとか。

The west terrace lit by the setting sun. The door to the right leads to the dining room, and the chair was Asplund's favorite.

三角形のトイレ小屋。ふたつの木製便器が並ぶ。

A triangular outhouse. There are two wooden toilets inside.

キッチンの外壁と岩山を仕切る板塀。岩の形状に合わせて隙間なく作られている。

A board fence divides the exterior wall of the kitchen and the crags. It was designed to fit the rock perfectly without any cracks.

リビングの扉を開けると、西日を受けたテラスが心地よい団欒のスペースとなる。
When opening the living room door, the terrace, bathed in the afternoon sun, has a comfortable atmosphere.

ダイニング。廊下に通じる左のドアは、階段2段分高い。室内の壁、天井はラフな仕上げの板張りとし、部位により微妙な色使いで塗り分けられている。

The dining room. The door on the left, which leads to the hallway, is two-steps high. The walls and ceiling in the room are paneled with roughhewn wood. The room is subtly divided into sections using different colors of paint.

キッチンから廊下を経てダイニング、そしてリビングへ下る。廊下、ダイニングの天井は西に向かってわずかに下り勾配。

The dining room and beyond it, the living room, as seen through the hallway from the kitchen. The ceiling in the hallway and dining room slopes gradually toward the west.

ダイニングよりリビングを見る。微妙な角度による接合がリビングへのアプローチを新鮮にする。

The living room as seen from the dining room. The slight angle of the joint gives the approach to the living room a refreshing quality.

一日中、南の窓から光が差し込む至福の空間。窓はサッシと網戸が天袋に収納され、フレームレスも可能なディテールとなっている。

A blissful space that is bathed in sunlight throughout the day via the windows on the south side. The sash and screens of the windows can be stored in a cupboard, and the windows can also be used without frames.

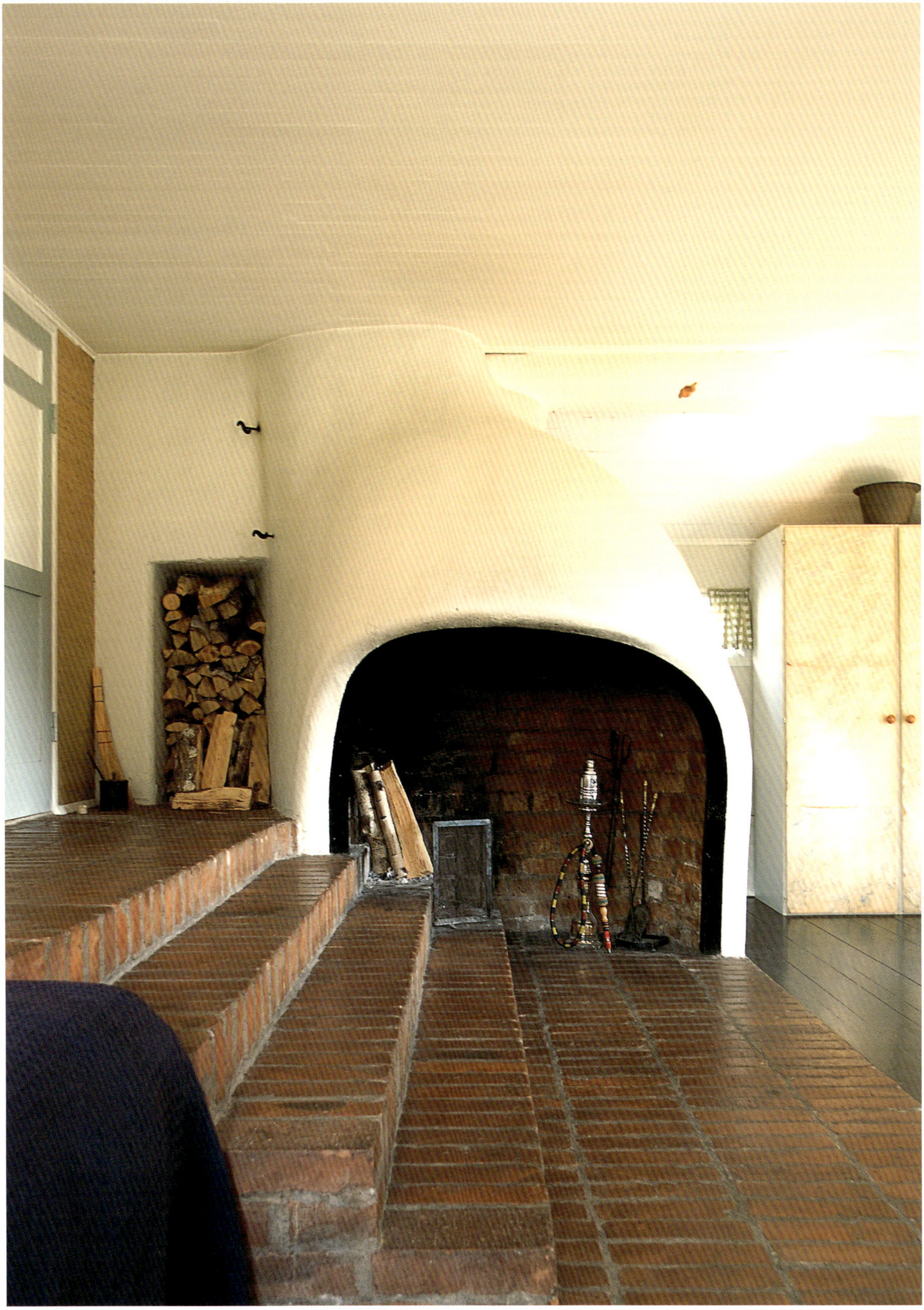

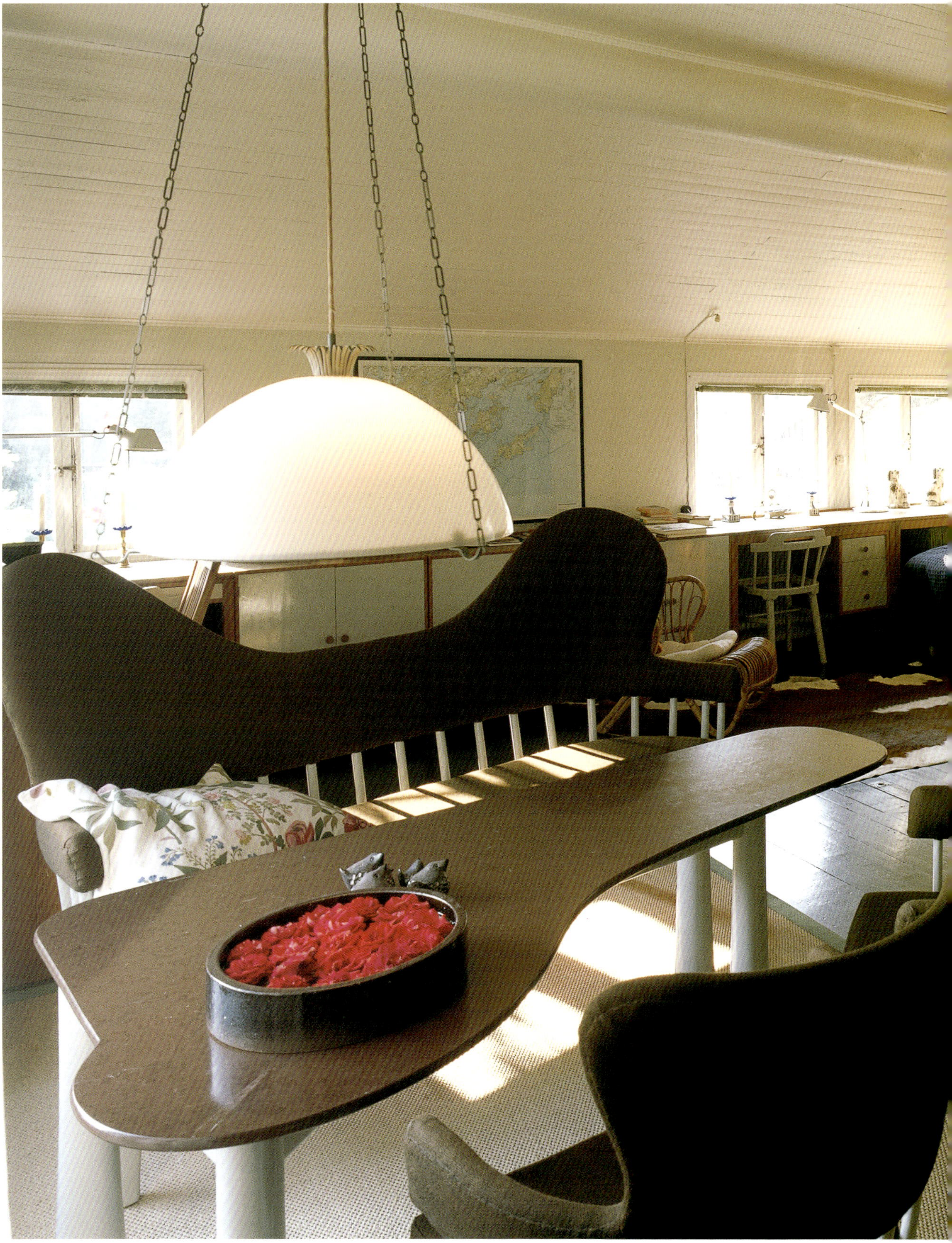

リビングルーム全景。2本の丸太梁が露出した船底天井。有機的な家具と暖炉がくつろぎの空間をユーモラスに演出している。壁にはアスプルンドが愛用した皮のジャケットと帽子。

A full view of the living room. The ceiling is curved with two exposed round beams. The organically-shaped furniture and fireplace add a humorous touch to the relaxed space. Hanging on the wall are Asplund's favorite leather jacket and cap.

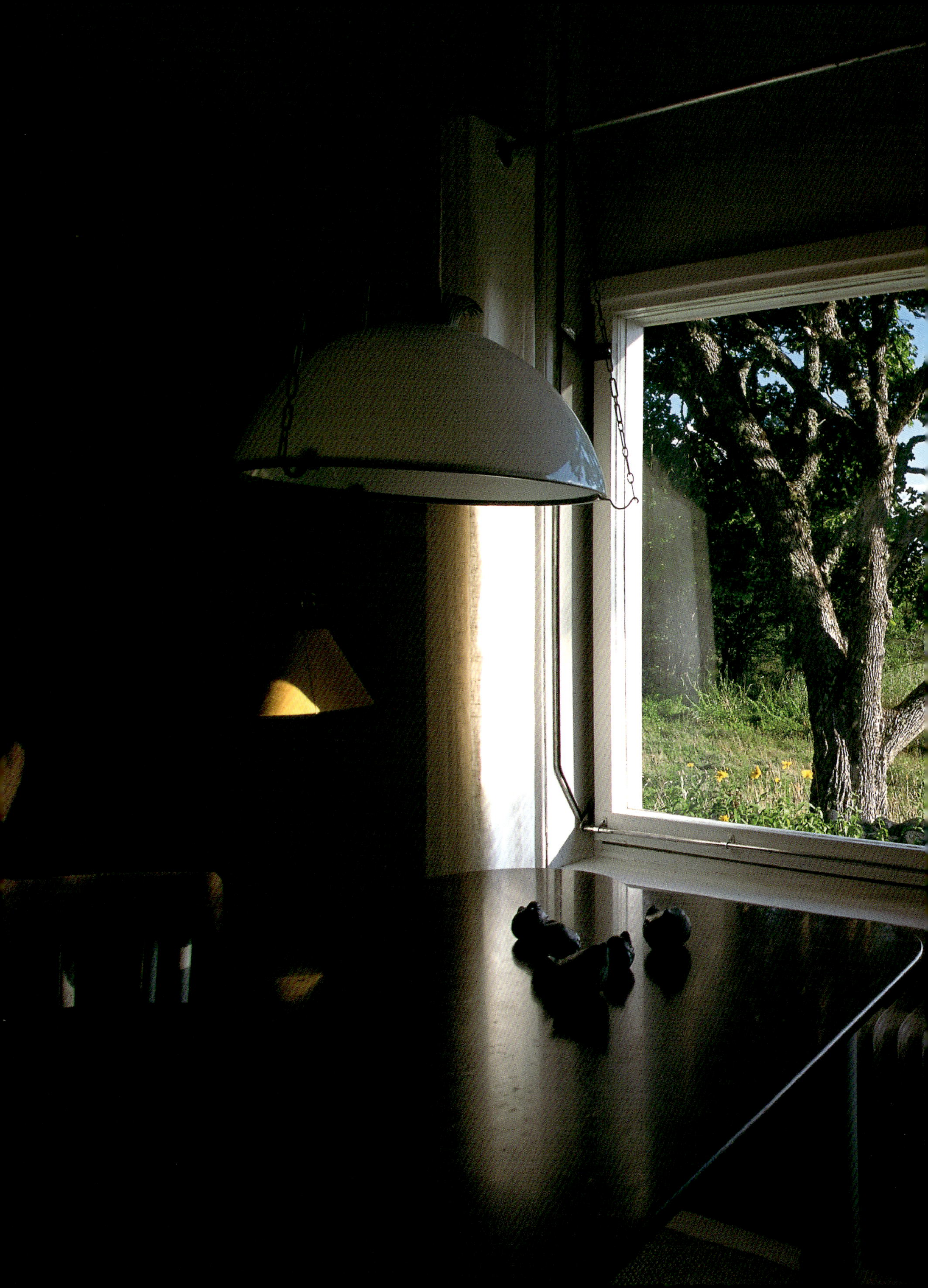

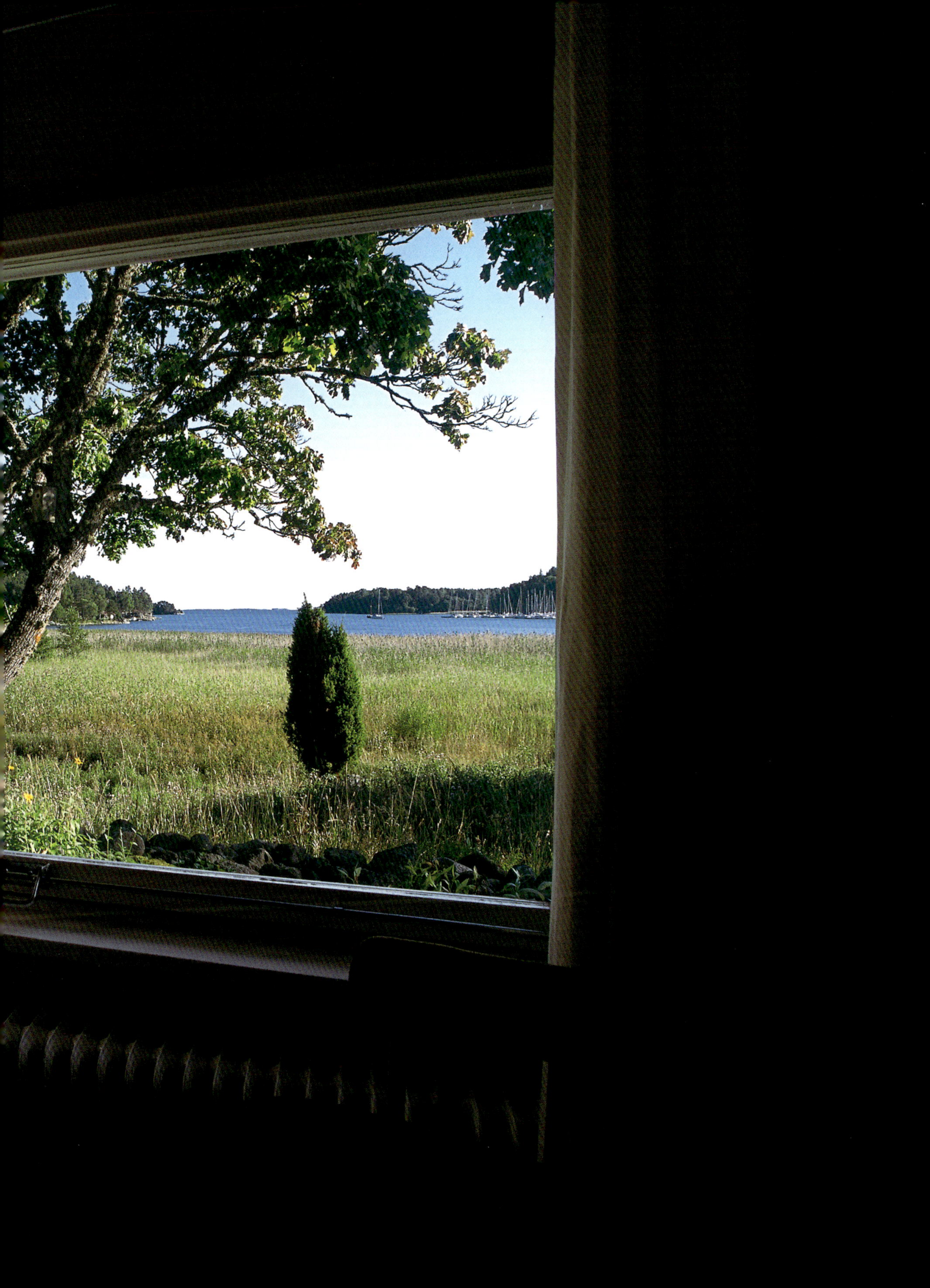

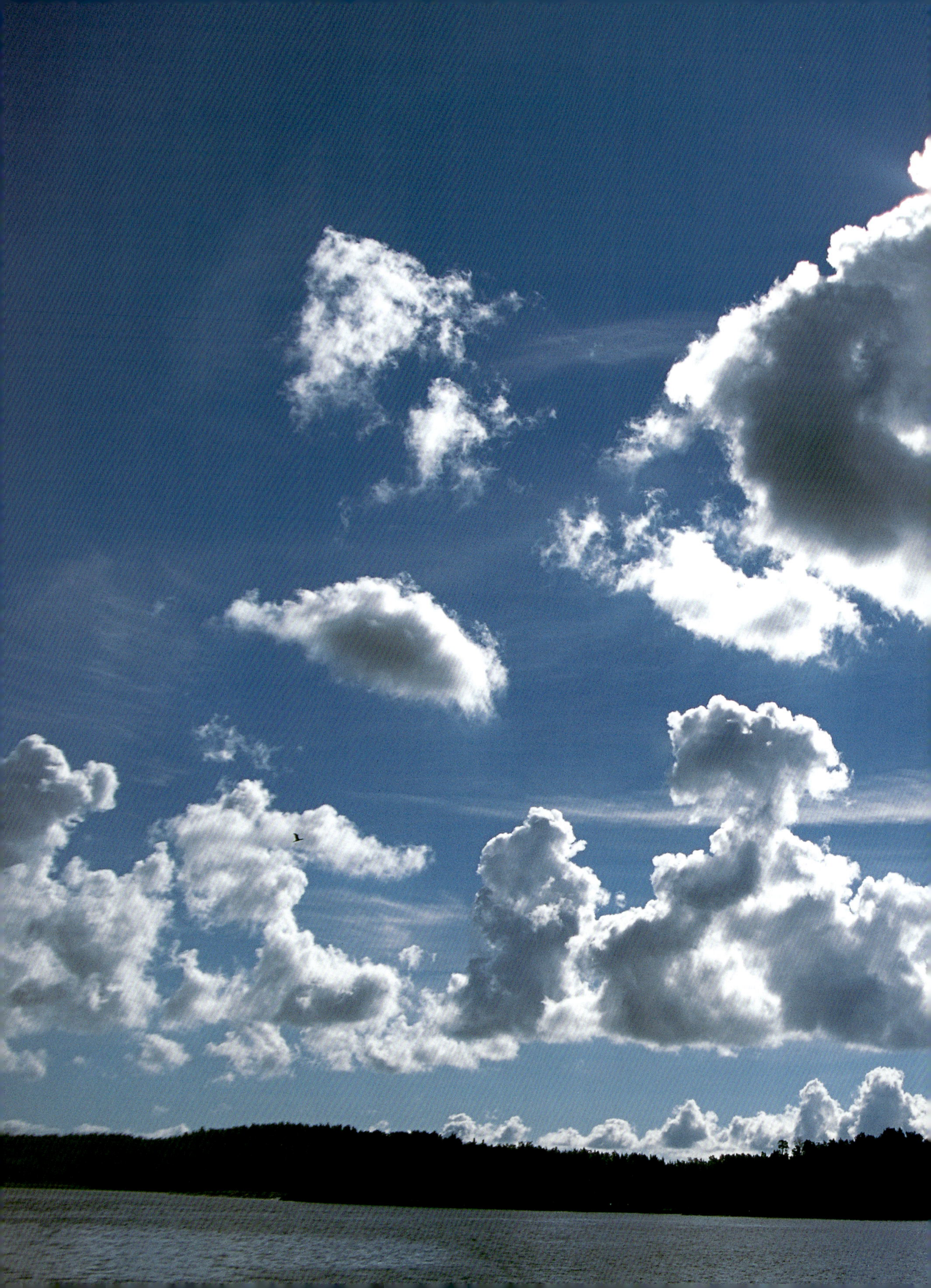

作品リスト　List of Works

年／Year	作品名／Project and Work	場所／Place	
1907	ヨーハンション邸（L. I. ヴァールマンの指導） Villa Johansson, under the supervision of the architect L. I. Wahlman	ロネビー Ronneby	○
1908	ヨーハンション邸（L. I. ヴァールマンの指導） Villa Johansson, under the supervision of the architect L. I. Wahlman	ロネビー Ronneby	○
1909	ヘルシングボリ小学校　コンペ応募案　選外 Elementary School in Hälsingborg, Competition Design, Rejected	ヘルシングボリ Hälsingborg	▲
1909	パリのスウェーデン教会　コンペ応募案　選外（佳作扱い） The Swedish Church in Paris, Competition Design, Rejected (Honorable Mention)	パリ（フランス） Paris (France)	▲
1911	イーヴァル・アスプルンド邸 Villa Ivar Asplund	リーディンイェ Lidingö	▲
1912	カルマルの小学校　コンペ応募案　2等 Elementary School in Kalmar, Competition Design, 2nd Prize	カルマル Kalmar	▲
1912	ローセンベリ邸 Villa Rosenberg	カールスハムン Karlshamn	▲
1912	大工組合　コンペ応募案　H. S. ベルヴェンと協同　買い上げ賞 Carpenters' Union Building, Competition Design, together with H. S. Berven, Purchase Prize	ストックホルム Stockholm	▲
1912-18	カールスハムンの中学校　コンペ応募案　1等 Secondary School at Karlshamn, Competition Design, 1st Prize	カールスハムン Karlshamn	○
1913	イェーテボリ裁判所増築　コンペ応募案　1等 Göteborg Law Courts, Rebuilding and Extension, Competition Design, 1st Prize	イェーテボリ Göteborg	○
1913	ヘデムーラ共学校　指名コンペ応募案　1等 Coeducational School in Hedemora, Invited Competition Design, 1st Prize	ヘデムーラ Hedemora	▲
1913	セーランデル邸 Villa Selander	エルンシェルズヴィーク Örnsköldsvik	○
1913	ストゥーレ邸 Sturegården	ニィーシェーピング Nyköping	○
1914	電報電話局 Telegraph and Post Office in Karlshamn	カールスハムン Karlshamn	○
1914	ルート博士邸 Dr. Ruth's Villa	クーサンコスキ（フィンランド） Kuusankoski (Finland)	○
1915	ハンマルビー運動場の入口棟 Entrance Buildings to Hammarby Sports Ground	ストックホルム Stockholm	○
1915	ホファー教会の聖餐器（銀細工師ヤコブ・エングマン制作） Communion Vessels for Hofors Chapel, executed by the silversmith Jacob Ängman		○
1915	エンシェーデの鉄道車庫 Train Sheds at Enskede	ストックホルム Stockholm	○
1915	南ストックホルム墓地　コンペ応募案（建築家シーグルド・レヴェレンツと協同）1等 Stockholm South Burial Ground (Woodland Cemetery), International Competition Design, together with architect Sigurd Lewerentz, 1st Prize	ストックホルム Stockholm	○
1915	複合居住施設と商店 Housing Complex and Village Shop	オルベルガ Ålberga	○
1915	集会施設と宿泊施設 Meeting Hall and Inn	オルベルガ Ålberga	▲
1915-24	カール・ヨーハン学校　コンペ応募案　2等 Elementary School (Carl Johan School), Competition Design, 2nd Prize	イェーテボリ Göteborg	○
1916	ロシア鋼索工業社の社宅 Houses for Russian Steel Rope Factory, Ltd.	エカテリノスラヴ（ロシア） Ekaterinoslav (Russia)	○

スウェーデン工芸協会事務所
The Swedish Society of Arts and Crafts

凡例 : ○実施 ●アスプルンドの没後、引き継いだ別の建築家の手で実施 ▲計画案
Explanatory Notes : ○executed ●executed by another architect after Asplund's death ▲unexecuted project

年／Year	作品名／Project and Work	場所／Place	
1916	ウプサラ・エーケビー社製タイル張暖炉 コンペ応募案 2等 Tiled Stove for Upsala-Ekeby Company, Competition Design, 2nd Prize		○
1917	労働者用住宅 Workers' Housing at Kv. Stativet and Tumstocken	ストックホルム Stockholm	○
1917	イェータ広場 コンペ応募案 選外 Göta Square, Competition Design, Rejected	イェーテボリ Göteborg	▲
1917	国営冷蔵穀物庫 Government Cold Storage Warehouse	ハルスベリ Hallsberg	○
1917	スウェーデン工芸協会主催住宅展に出品のインテリアデザイン Interior Design, Home Exhibition of Swedish Society of Arts and Crafts	ストックホルム Stockholm	○
1917-18	スネルマン邸 Villa Snellman	ユーシュホルム Djursholm	○
1917-18	国営穀物サイロ（カール・フォーセル教授とエーリック・フーベンディック教授と協同） Government Silos, together with Professor Carl Forssell and Erik Hubendick	イースレーヴ、エスキルトゥーナ、リンシェービング、オストルプ、トーメリッラ Eslöv, Eskiltuna, Linköing, Åstorp, Tomelilla	○
1917-18	ティーセンフルト領主館の改修 Tisenhult Manor, Restoration	カトリーネホルム Katrineholm	○
1917-21	リステール州裁判所 Lister County Courthouse	セルヴェスボリ Sölvesborg	○
1918	労働者用住宅 Workers' Housing	ティーダホルム Tidaholm	○
1918	ブローキンド領主館の改修と増築 Brokind Manor, Restoration and Extension	エステルゴットランド Östergotland	▲
1918 1919-20 1924-25	グスタフ・アドルフ広場の整備計画と裁判所と証券取引所の増改築計画 指名コンペ応募案 1等 Gustaf Adolf Square in Göteborg, Arrangement of the Square with Reconstruction and Extention of the Law Courts and the Stock Exchange Quarter, Invited Competition Design, 1st Prize	イェーテボリ Göteborg	▲
1918	ヴェステロースの墓地 Cemetery in Västerås	ヴェステロース Västerås	▲
1918-20	森の礼拝堂 Woodland Chapel at Woodland Cemetery	ストックホルム Stockholm	○
1919	エリクス広場の鉄道貨物駅（テューレ・ティーデブラッドと協同） Railway Goods Station at Eriksplan, together with Ture Tidebald	ストックホルム Stockholm	▲
1919	聖ペトリ教会の洗盤台 指名コンペ応募案（銀細工師ヤコブ・エングマン制作） Font for St.Petri Church, Invited Competition, executed by silversmith Jacob Ängman	マルメ Malmö	○
1920	スウェーデン工作連盟展に出品のインテリアデザイン Interior Design, Exhibition of the Workshop Society	ストックホルム Stockholm	○
1920-28	ストックホルム市立図書館 Stockholm City Library	ストックホルム Stockholm	○
1921	アルムンイェ墓地拡張計画 Almunge Cemetery, Extension	アルムンイェ Almunge	○
1921	ヘルイェアンズホルメン コンペ応募案 2等 Helgeandsholmen, Competition Design, 2nd Prize	ストックホルム Stockholm	▲
1921	ストックホルム市庁舎の家具 Furniture for Stockholm City Hall	ストックホルム Stockholm	○
1921	オスカール・ベルナドッテ王子家の納骨堂 Prince Oskar Bernadotte's Family Vault in North Cemetery	ストックホルム Stockholm	○

ブレーデンベリ・デパート
Bredenberg Department Store

オクセレースンド墓地の礼拝堂
Chapel in Oxelösund Cemetery

年／Year	作品名／Project and Work	場所／Place	
1922	クレヴァリーデン　橋と道路 Klevaliden, Brige and Road Approaches	ヒュースクヴァルナ Huskvarna	○
1922	国政庁舎　コンペ応募案（建築家トゥーレ・リーベリと協同）2等 Royal Chancellery Buildings, Competition Design, together with architect Ture Ryberg, 2nd Prize	ストックホルム Stockholm	▲
1922	バローン・オーケルヘイム家墓石 Baron Åkerhielm Family Tomb		▲
1922-23	スカンディア・シネマ Skandia Cinema	ストックホルム Stockholm	○
1922-24	森の墓地の管理棟 Offices at Woodland Cemetery	ストックホルム Stockholm	○
1923	オブセルヴァトーリエキューレン周辺の街区計画 Town Plan for the Area around Observatoriekullen	ストックホルム Stockholm	○
1924	パリ万国博覧会のスウェーデン館　指名コンペ応募案　選外 Swedish Pavilion for Paris Exhibition 1925, Invited Competition Design, Rejected	パリ（フランス） Paris (France)	▲
1924-25	パリ万国博覧会スウェーデン館のインテリアデザイン Interior Design for the Swedish Pavilion at Paris Exhibition 1925	パリ（フランス） Paris (France)	○
1924-25	ステーン・アンカルクローナ提督家の納骨堂 Admiral Sten Ankarcrona's Family Vault in North Cemetery	ストックホルム Stockholm	○
1924-26	ギレットホテルのレストランのインテリアデザイン Interior Design for the Restaurant in Gillet Hotel	ストックホルム Stockholm	○
1924-29	オクセレースンドの墓地 Cemetery at Oxelösund	オクセレースンド Oxelösund	○
1925	イェーテボリのグスタフ・アドルフ広場の旗棒 Flagpoles for Gustaf Adolf Square in Göteborg	イェーテボリ Göteborg	▲
1926	ダネリウス財団コンペによるストックホルム市立図書館の公園のパブリックアート（彫刻家イーヴァル・ヨーンションとの協同）買い上げ賞 Danelius Fund Competition for Public Art Work in the Park around Stockholm City Library, together with sculptor Ivar Johnsson, Purchase Prize	ストックホルム Stockholm	○
1926	クヴィーベリ墓地　コンペ応募案　1等 Cemetery at Kviberg, Competition Design, 1st Prize	イェーテボリ Göteborg	○
1926	クヴィーベリ墓地に隣接の居住地区計画 Planning of Housing Area beside Kviberg Cemetery	イェーテボリ Göteborg	▲
1926	オーデンハッレン　ストックホルム市立図書館に隣接の市場 Odenhallen, Market Hall beside Stockholm City Library	ストックホルム Stockholm	▲
1926-28	レッティングス大臣家の納骨堂 Secretary of State Hj. Rettig's Family Vault in North Cemetery	ストックホルム Stockholm	○
1927-35	ストックホルム市立図書館の公園のランドスケープデザイン Landscape Design for the Park around Stockholm City Library	ストックホルム Stockholm	○
1928	アルヴフルステン　皇太子宮殿の増改築計画 Arvfursten (Crown Prince's) Palace, Reconstruction and Extention	ストックホルム Stockholm	▲
1928-30	ストックホルム博覧会 Stockholm Exhibition 1930, Principal Architect of the Exhibition	ストックホルム Stockholm	○
1929-36	カールスハムンの中学校増築 Extention to Secondary School at Karlshamn	カールスハムン Karlshamn	○
1931	スウェーデン工芸協会事務所のインテリアデザイン Interior Design for the Office of The Swedish Society of Arts and Crafts at Nybrogatan 7	ストックホルム Stockholm	○

クヴィーベリ火葬場
Kviberg Crematorium

シェヴデ火葬場
Skövde Crematorium

年／Year	作品名／Project and Work	場所／Place	
1932	ノール・メーラルストランド街の集合住宅　指名コンペ応募案　特別賞 Block of Flats in Norr Mälarstrand, Invited Competition Design, Extra Prize	ストックホルム Stockholm	▲
1932	クヴィーベリ墓地の礼拝堂　指名コンペ応募案 Chapel at Kviberg Cemetery, Invited Competition Design	イェーテボリ Göteborg	▲
1932	マルメ博物館　コンペ応募案　選外 Malmö Museum, Competition Design, Rejected	マルメ Malmö	▲
1933	画家グスタフ・カールストレムの住居船 Houseboat for artist Gustaf Carlström		▲
1933	国立美術館の一室のインテリアデザイン Interior Design for the Room at National Museum	ストックホルム Stockholm	▲
1933	レーダ・クヴァーンの肘掛椅子 Armchairs for Röda Kvarn	ストックホルム Stockholm	○
1933-35	ブレーデンベリ・デパート Bredenberg Department Store	ストックホルム Stockholm	○
1933-37	国立バクテリア研究所　指名コンペ応募案　1等 State Bacteriological Laboratory, Invited Competition Design, 1st Prize	ソルナ Solna	○
1934	ブロンマ空港　指名コンペ応募案　選外 Bromma Airport, Invited Competiton Design, Rejected	ストックホルム Stockholm	▲
1934	B. ベックストレムの夏の家 Summer House for B. Beckström	スタヴスネース Stavsnäs	○
1934-37	イェーテボリ裁判所増築 Göteborg Law Courts, Reconstruction and Extension	イェーテボリ Göteborg	○
1935	スカンセン入口のストックホルムタワー Stockholm Tower at Entrance to Skansen	ストックホルム Stockholm	▲
1935-37	オクセレースンド墓地の礼拝堂 Chapel in Oxelösund Cemetery	オクセレースンド Oxelösund	○
1935-40	森の火葬場 Woodland Crematorium in Woodland Cemetery	ストックホルム Stockholm	○
1936	ストックホルム出身学生寮 Building for the Students of Stockholm Nation at Upsala	ウプサラ Upsala	▲
1936-40	クヴィーベリ火葬場　指名コンペ応募案　1等 Kviberg Crematorium, Invited Competition Design, 1st Prize	イェーテボリ Göteborg	●
1936-37	アスプルンドの夏の家 E. G. Asplund's Summer House	ステンネース Stennäs	○
1936-40	海事博物館前の広場とストックホルムタワー Stockholm Tower and Square at Maritime Museum	ストックホルム Stockholm	▲
1937-40	シェヴデ火葬場 Skövde Crematorium	シェヴデ Skövde	●
1937-41	国立獣医学バクテリア研究所 State Veterinary Bacteriological Laboratory	ストックホルム Stockholm	●
1938-39	社会福祉局　指名コンペ応募案　1等 Social Welfare Office, Invited Competition Design, 1st Prize	ストックホルム Stockholm	▲
1939	マルムシルナッズ通りの集合住宅 Block of Flats at Malmskillnadsgatan	ストックホルム Stockholm	▲
1939-40	ストックホルム資料局　指名コンペ応募案　1等 Stockholm City Archives, Invited Competition Design, 1st Prize	ストックホルム Stockholm	●

ストックホルム資料局
Stockholm City Archives

作品リスト参考文献　Reference
・*Teknisk Tidskrift Arkitektur, Byggmästaren* and *Arkitektur*, Stockholm, 1900-1990.
・Gustaf Holmdahl et al.ed., *Gunnar Asplund Architect*, Stockholm, 1950.
・Stuart Wrede, *The Architecture of Erik Gunnar Asplund*, Cambridge and London, 1980.
● 注記：写真6点は、1930年代以降の作品のうち、現存しており本章で紹介できなかったもの。(家具や個人住宅を除く)
Note : These six photographs, showing works dating from the 1930s, are not discussed in this chapter (with the exceptionof furniture and private residences).

略歴　Profiles

吉村行雄 ［よしむら ゆきお］
建築写真家

1946年大阪府生まれ。1971年武蔵野美術大学造形学部建築学科卒業後、竹中工務店入社。設計本部、本社広報を経て設計本部部長。2006年吉村行雄写真事務所開設。1998年ニューヨーク、2001年ストックホルムにて個展を開催。国内では個展・グループ展、講演会を多数開催。2006年「建築家グンナール・アスプルンド―癒しのランドスケープ」展企画・演出。2007年武蔵野美術大学・芦原義信賞受賞。北欧建築・デザイン協会理事、北欧文化協会正会員、日本建築写真家協会会員。
主な写真集に、『Light/Space/Architecture スウェーデンの近代建築』、『TAKENAKA-A book of Buildings』、私製『建築カレンダー』などがある。

Yukio Yoshimura
Architectural Photographer

Profile: Born in Osaka in 1946. After graduating from the Department of Architecture at Musashino Art University in 1971, began working in the Design Department at Takenaka Corporation. Senior Manager of the Design Management Department at Takenaka. Established Yukio Yoshimura Photography in 2006. Held solo exhibitions of photography in New York in 1998, and in Stockholm in 2001. Has participated in many solo and group exhibitions and lectures in Japan. Direction of Exhibition "E. G. Asplund : Healing Landscape" in Japan in 2006. Received the Musashino Art University / Yoshinobu Ashihara Award in 2007.

Positions: Director of the Scandinavian Architecture & Design Institute of Japan, Member of the Nordic Cultural Society of Japan, and the Japan Architectural Photographers Society.

Publications: *Architecture Calendar* (privately published photo collection published annuary since 1972), *Takenaka - A Book of Buildings* (photo collection; 1994), *Kenchiku Bunka* (Architectural Culture; article and photos; 2000), *Light/Space/Architecture* (photo collection; 2001), "Asplund: Woodland Cemetery," (photos for feature article; *approach* 2001), "Asplund: The Summer House" (photos for feature article; *approach* 2004).

川島洋一 ［かわしま よういち］
建築家・建築史家

1962年大阪府生まれ。1988年千葉大学工学部建築学科卒業。1989-90年および92-93年スウェーデン国立ルンド大学大学院留学。1997年京都工芸繊維大学大学院博士後期課程修了。博士（学術）。1996-98年日本学術振興会特別研究員PD。1999年川島洋一建築研究所設立。国立石川高専建築学科助教授を経て、現在福井工業大学デザイン学科教授。2006年「建築家グンナール・アスプルンド―癒しのランドスケープ」展企画・監修。
主な共著書として、『近代建築史』（1998年／昭和堂）、『ヨーロッパ建築史』（1998年／昭和堂）、『Light／Space／Architecture スウェーデンの近代建築』（2001年）、『作家たちのモダニズム』（2003年／学芸出版社）、『建築史論聚』（2004年／思文閣出版）などがある。

Yoichi Kawashima
Architect/Architectural Historian

Profile: Born in Osaka in 1962. Graduated from the School of Architecture at Chiba University in 1988. Studied at the Graduate School of Architecture at the University of Lund, Sweden from 1989 to 1990 and 1992 to 1993. Completed Ph.D. at the Graduate School of Architecture at the Kyoto Institute of Technology, in 1997. Supervision of Exhibition "E. G. Asplund : Healing Landscape" in Japan in 2006.

Positions: Research Fellow, Japan Society for the Promotion of Science from 1996 to 1998. Founded Atelier Yoichi Kawashima in Kyoto in 1999. Associate Professor, School of Architecture, Ishikawa National College of Technology from 2001 to 2002. Assistant Professor, Associate Professor, Professor School of Architecture, Fukui University of Technology from 2002 to 2009, Professor, School of Design, Fukui University of Technology from 2009 to the present.

Publications: *History of Modern Architecture* (1998), *History of European Architecture* (1998), *Light/Space/Architecture* (2001), *Modernism in 14 Architects* (2003), *Kenchiku Shironshu* (2004).

謝辞　Acknowledgments

本書の刊行は、多くの方々のご好意とご協力に支えられて実現した。ここに一部の方のお名前をあげて、感謝の気持ちを表したい。

吉村は、スウェーデン訪問のたびにお世話になり、ストックホルムでの写真展の実現にご尽力いただいたエイコ＆クリステル・デュークご夫妻、そしてご夫妻の紹介とスウェーデン取材のきっかけをつくって下さった鳥巣元太氏に感謝申し上げる。アスプルンドご子息のインゲマール・アスプルンド氏の献身的なご支援なくして本書は実現しなかった。そのアスプルンドご夫妻を紹介してくださった、ストックホルム市立美術館の館長ベーリット・スヴェッドベリ女史、同美術館でご担当いただいたアネット・オーストレム女史にも感謝する。アスプルンド財団会長グンヴォール・エングストレム女史のご厚意にも感謝の意を表したい。また長年にわたり私の写真活動を見守り、精神的な支えであった故平生舜一氏、そして竹中工務店の懐深いご厚情に感謝申し上げたい。そして私事ながら長年にわたる私のわがままを温かく見守ってくれた妻・保子にも感謝の気持ちをささげたい。

川島が、このたび思いがけずアスプルンド論を書く機会に恵まれたのは、吉村行雄氏のご高配のおかげである。スウェーデン留学の際には、ルンド大学のペーター・シェーストレム氏とヴィベケ・ダルガス氏にお世話になり、心の財産をいただいた。またレナ・エークルンド氏にはご温情をいただいた。あらためて中村昌生、日向進、大河直躬の各先生に受けたご学恩に想いをめぐらせる。スウェーデン政府、ルンド大学、花王芸術文化財団、日本学術振興会科学研究費には奨学金と研究費をいただいた。妻・麻柚には貴重なアドバイスをもらった。以上、記して感謝したい。

最後になったが、本書の実現にご尽力いただいた水上町子氏にお礼申し上げたい。デザイナーの太田徹也氏には、アスプルンドの魅力を引き出す見事な仕事をしていただいた。本書の出版の意義を評価し、編集の指揮を取っていただいたTOTO出版の遠藤信行編集長と、粘り強く編集作業を続けてくださった清水栄江氏に心より感謝申し上げる。

The publication of this book could not have been realized without the goodwill and cooperation of a great number of people. We would like to express our appreciation to some of these important individuals.

Yukio Yoshimura : I would like to thank Eiko and Christer Duke for their kindness, and also to Genta Torisu for helping with many things when I first began interested in Sweden. Without the dedicated support of E. G. Asplund's son, Ingemar Asplund, the book would have been impossible. I would also like to thank Berit Svedberg, the director of the Stockholm City Museum, and Annette Aström. I would like to express my appreciation to Gunvor Engström, chairperson of the Asplund Foundation. And I must mention the late Shunichi Hirao and the Takenaka Corporation. Finally, I would like to thank my wife, Yasuko, for taking such good care of me over the years.

Yoichi Kawashima : I would like to express my gratitude to Yukio Yoshimura, who made it possible for me to write this book. I would also like to thank Peter Siöström and Vibeke Dalgas of the University of Lund for their help and kindness during my time as a student in Sweden, Lena Eklund for her affection, and also to my teachers, Masao Nakamura, Susumu Hyuga and Naomi Ookawa. For financial support, I am indebted to the Swedish institute, the University of Lund, the Kao Foundation for Arts and Sciences, and the Japan Society for the Promotion of Science. Finally, I would like to thank my wife, Mayu, for all of her invaluable advice.

Both of us would like to express our appreciation to Machiko Mizukami, and to the designer Tetsuya Ohta for his outstanding work, and also to Nobuyuki Endo, head editor at TOTO Publishing, for overseeing the project, and to Sakae Shimizu for her perseverance in the editorial process.

Credits　クレジット

Photography / Drawing Credits　写真・図版クレジット

All photographs and captions by Yukio Yoshimura except the following :

Arkitekturmuseet
p.4, p.16-18, p.20-24, p.26-30, p.37-39(bottom), p.42(bottom),
p.52-53(bottom), p.56-57, p.62(bottom), p.81(bottom), p.148(bottom),
p.152-153(top), p.170(bottom), p.212(bottom), p.248(bottom), p.249(top)

Courtesy of Takenaka Corporation *approach*
p.36, p.48-49

The Cemeteries Administration
p.19

Yoichi Kawashima
p.12, p.265(right), p.266-267

Production Cooperation　制作協力者

Architectural Drawings　図版制作
Masahiro Eigen　　　　　栄元正博(神戸芸術工科大学)
Shuji Yamamoto　　　　　山本修司
Mitsuhiro Okamura　　　　岡村光洋

English Translation　英訳
Christopher Stephens　　　クリストファー・スティヴンズ
Japanese Translation　和訳
Jun Doi　　　　　　　　　土居　純

Research Cooperation (alphabetical order)　取材協力

Bo Andrén
Arkitekturmuseet
Asplund Foundation
Anne Asplund
Ingemar Asplund
Annette Åström
Christer Duke
Eiko Duke
Catrin Ek
Embassy of Sweden in Japan
Gunvor Engström
Inger Enlund
Leif Gustafson
Charlotta Hagerud
Ivar Hagerud
Torun Herlöfsson
Bengt O. H. Johansson
Börje Olsson
Kaj Reinius
Berit Svedberg
Anna-Lena Wibom

E.G. ASPLUND
アスプルンドの建築 1885–1940

2005年8月30日　　初版第1刷発行
2021年3月30日　　初版第4刷発行

写真 ················ 吉村行雄

文 ···················· 川島洋一

発行者 ············ 伊藤剛士

発行所 ············ TOTO出版（TOTO株式会社）
〒107-0062
東京都港区南青山1-24-3
TOTO乃木坂ビル2F
[営業] TEL : 03-3402-7138
　　　 FAX : 03-3402-7187
[編集] TEL : 03-3497-1010
URL : https://jp.toto.com/publishing

デザイン ········· 太田徹也

印刷・製本 ········ 株式会社東京印書館

落丁本・乱丁本はお取り替えいたします。
本書の全部又は一部に対するコピー・スキャン・
デジタル化等の無断複製行為は、
著作権法上での例外を除き禁じます。
本書を代行業者等の第三者に依頼してスキャンや
デジタル化することは、たとえ個人や家庭内での
利用であっても著作権法上認められておりません。
定価はカバーに表示してあります。

Printed in Japan
ISBN978-4-88706-257-3